# The Scourge
# of
# WAR

*The Scourge*

*of*

# WAR

## New Extensions on an Old Problem

Edited by Paul F. Diehl

The University of Michigan Press
*Ann Arbor*

Copyright © by the University of Michigan 2004
All rights reserved
Published in the United States of America by
The University of Michigan Press
Manufactured in the United States of America
∞ Printed on acid-free paper

2007   2006   2005   2004      4   3   2   1

*A CIP catalog record for this book
is available from the British Library.*

Library of Congress Cataloging-in-Publication Data

The scourge of war : new extensions on an old problem / edited
by Paul F. Diehl.
p.   cm.
Includes bibliographical references.
ISBN 0-472-11395-X (cloth : alk. paper)
1. War.   2. War, Causes of.   3. War—Mathematical models.
I. Diehl, Paul F. (Paul Francis)

U21.2.S4   2004
355.02—dc22                                    2004004962

To J. David Singer
Scholar, Mentor, Activist

# CONTENTS

## Contents

III. DYADIC FACTORS AND INTERACTIVE EFFECTS

# PREFACE

In the first part of the last century, the study of international relations, and international conflict in particular, was indistinguishable from diplomatic history. Major scholarly concern was with describing the events that led to the two world wars and in providing idiosyncratic explanations for those events. There were pioneering scholarly efforts by Lewis Fry Richardson, Pitirim Sorokin, Quincy Wright, and others that departed from this tradition. Yet these were clearly exceptions, however notable they now appear in retrospect. The study of international relations changed dramatically in the second half of the twentieth century as the political science discipline as a whole adopted the scientific method. At the forefront of this movement in international relations were J. David Singer and the Correlates of War (COW) Project. In the history of the international relations discipline, and indeed within political science as a whole, few have made more important contributions.

Begun in 1963, and directed by Singer for thirty-eight years, the COW Project was one of the first of several data-based projects in international relations. Yet of the four leading data-based projects (COW, Dimensionality of Nations [DON] Project, 1914 Project, and Inter-Nation Simulation Project) reviewed by Hoole and Zinnes (1976), only the COW Project survives today. The most obvious contribution of the COW Project has been in the area of data collection and dissemination. The project currently has eleven data sets (e.g., on war, militarized disputes, geographic proximity) that include information on events and national attributes from 1816 to modern times. Indicative of the importance of the data is its widespread use by scholars around the world. Two systematic analyses (McGowan et al. 1988; Diehl et al. 2000) concluded that Correlates of War data have been used by more international relations scholars than any other collection, and this is true by a wide margin.

There is a tendency to forget that J. David Singer and Correlates of

War Project members also produced some of the most significant research on international conflict over the past four decades. Singer himself was the author, coauthor, or editor of many books, articles, and chapters that generated empirical findings from COW Project data. These extend over a long time-frame, from his early work on alliance aggregation (Singer and Small 1968) to more recent studies on civil war (Henderson and Singer 2000); these number more than 25 books and 150 journal articles or book chapters. Many of these studies represented important empirical findings, often well ahead of their time. For example, the first key empirical findings on the democratic peace were contained in an article by Small and Singer (1976) over a quarter of a century ago, presaging the field's fascination with the subject in the 1990s. Similarly, the original Wallace and Singer (1970) article on international organizations and war was one of the first to explore the intersection of the two. Yet COW research was always more than centered around one individual. Members of the Correlates of War Project produced hundreds of other books and articles on international war and conflict short of the war threshold (for a listing, see Suzuki, Krause, and Singer 2002). These include pathbreaking works on expected utility theory, the democratic peace, enduring rivalries, and many other subjects that now constitute the mainstream of international relations research.

It is tempting to simply sit back, reflect on Singer and COW's accomplishments, and give them the accolades that they deserve. Indeed, both have received many honors over the past decade. Yet the contributors to this volume have taken another tack. They begin with the premise that the data collection efforts of the COW Project and Singer's early empirical and theoretical work contain important paths for research into issues and problems vital to our understanding of international war processes. Some of these paths come from applying new techniques and approaches to the well-mined data sets on war and militarized disputes. Other paths stem from ideas that have been mistaken, ignored, or underdeveloped, but nevertheless have significant heuristic value. Still others derive from extending the work of Singer and COW further down the roads he helped establish or onto new venues.

All the contributors take an empirical finding, idea, or argument (or multiples of the same) first developed by J. David Singer and the Correlates of War Project as a starting point for their analyses. Except for the concluding chapter, which provides a theoretical and empirical synthesis of the Singer and COW legacies, all contributions to this volume provide empirical analyses using Singer and COW ideas and COW data. A few use some forgotten ideas or models (e.g., the internation influence model) developed forty years ago and apply it to new venues. Others revisit empirical findings from decades ago (e.g., on capabilities and dispute outcomes) that benefit from some reevaluation and extension. Still others take the standard COW data sets and subject them to new theoretical notions (e.g., power laws) or cutting-edge analyses (e.g., neural network analysis). The chapters in the collection represent many strands from the forefront of international conflict research, whether it be in the methods employed or the subject matters addressed (e.g., democratic peace, territory, intervention). What they have in common is a reflection that much can be learned by looking back at the work of J. David Singer and the COW Project. Yet they also recognize that such understanding is only enhanced by further empirical research using those ideas and data. That is, this collection is one in which leading scholars look back in order to move the study of international conflict forward.

## CONTENTS

J. David Singer and the COW Project are perhaps most widely known for producing the definitive data sets on war and related conflict. First published as *The Wages of War* (Small and Singer 1972) and then revised and updated as *Resort to Arms* (Small and Singer 1982), these collections provided a comprehensive listing of wars since 1816 as well as providing descriptive overviews of the patterns and changes in the evolution of interstate war. The second book also included a comprehensive listing of civil wars. The first section of this collection is dedicated to a reexamination of those and related data, with an eye to uncovering theoretically important patterns, few or none of which are evident in standard COW analyses.

Claudio Cioffi-Revilla and Manus Midlarsky explore the war data and seek to demonstrate that they obey a uniform class of power laws with respect to onset, fatalities, and duration. Unlike past efforts, these look at civil and interstate wars jointly as well as examine new hypotheses not found in Singer and Small's work or that of other scholars who have sought to uncover various patterns in warfare. The second chapter in this section also explores data patterns from perhaps the most widely used COW data set: militarized interstate disputes. Recently described in Jones, Bremer, and Singer (1996), militarized disputes are the interstate conflicts that have the potential to escalate to war. Monica Lagazio and Bruce Russett take this data set and apply neural network analysis to understand the initiation of disputes. The interactive and nonlinear influences postulated by the authors challenge conventional treatments, including by Singer and his associates, of dispute behavior.

Singer's own conceptual framework and much of the design of the Correlates of War Project was centered on the concept of levels of analysis (Singer 1961b). Empirical work was frequently divided according to whether the variables thought to influence war were at the subnational, national, dyadic, or systemic level of analysis. The next two sections of the book offer empirical studies of conflict at several of those levels of analysis; although the COW Project's initial work was set at the systems level, empirical research has increasingly moved away from such explanations in accounting for the onset and escalation of war, and system factors are accordingly not addressed here.

The second section of the book explores conflict factors at the national and subnational levels. J. David Singer recognized that leadership and domestic political factors were important in national decisions for war. Nevertheless, very little COW data gathering and empirical analysis focused on these concerns; of course, this was largely true of the quantitative study of international conflict in general, at least until the last decade. Zeev Maoz adopts and updates an approach to understanding decision makers' views used by Singer and Small (1974) to discern indicators of war and peace from the U.S. president's State of the Union messages. Maoz applies the same technique to statements made by world leaders at the 2000 UN Millennium Summit. He tries to match those statements on the events and conditions that led to war with historical reality. This provides insights into whether leaders' perceptions match such reality, a basic assumption of most models of war.

Bruce Bueno de Mesquita and James Lee Ray look beyond the concept of national interest, central to most realist approaches but widely criticized by Singer. This may seem somewhat surprising in that the COW data and research largely reflect a concern with testing realist propositions. They note that domestic political objectives of leaders have currency in explaining foreign policy actions, and discuss the implications of two-level games for conflict studies and levels of analysis. Finally, Volker Krause expands on the original Wayman, Singer, and Goertz (1983) article that sought to account for success in militarized disputes. He takes the finding that national capabilities and allocations to the military in particular are effective predictors of success, and then disaggregates them, exploring whether relying on alliances is more effective than building up one's arms.

In third section of the volume, the focus shifts to the dyadic level of analysis and interactions between different factors. At the dyadic level, joint characteristics or relationships of the two states involved in conflict are used to explain conflict behaviors. In Singer's work, and in the COW Project more broadly, this has often led scholars to concentrate on alliances, arms races, and the like. Douglas Lemke and Patrick Regan take Singer's (1963) internation influence model and apply it to military interventions. The model is used to generate hypotheses in a different and increasingly important context. This chapter is another illustration of how old ideas can be adapted to generate new insights. A second chapter in this section focuses on the democratic peace. Although there have been hundreds of articles and a number of books on this subject in the past decade, perhaps the first systematic empirical finding on democracies and war came from Small and Singer (1976). Subsequently, Singer has adopted a skeptical view toward claims of a democratic peace. Errol Henderson starts with the original Small and Singer article and uses some of Singer's later criticisms to construct hypotheses and test them. He hopes to demonstrate that Singer was correct about the limitations of the democratic peace. In the final chapter of this section, Paul Senese and John Vasquez refine some of the earlier work by Singer and other COW Project members on alliances and war. Rather than looking at alliances in isolation, as was characteristic of previous work, Senese and Vasquez show that alliances have an escalatory impact in the context of territorial disputes between states. This is evident only when combining the two factors: alliances and territorial conflict.

The final section of the book consists of a chapter by Daniel Geller and is intended as a synthetic treatment of Singer and the Correlates of War Project's research on war. Geller reviews and assesses the theoretical contributions that Singer and COW have made to the study of war, as well as summarizing the key empirical findings in that work. He concludes with an analysis of the likely scholarly legacy for the study of war and international relations in general. We hope that these findings will inspire future research similar to that reflected in this collection.

The genesis of this collection came from a desire to find new ideas and approaches to understanding international war. Surprisingly (or maybe not), the stimulus came from the past work of J. David Singer and the Correlates of War Project, some it more than forty years old. We thank David Singer for a lifetime of contributions to the study of international conflict and his colleagues in the Correlates of War Project for building on that distinguished tradition. Accordingly, this collection is dedicated to J. David Singer.

Several colleagues read proposals and draft chapters for this collection; I would like to thank Paul Hensel, D. Scott Bennett, Jack Levy,

and Russell Leng for their efforts and sage advice. Two anonymous reviewers for the University of Michigan Press gave excellent feedback on
an earlier version of this manuscript, and the improvement in the final
version is attributable, in part, to their recommendations. Jeremy Shine
and his successor James Reische provided encouragement at all stages of
the project. Finally, my indispensable assistant Delinda Swanson made
sure that all the details of final manuscript preparation were handled
with care and precision.

# PART I PATTERNS IN THE EVOLUTION OF WAR AND CONFLICT

# POWER LAWS, SCALING, AND FRACTALS IN THE MOST LETHAL INTERNATIONAL AND CIVIL WARS

*Claudio Cioffi-Revilla and Manus I. Midlarsky*

The most lethal international and civil wars in modern history (1816–present) have caused tens of millions of fatalities ($\sim 10^7$) measured in battle deaths alone. The even more catastrophic loss of human life in terms of total casualties and war-related civilian deaths caused by these interstate and domestic conflicts combined during the past two centuries has been even greater (perhaps $\sim 10^8$, in the hundreds of millions range). In spite of their theoretical and policy significance (Clemens and Singer 2000), an in-depth analysis of the set of highest-magnitude international and civil wars has never been conducted, although several decades have passed since the Correlates of War Project has been reporting extensive systematic data and numerous findings on other types of wars (Singer and Small 1972; Small and Singer 1982; Vasquez 2000).

In this study we use complexity theory to analyze and compare the so-called power law behavior of the highest-magnitude international wars and civil wars along dimensions of onset (time between onsets), fatalities (battle deaths or intensity) and duration, testing specific hypotheses and quantitative models that account for their occurrence. To clarify matters at the outset, the term *power law* has no connection of any kind with the conventional usage of the term *power* in political science. Instead, it is a verbal description of a mathematical function describing the uniform decline in values according to a numerical power $(2, 3, \ldots)$. Small and Singer (1982) and subsequent studies (summarized in Geller and Singer 1998) report numerous analyses of war, but power law analyses focused on this specific class of most lethal wars have never before been conducted. Among other findings, we demonstrate that the

3

most lethal international and civil wars obey a uniform class of power laws with respect to onset, fatalities, and duration. The power law, therefore, is a description of conflict behavior intrinsic to the conflict process itself.

These new results, based solely on Correlates of War Project data produced by J. David Singer and his collaborators, are significant for several reasons: (1) they provide the first solid replication of Lewis F. Richardson's (1948, 1960) original discovery of the power law behavior of war magnitude, which until now had been based exclusively on Richardson's much older "deadly quarrels" data; and (2) they extend the power law behavior of warfare to other theoretically important spatiotemporal dimensions of warfare, such as time-between-onsets and duration, not just the single magnitude dimension tested by Richardson. Thus, the power law pattern of warfare is now shown to govern not just one (magnitude), but a minimum of three spatiotemporal dimensions of warfare: time of onset, magnitude, and duration. In turn, this finding is significant because the so-called scaling property of these highly lethal wars, associated with their power law behavior, reveals previously unknown fractal properties that have implications for theoretical research as well as for early warning and mitigation policies. Inter alia, our findings account for the "long peace" phenomenon, which we demonstrate is infrequent but certain, given a sufficiently long historical epoch. As we discuss in this chapter, the multidimensional scaling of high-magnitude warfare according to uniform power laws may also indicate that the international system produces these highly lethal events as a result of "self-organized criticality" (Bak 1996), a previously undiscovered phenomenon in international relations. The high scientific reliability and validity of the modern COW data sets available today make these and other significant inferences possible, by combining the precision of systematic empirical observation with the power of estimated formal models.

This chapter contains five sections. The first provides theoretical and empirical background on power laws, explaining what they are and how complexity theory provides some insightful conceptual, modeling, and empirical tools for advancing our understanding of warfare. The purpose here is not to provide a primer on complexity theory (Badii and Politi 1997; Bak 1996; Meakin 1998; Richards 2000; Schroeder 1991; Waldrop 1995) but rather to highlight the theoretical implications of empirical power laws that are observed in distributions of data. The second section explains the methods used in this study. Our findings are reported in the third section, followed by a discussion of findings. The last section provides a summary.

4

## BACKGROUND

### Power Law Behavior and Complexity Concepts

What is a power law? Informally, a *power law* describes a variable *X* that has *many* (a high frequency of) *small* values, *some mid-range* values, and only a *few large* values, as opposed to the opposite (many large and few small) or some other pattern (Cioffi-Revilla 2003). By contrast, a "normal" (Gaussian) variable has a distribution with many midrange values and few extreme values at both high and low ends; a "uniform" variable has a distribution with the same number of values across the entire range. Therefore, a power law is characterized by the unique "many-some-few" pattern of symmetry (Schroeder 1991). In the social sciences, power laws were first discovered in areas such as linguistics (Zipf 1949), economics (Pareto 1927), sociology (Simon 1957), conflict analysis (Richardson 1941; see also Midlarsky 1989), and geography (Berry and Pred 1965). However, it was not until the recent formulation of *complexity theory* (Badii and Politi 1997; Bak 1996; Schroeder 1991; Waldrop 1995) that power laws acquired increased theoretical relevance for the insights they provide into the underlying (latent) causal dynamic mechanisms that produce the unique or "signature" pattern of "many-some-few" frequencies.

More rigorously, a power law distribution is a nonlinear mathematical model from complexity theory that specifies that the frequencies associated with values of a given variable *X* are distributed according to an *inverse function*, such that increasing values of *X* occur with decreasing frequency. Formally,

$$N_c = a'/10^{bX}, \qquad (1)$$

where $N_c$ is the *cumulative frequency* of values of *X*, and $a'$ and $b$ are constants that determine the *range* of values and the *scaling* proportion for $x \in X$, respectively. The nonlinear form of equation (1), or hyperbolic distribution, is *linearized* by taking common logarithms on both sides and rearranging terms, yielding

$$\log N_c = a - b\,X, \qquad (2)$$

where $a = \log a'$. The graphs of equations (1) and (2) are shown in figure 1. (Throughout this chapter, "log" denotes $\log_{10}$.) Note that whereas the original power law, equation (1), is *nonlinear* (fig. 1a), the transformed power law, equation (2), is *linear* (fig. 1b).

5

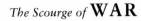

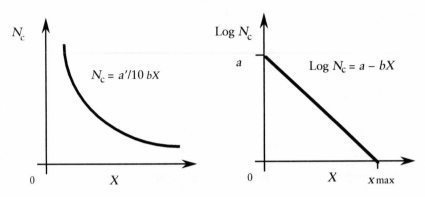

Fig. 1.   Graphs of a power law

A power law, or a given variable $X$ obeying a hyperbolic distribution, has the following distinctive properties associated with *complex systems* that are governed by underlying *nonlinear dynamics:* (1) self-similarity, (2) scaling, (3) fractal dimension, (4) criticality and underlying driven threshold systems, and (5) long-range interactions.

*Self-similarity.*   When $X$ obeys a power law, a recurring pattern of *constant proportion* occurs across the entire range of values of $X$, as highlighted by the linear graph in figure 1b. The graph of the frequency function is as linear in the low range of values as it is in the high range, and everywhere in between. This type of global symmetry is known as *self-similarity* in complexity theory. Self-similarity is also said to be an *emergent* property because it applies to the whole set of values, to an entire distribution of observations, not to individual values or elements.

*Scaling.*   The property of self-similarity is also known as *scaling.* Lewis F. Richardson (1948, 1960) discovered that "deadly quarrels" scale with respect to *magnitude* $\mu$ (see also Midlarsky 1989). Do the highest-magnitude wars measured by the Correlates of War Project also scale? (Note that "deadly quarrels" and "COW wars" constitute different sets of sample points, so there is no a priori guarantee that they both scale.) More generally, do other dimensions besides $\mu$, such as *time of onset* and conflict *duration,* also scale? Do different *types* of warfare (interstate, extrasystemic, international, civil, combined) also scale, or scale differently? Note that scaling occurs if and only if a variable obeys a power law. (Most biological organisms do *not* scale.) Is it possible for scaling to occur in the behavior of highest-magnitude warfare, in spite of major changes in technology, population patterns, international system composition, and other arguably significant changes that have occurred during the past two centuries? Intuition would say "no."

*Fractal dimension.* If the slope $b$ in equations (1) and (2) were allowed to assume only integer values $(1, 2, 3, 4, \ldots)$ then the frequencies associated with each value would decrease inversely by the power of such integer proportions, as in equation (1). However, when $b$ assumes fractional values then the range of proportions is itself continuous, no longer discrete as in Euclidean space. Thus, the $b$-value in a power law is called the *fractal dimension* (Mandelbrot 1977; Meakin 1998). Note that scaling vanishes as the slope decreases $(b \rightarrow 0)$, because all values of $X$ assume the same frequency when $b = 0$, so from a scaling perspective a uniform random variable exists in a 0-dimensional space. A hyperbolic power law $(b = 1)$ yields a 1-dimensional space. A quadratic power law $(b = 2)$ yields a 2-dimensional space. In general, a $b$-power distribution yields a $b$-dimensional space, and fractional values of $b$ yield fractal dimensions embedded within Euclidean space. Thus, for $0 < b < 1$ (as we will demonstrate for warfare) the fractal dimensionality is between a point and a line; for $1 < b < 2$ it is between a line and a plane; for $2 < b < 3$ it is between a plane and something else.

*Criticality and underlying driven threshold systems.* Scaling phenomena are produced by an underlying system that is *driven* by slowly evolving input processes to a phase of criticality (Rundle et al. 1996, 2000). Although the input driving the system can behave continuously, the state variables can change abruptly inside what is called a critical *bifurcation* region, producing scaled phenomena. Is the international system a "driven threshold" system in the sense of complexity theory (Cioffi-Revilla and Rundle 1999, 2000)? The demonstration of extensive scaling for multiple dimensions of warfare—such as time between onsets, magnitude, and duration—would provide significant support for such a conjecture. As discussed later, in the case of the international system the driving dynamics can be interpreted as slowly evolving changes in national attributes (for example, military budgets and capabilities), power distributions, or technological changes, which are known to affect decision-making calculations on war and peace.

*Long-range interactions.* Scaling phenomena are produced by systems that evolve into a critical phase where *long-range interactions* occur. A system governed by only nearest-neighbor or *local* interactions will tend to produce mostly normally distributed phenomena, not power law phenomena with significant left-skewness (long or "thick" right tail). Long-range interactions involving alliances, remote force deployments, power projection, and significant loss-of-power gradients are well-documented for many of the highest-magnitude wars in the international system. Conversely, long-range interactions are rare for lower-magnitude wars. This could explain why most "world wars" are also "global wars," and vice versa. However, most wars among neighbors (short-range interactions) are neither world wars nor global wars.

The preceding concepts from complexity theory are all related to power laws, such that when a power law behavior is observed in a given empirical domain—such as warfare—these ideas may suggest new insights on the phenomenon under investigation. Thus, power laws can be interpreted as diagnostic indicators of self-similarity, scaling, fractals, criticality, driven threshold dynamics, long-range interactions, and other complex phenomena.

### Power Laws of Warfare

Given the preceding concepts, in this study we examine the power law behavior of highest-magnitude warfare with respect to three separate (putatively independent) dimensions of warfare:

- Time between consecutive onsets $T$
- Richardson magnitude $\mu$
- Duration $D$

As detailed later, our hypothesis is that all three of these key spatiotemporal dimensions of war—not just Richardson's magnitude—obey uniform power laws, that is, equations (1) and (2). If so, then the preceding insights and implications from complexity theory—the properties of self-similarity, scaling, fractal dimension, criticality, driven threshold systems, and long-range interactions—become relevant for better understanding high-magnitude warfare. The general idea is analogous to that which occurs when exponential behavior is observed in the aggregate behavior of a given population; additional insights can be derived from the exponential laws to advance one's understanding of the population's behavior. Conversely, if power laws do *not* govern key dimensions of high-magnitude warfare such as onset time, magnitude, and duration, then these ideas become less relevant for understanding these conflicts, and a different set of concepts should be developed.

## METHOD

The previous section provided theoretical motivation and foundations for modeling high-magnitude warfare with power law models. In this section we explain the data, methods, and standards of inference used in this study.

8

## Data

The data sets used in this study were obtained from the three main original warfare files of the Correlates of War Project:

1. the Inter-State War Data, 1816–1997, version 3.0, taken from http://pss.la.psu.edu/ISWarFormat.htm;
2. the Extra-State War Data, 1816–1997, version 3.0, taken from http://pss.la.psu.edu/ESWarFormat.htm; and
3. the Civil War Data, 1816–1980 ($N$ = 106), taken from Small and Singer (1982).

These are the standard war files of the Correlates of War Project; the same ones that are used by most of the chapters in this book. The availability of these data sets through the Internet marks a significant scientific improvement with respect to earlier modes of dissemination. Accordingly, each of the analyses conducted in our study can be replicated with the same data downloaded from these URLs.

In comparative terms, the earlier Richardson discovery of the power law of war magnitude $\mu$ was based on his earlier "deadly quarrels" data set, which would have been a sample roughly equivalent to the sum total (union) of all three of the modern COW data sets. Hence, this is a more focused and targeted analysis aimed at both (1) replicating Richardson and (2) extending the domain of power laws to temporal dimensions (onset and duration) and the separate and specific set of high-magnitude wars (international and civil wars).

### Variables

For each war sample (international, civil, and combined) we used the following variables: onset year $\tau$, fatalities $F$, and duration $D$. In turn, based on the COW-defined variables (Small and Singer 1982; Geller and Singer 1998) we derived the following additional variables: (1) *time between onsets T,* defined as

$$T = \tau_{i+1} - \tau_i,$$

where $i = 1, 2, 3, \ldots, N$; (2) *Richardson magnitude* $\mu$, defined as

$$\mu = \log F; \text{ and}$$

(3) *war duration D*, defined as the length of time a war lasts.

In the statistical analyses reported in the next section we used the Richardson magnitude $\mu$ and not $F$, because the latter ranges across several orders of magnitude, so it is more appropriate to use the logarithmic scale of $\mu$ rather than values of $F$ to test for a given power law. In addition, as noted by Richardson (1960, 6), values of $\mu$ are less susceptible to measurement error than values of $F$.

### Hypotheses

Our general research hypothesis is that each of the three basic dimensions of warfare ($T$, $\mu$, and $D$) conforms to a power law with constant $a$ and fractal slope $b$, as in equations (1) and (2). Accordingly, our specific research hypotheses were formulated as follows.

$$H_1: \quad \log N_c(T) = a_1 - b_1\, T, \tag{3}$$

$$H_2: \quad \log N_c(\mu) = a_2 - b_2\, \mu, \tag{4}$$

$$H_3: \quad \log N_c(D) = a_3 - b_3\, D. \tag{5}$$

The corresponding null hypothesis $H_0$ for a given dimension $X$ was that $X$ does not follow a power law. Empirically, this would mean that a poor fit would result between the ranked-log frequency data and the linearized power law (eqs. 3–5).

### Analysis

The power law analysis conducted in this study aimed at replicating and extending earlier analyses of the scaling properties of warfare dimensions (Richardson 1948, 1960; Cioffi-Revilla 2000b) to the specific class of highest-magnitude wars. The power law analysis consisted of testing equations (3)–(5) on the three sets of COW Project data (international wars, civil wars, and all wars combined). The standard procedure for testing the power law behavior of a variable $X$ with a set of values $x_1, x_2, x_3, \ldots, N = \{x_j\}$, consists of (1) ranking the values of $X$ to obtain a ranked set of values $\langle x_j \rangle \in X$; (2) calculating the cumulative frequency $N_c = \Sigma_j f_i$ for increasing values of $X$, where $f_i$ is the frequency of the $i$th ordered value; and (3) regressing the log $N_c$ values against values of $X$. Examples of this basic procedure may be found in Axtell (1999), Barabási and Albert (1999), Nishenko and Barton (1996), Richardson (1960, 149), Weiss (1963), and Wyss and Wiemer (2000, 1337).

All statistical calculations were performed with Statistica™ version 4.1 for Macintosh (see www.statsoft.com) running Mac OS 9.1.

## *Inference*

For purposes of establishing valid inferences, we used standard goodness-of-fit criteria for linear models, given that equations (3)–(5) are rendered in linear form: *t*-ratios of *a* and *b* estimates, coefficient of determination $R^2$, the *F*-ratio, and significance levels of the preceding statistics. By convention, the .05 level of significance is taken as sufficient, with lower levels indicative of increasingly high significance. Surprisingly, much of the extant literature relies solely on the $R^2$ value, which provides a weak or ambiguous standard when used as the sole criterion (King 1986).

We also compared results derived from the empirical data sets with nonscaling results obtained from a simulated (synthetic) set of independent and identically distributed (i.i.d.) uniform random variables $U_i$. As we demonstrate in the next section, a uniform random variable (r.v.) yields a set of baseline estimates that facilitate the interpretation of results derived from real data. A uniform r.v. *U* has the following distinguishing properties, which are different from a power law:

1. Every value $u \in U$ is equiprobable (i.e., a low frequency of high values, or a high frequency of low values, is not possible);
2. No scaling occurs (the c.d.f. $G(x)$ is monotonic, $d^2G/dx^2 = 0$); and
3. The fractal slope is equal to zero ($b = 0$). Formally, $b \to 0$ as $p(x) \to p(u)$, where $p(\cdot)$ is the p.d.f. for the r.v. *X* and the r.v. *U*, respectively.

In particular, the occurrence of the third property in empirical data is a sufficient condition for rejecting the research hypothesis ($H_r$: warfare dimension *X* scales with slope *b*, where $X = T$, $\mu$, or *D*) and accepting the null hypotheses ($H_0$: $X = U$), regardless of the associated $R^2$ value. Conversely, we accept the research hypothesis that *X* scales with slope *b* whenever $b \neq 0$, with high *t*-ratio, and the *F*-ratio is significant at $p < .05$.

## RESULTS

First, we examine results from the total set of all wars consisting of the combination of the interstate, extrastate, and civil war data (Cioffi-Revilla 2000b). These findings are presented in figure 2, which shows the power law plots for the time between onsets ($\tau$), Richardson magnitude

($\mu$), and duration ($D$) for wars of all magnitude (low and high). As shown in figure 2, some of the curves exhibit a less than perfect fit. Specifically, that segment of the plot containing the largest wars (i.e., highest magnitude range) does not appear to conform to the pattern exhibited by the remainder. This is especially true for fatalities and duration. This upper-range "bending" of the data at the bottom of these plots requires explanation and a separate analysis to determine if indeed these large wars conform to a power law with somewhat different parameters or to some other as yet unspecified pattern.

"Highest-magnitude wars" are operationally defined as those wars that rank within the upper decile (top 10 percent) of the distribution of fatalities, as shown in table 1. The cumulative number of fatalities produced by these twenty-four wars alone, the highest-magnitude outbreaks in the international system since 1816, totals approximately

TABLE 1. Largest International and Civil Wars Ranked by Fatalities (intensity), 1816–Present

| COW No. | War Name | Onset Year $\tau$ | Duration $D$ (days) | Fatalities $F$ | Richardson Magnitude $\mu = \log F$ |
|---|---|---|---|---|---|
| 139 | World War II | 1939 | 2,175 | 16,634,907 | 7.22 |
| 106 | World War I | 1914 | 1,567 | 8,578,031 | 6.93 |
| 652 | China CW | 1860 | 1,650 | 2,000,025 | 6.30 |
| 199 | Iran-Iraq | 1980 | 2,890 | 1,250,000 | 6.10 |
| 163 | Vietnamese | 1965 | 3,735 | 1,021,442 | 6.01 |
| 868 | Nigeria CW | 1967 | 906 | 1,000,000 | 6.00 |
| 784 | China CW | 1946 | 1,476 | 1,000,000 | 6.00 |
| 130 | Sino-Japanese | 1937 | 1,615 | 1,000,000 | 6.00 |
| 151 | Korean | 1950 | 1,130 | 909,833 | 5.96 |
| 778 | Spain CW | 1936 | 972 | 658,300 | 5.82 |
| 658 | USA CW | 1861 | 1,440 | 650,000 | 5.81 |
| 421 | Fr.-Indochinese | 1945 | 3,105 | 600,000 | 5.78 |
| 745 | Russia CW | 1917 | 1,026 | 502,225 | 5.70 |
| 880 | Pakistan CW | 1971 | 249 | 500,000 | 5.70 |
| 049 | Lopez | 1864 | 1,936 | 310,000 | 5.49 |
| 835 | Vietnam CW | 1960 | 1,836 | 302,000 | 5.48 |
| 381 | Spanish-Cuban | 1895 | 1,152 | 300,000 | 5.48 |
| 317 | Franco-Algerian | 1839 | 2,975 | 300,000 | 5.48 |
| 802 | Columbia CW | 1949 | 4,788 | 300,000 | 5.48 |
| 061 | Russo-Turkish | 1877 | 267 | 285,000 | 5.46 |
| 022 | Crimean | 1853 | 861 | 264,200 | 5.42 |
| 853 | Sudan CW | 1963 | 3,027 | 250,000 | 5.40 |
| 727 | Mexico CW | 1910 | 3,285 | 250,000 | 5.40 |
| 058 | Franco-Prussian | 1870 | 223 | 204,313 | 5.31 |

*Source:* Correlates of War Project, files cited in the Methods: Data section.
*Note:* CW = civil war. $N$ = 24 wars.

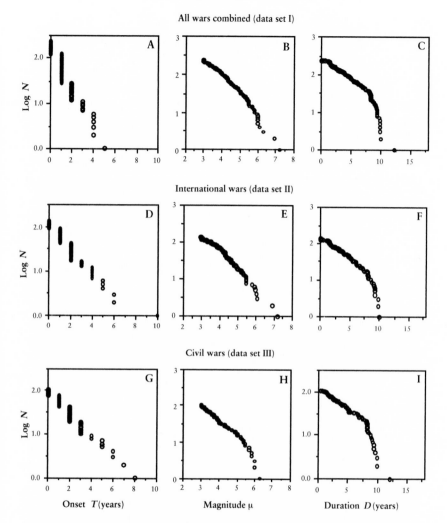

Fig. 2. Power law plots of onset $T$, magnitude $\mu$, and duration of warfare based on Correlates of War Project data. (Adapted from Cioffi-Revilla 2000a.)

39,070,276 or $\approx 4 \times 10^7$ fatalities. With few exceptions, this class of high-intensity wars corresponds to those recently highlighted by Clemens and Singer (2000). As a class, these highest-magnitude cases account for the overwhelming majority of loss of human life by organized violence in modern history.

Do the high-magnitude wars shown in table 1 obey power laws with respect to the three basic dimensions of onset, magnitude, and duration? This is an important puzzle to address, given the devastating nature of these wars and the special properties of power laws and related behavior. Note that while some of these dimensions of warfare have been studied from a stochastic perspective (extensive references found in Cioffi-Revilla 1998, 52–53), only the magnitude μ variable has been analyzed for power law behavior—the others have not. Lewis F. Richardson (1941, 1960) was the first to discover the power law behavior of warfare magnitude , based on his data set of "deadly quarrels." Surprisingly, no one in the past fifty years has investigated the power law behavior of warfare using data from the Correlates of War Project, nor has a focused study been conducted on warfare in the high-magnitude range.

With respect to the wars in table 1, a power law model of such wars would capture the pattern (first discovered by Richardson for "deadly quarrels") that there have been very few wars as intense as World War II, but there have been many wars with lower magnitude. In fact, table 1 shows that since 1816 there has been only one large war at magnitude 7, only seven wars at magnitude 6, and many more at magnitude 5. This is precisely the power law pattern, which is neither "normal" nor "uniform."

The purpose of this study is to analyze and compare the power law behavior present (or absent, as the case may be) in the occurrence of these highest-magnitude wars, as measured by the Correlates of War Project. Given the implications of power law behavior, the puzzling pattern of highest-magnitude warfare is of fundamental and enduring scientific interest.

Based on table 1, we used the following three data sets in this study.

Data set I. *Most lethal international wars* (N = 13), produced by combining interstate wars and extrastate wars, ranking them by fatalities, and taking those cases in the top decile of the distribution;

Data set II. *Most lethal civil wars* (N = 11), produced by ranking all the civil war cases by fatalities, and taking those cases in the top decile of the distribution; and

Data set III. *Most lethal wars* (N = 24), combining data sets I and II), produced by merging the largest international wars with the largest civil wars, rank ordering them by fatalities, and taking those cases in the top decile of the distribution.

Note that the war cases included in our third data set (see table 1), containing international wars and civil wars combined, most closely resembles Richardson's (1960; see also Wilkinson 1980) pioneering data set of "deadly quarrels"—but only the top decile of cases when ranked by magnitude. Our third data set also resembles, both in content and size, the recent Clemens and Singer combined sample of international wars and civil wars (2000).

Table 2 and figures 3 (a–c), 4, and 5 show the parameter estimates

TABLE 2. Scaling Parameter Estimates ($a$, $b$) for Power Laws of Onset $T$, Magnitude $\mu$, and Duration $D$ Dimensions of Largest-Scale Warfare, 1816–Present

| Warfare Dimension X | Intercept $a$ | Fractal Slope $b$ | N | $R^2$ | F | Power Law Plot |
|---|---|---|---|---|---|---|
| **I. Largest International Wars** | | | | | | |
| T | 1.28 | −0.05 | 12 | 0.91 | 96.48 | Figure 3A |
| | (19.86) | (9.82) | | | | |
| $\mu$ | 3.98 | −0.55 | 13 | 0.95 | 202.17 | Figure 3B |
| | (17.46) | (14.22) | | | | |
| D | 1.27 | −0.10 | 13 | 0.91 | 115.86 | Figure 3C |
| | (22.75) | (10.76) | | | | |
| **II. Largest Civil Wars** | | | | | | |
| T | 0.88 | −0.02 | 10 | 0.85 | 45.11 | Figure 4A |
| | (16.51) | (6.72) | | | | |
| $\mu$ | 6.94 | −1.09 | 11 | 0.95 | 165.54 | Figure 4B |
| | (14.27) | (12.87) | | | | |
| D | 1.25 | −0.10 | 11 | 0.98 | 608.69 | Figure 4C |
| | (48.53) | (24.67) | | | | |
| **III. Largest Wars (international and civil combined)** | | | | | | |
| T | 1.37 | −0.06 | 23 | 0.97 | 736.05 | Figure 5A |
| | (70.93) | (27.13) | | | | |
| $\mu$ | 5.31 | −0.74 | 24 | 0.95 | 448.11 | Figure 5B |
| | (25.94) | (21.17) | | | | |
| D | 1.54 | −0.11 | 24 | 0.96 | 486.23 | Figure 5C |
| | (52.33) | (22.05) | | | | |
| **IV. Uniform Random Data (Monte Carlo simulation)** | | | | | | |
| U | 3.20 | 0.00 | 1,000 | 0.77 | 3,317.7 | Figure 6 |
| | (250.19) | (57.60) | | | | |
| **V. Richardson's Deadly Quarrels** | | | | | | |
| $\mu$ | 4.13 | −0.54 | 5 | 0.997 | 874.61 | Richardson |
| | (43.27) | (29.57) | | | | (1960, 149, fig. 4) |

Source: Calculated by the authors.
Note: $t$-ratios of estimates are given in parentheses.
All estimates of $a$ and $b$, as well as values of $R^2$ and $F$, are significant, $p < .01$. Most estimates are highly significant, $p < .001$, as seen from the high $t$-ratios given in parentheses below the values of $a$ and $b$.
$N = 5$ for Richardson's deadly quarrels because of aggregation.

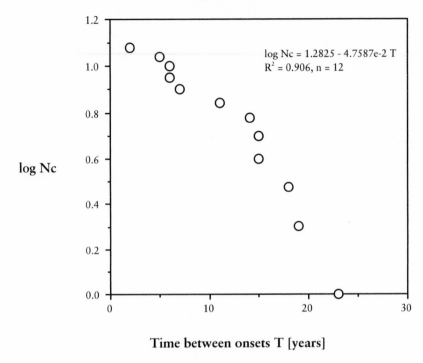

$$\log Nc = 1.2825 - 4.7587e\text{-}2\ T$$
$$R^2 = 0.906, n = 12$$

**Time between onsets T [years]**

Fig. 3a.   Time between onset of largest international wars

obtained for power law models of warfare dimensions $T$, $\mu$, and $D$, that is, equations (1) and (2). The table reports results for each of the five different samples of war cases described earlier in the Methods section. Figure 6 shows the results from the Monte Carlo experiment with uniformly distributed random data.

Section I in table 2 (and fig. 3a–c) reports results for the thirteen most lethal international wars, or top decile of international wars. Section II (and fig. 4a–c) shows findings for the eleven most lethal civil wars, or top decile of civil wars. Section III (and fig. 5a–c) reports results for all twenty-four most lethal wars combined, simultaneously the largest sample examined in this study and the wars in the top decile listed in table 1. For reference, section IV in table 2 provides baseline estimates generated by the Monte Carlo simulation. Recall that $U$ obeys a power law with zero fractal slope ($b = 0$) and, consequently, no scaling (n.s.). Note that the $R^2$ value for the random variable $U$ is the lowest (0.77) albeit significant, a clear indication that the coefficient of determination should never be used alone to assess the goodness of fit of a power law.

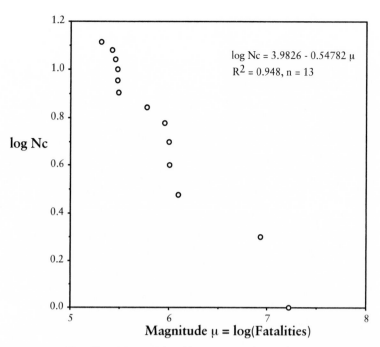

Fig. 3b.   Magnitude of largest international wars

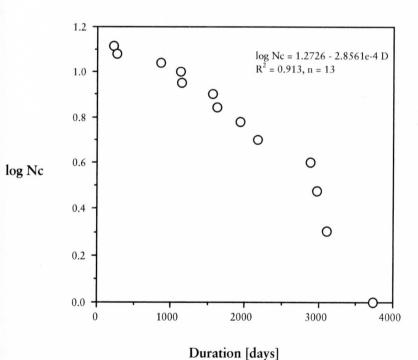

Duration [days]

Fig. 3c.   Duration of largest international wars

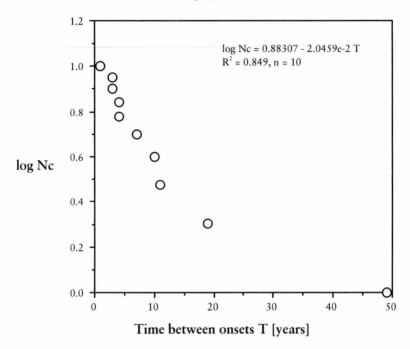

Fig. 4a.   Onset of largest civil wars

Section V in table 2 provides an additional set of comparative statistics, consisting of the original scaling parameter estimates first discovered by Richardson (1948, 1960) for cases of "deadly quarrels." Recall that the composition of the Richardson sample ($N = 282$ deadly quarrels) most closely resembles our third sample, because both combine international and civil wars, although our sample size is smaller ($N = 24$ highest-magnitude wars).

For each sample (data sets I–V) and warfare dimension ($T$, $\mu$, $D$), table 2 also reports the corresponding estimate for the intercept $a$, the fractal slope $b$, the sample size $N$, the variance explained by the power law, or coefficient of determination $R^2$, the F-ratio, and a reference to the corresponding power law plot (figs. 3–6) for each war dimension. Note that all estimates are OLS and ML, because the linearized form, equation (2), of the power law, equation (1), was used for each dimension. In each sample the estimates for onset time $T$ have $N - 1$ cases, not the original $N$ in the decile, because one case is lost when calculating war outbreaks between consecutive events.

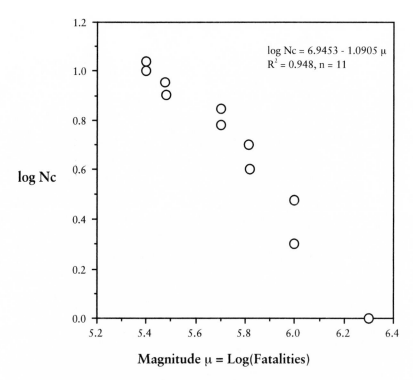

**Magnitude μ = Log(Fatalities)**

Fig. 4b.   Magnitude of largest civil wars

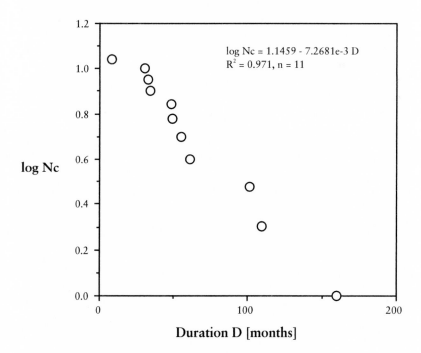

**Duration D [months]**

Fig. 4c.   Duration of largest civil wars

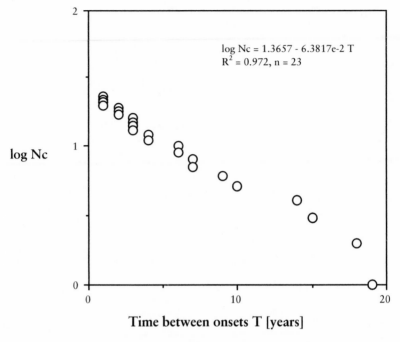

Fig. 5a.   Onset of all wars combined (international and civil)

## DISCUSSION

In this section we discuss the main results obtained in this study, some implications for current ideas on high-magnitude warfare, and some directions for future research.

### *Findings*

Is high-magnitude warfare governed by power laws? The main findings produced by this study can be summarized as follows.

*Power law behavior.*   Every empirical estimation (table 2, sections I–III) yielded positive results, as shown by the high statistical significance of the estimates. Specifically, all estimates of $a$ and $b$ (note the consistently high $t$-ratios in parentheses below each estimate), as well as the $F$ and $R^2$ values are significant ($p < .05$), in most cases *highly* significant ($p < .001$). This pattern across different samples of highest-magnitude wars (international, domestic, and combined), as well as different dimensions

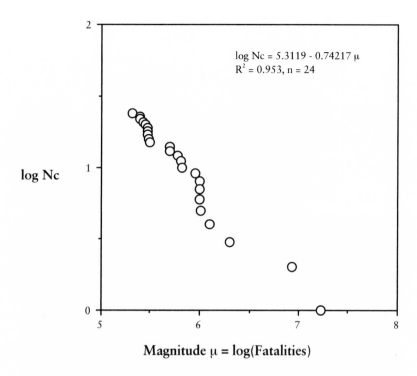

$$\log Nc = 5.3119 - 0.74217\,\mu$$
$$R^2 = 0.953,\ n = 24$$

Fig. 5b.   Magnitude of all wars combined (international and civil)

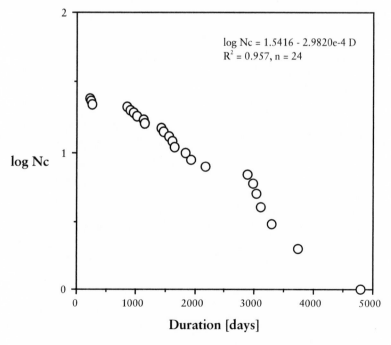

$$\log Nc = 1.5416 - 2.9820e\text{-}4\ D$$
$$R^2 = 0.957,\ n = 24$$

Fig. 5c.   Duration of all wars combined (international and civil)

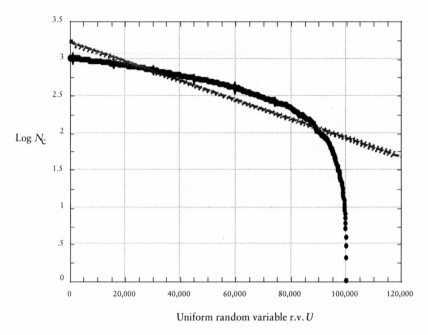

Uniform random variable r.v. *U*

Fig. 6. Power law plot for *N* = 1,000 synthetic realizations of a uniform random variable *U*(0, 100,000)

(onset, magnitude, and duration) provides the strongest confirmation so far for the power law behavior of largest-magnitude warfare.

Yet the parameters for the highest magnitude wars differed from those of the full set reported by Cioffi-Revilla (2000b) (compare figs. 2 and 3–5). This was especially true for fatalities and duration. Why? There are two explanations for this phenomenon. One answer may lie in the "democratization" of war. As a war continues without end in sight, fatalities grow in number, and an increasing proportion of the population is drawn into the war. Germany between 1916 and 1918 is a classic case in point, with its strikes, industrial sabotage, severe food shortages, and naval mutiny. Indeed, it is inconceivable that the Weimar Republic could have emerged in such liberal form (for its time) without the revolutionary sentiments sweeping the country in reaction to the war. National policy during such a high-magnitude war is increasingly affected by large segments of the population that seek to end the war or at least to reduce the casualty level. Wars with potentially shorter durations and lower casualty levels are less subject to such popular influences and are found to the left of the plots in figure 2. Those that have been "democratized" (e.g., also Vietnam) are found on the bottom right of the plot.

Another explanation for the steeper slope of these highest-magnitude power laws lies in the empirical finite size of the international system producing these severe events: there are just so many belligerents, so many possible war alliances, so much armament, so many combat fronts that can be managed simultaneously, and so forth. As a result, the theoretically possible largest magnitudes of warfare are never actually realized due to the underlying finite dynamics.

*Warfare magnitude scales.* Every set of estimates for the power law of warfare magnitude $\mu$ shows a close fit, with highly significant departure from the uniform distribution (compare empirical $b$ slopes for $\mu$ with the Monte Carlo slope in table 2, section IV), indicative of strong scaling behavior. This finding is also consistent across samples I, II, and III. Recall that, as noted in the Methods section, the scaling property is not additive—because it is nonlinear—so results from data set III (all wars combined) would not necessarily scale just because results for I (international wars) and II (civil wars) show scaling. This finding therefore replicates and confirms Richardson's original discovery for "deadly quarrels," extending it to all types of high-magnitude warfare measured by the COW data: interstate wars, extrasystemic wars, and civil wars. All high-magnitude wars, not just deadly quarrels, obey the property of self-similarity. Thus, for example, we would expect "major power wars" (Levy 1983), as well as high-magnitude warfare in earlier international systems (Cioffi-Revilla 1991, 1996; Cioffi-Revilla and Lai 1995, 2001; Eckhardt 1992) to follow similar scaling patterns with respect to magnitude.

*Onset and duration have weaker scaling symmetry.* For both onset and duration the fractal slope estimate is closer to 0, even if the coefficients of determination $R^2$ and $F$ are high, meaning that the distributions of onset and duration values are closer to a uniform distribution (somewhat weaker scaling). Recall that a uniform random variable $U$ has fractal slope equal to 0. Thus, the temporal variables of high-magnitude warfare, involving the timing of onset and termination, follow a more haphazard pattern with greater uncertainty or higher entropy. This finding is consistent with earlier studies that have emphasized the stochastic nature of war onset and duration (Cioffi-Revilla 1998; Midlarsky 1981). Interestingly, the stochastic approach to the study of war onset was also pioneered by Richardson (1941, 1945a, 1945b, 1960). Our results can now be used to link extant probabilistic models with these new scaling models from complexity theory.

*Implications*

What does the power law behavior of highest-magnitude warfare imply? The preceding results, together with the concepts from complexity theory discussed earlier, hold the following new implications for high-magnitude warfare in the international system.

*Emergence.* The power law results from this study hold in the aggregate, regardless of the individual type of war (international or civil), the specific epoch of occurrence (in this case nineteenth century or twentieth century), the identity of participant actors (major powers or minor powers), the nature of decision making involved (rational or not), or other individual characteristics (for instance, weapons technology or firepower). Power law behavior is a global, emergent property of the class of high-magnitude wars. Significantly, this property supports an early claim by J. David Singer, other collaborators in the Correlates of War Project (Singer 1961b; Singer and Small 1972), and other independent researchers (Horvath 1965; Horvath and Foster 1963; Weiss 1963; Wesley 1962) upholding the autonomy of systemic-level theories and models, independent of lower-level explanations. The existence of power laws for high-magnitude wars strongly supports such a claim.

*Evolution.* The bending of the curves in figure 1 and different power law parameters found in figure 2 suggest an evolutionary pattern to modern warfare. The highest magnitude wars in table 1 (ranked by magnitude) are almost exclusively twentieth-century wars. Indeed, of the top fourteen wars in that table, only two occurred in the nineteenth century. Power law behavior, or what is essentially the same thing—fractal patterns of expansion—have been associated with the rise of states and, under somewhat different conditions, with their dissolution (Midlarsky 1999). Thus, the temporal evolution of warfare to higher magnitudes parallels other societal processes, also intrinsic to state behavior. Perhaps this evolutionary process may have reached a critical point in mutating to such a highly destructive level that it may have become all but obsolete, especially among major powers (Mueller 1989).

*Long peace.* Some researchers have found the recent "long peace" remarkable (Kegley 1991). However, given the property of scaling for the onset $T$ of high-magnitude warfare, as demonstrated by results in table 2 (sections I, II, and III), it follows that every now and then there *must* be a very high value (realization) of $T$, or long peace between high-magnitude onsets. The power law predicts this phenomenon in terms of scaling and self-similarity, given that high-magnitude warfare conforms to power laws. For high-magnitude international wars (fig. 3A), our model predicts an upper bound $T_{max} \approx$ 25–30 years, meaning that this is the longest peace that can be expected for this kind of warfare.

*Hierarchical equilibrium.* Our results parallel earlier findings regarding the hierarchical equilibrium nature of warfare in the international system, at least in recent epochs (Midlarsky 1988). Scaling is a form of hierarchical equilibrium. Conversely, hierarchical equilibrium also scales.

*Early warning and conflict management.* Another concern of the Correlates of War Project has been the design and calibration of early warning (EW) indicators. Our results produce some progress in this area, given the strong scaling patterns reported in this study. More specifically, the onset, magnitude, and duration patterns demonstrated in this study can be used in conjunction with EW indicators derived from probabilistic studies, such as distribution moments and hazard force models (Cioffi-Revilla 1998). For example, based on the ratio $a/b$ from the estimates in table 2, or by finding the intercept $(x_{max}, 0)$ of the fitted lines with the horizontal axes in figures 3–5, it is possible to project maximum values of magnitude and duration for each type of high-magnitude event. Estimates of maxima can then be used in calculations of risk assessment and emergency mitigation preparedness. Although preparedness policies may be futile in the case of purely international events, international agencies may be able to profit from such assessments in the case of high-magnitude civil wars. Our theoretical analysis indicates that civil wars yield a maximum of $\mu_{max} \approx 6.4 \approx 2.3 \times 10^6$ fatalities, just slightly higher than the 1860 Chinese (internationalized) civil war. Beyond such a level we would observe a violation of the power law, which is unlikely. Confidence intervals can also be calculated from table 2.

### Further Research

This study suggests a number of potentially fruitful research directions, given the nature of high-magnitude warfare and power laws.

*Long-range data.* An important extension of power law analysis is to long-range warfare data covering earlier historical periods and a greater variety of belligerents (Cioffi-Revilla 1991, 1996, 2000; Midlarsky 2000a). When did high-magnitude warfare begin to scale? What were the characteristics of the first systems of belligerents that produced such phenomena? What is the relationship, if any, between the scaling pattern of warfare and other long-term social and environmental processes? These and other research directions are being actively investigated in the Long-Range Analysis of War (LORANOW) Project, which will shed new light on the power laws of high-magnitude warfare, especially when compared with parallel results obtained for modern data.

*Systematized mass murder.* Genocide, a topic not often examined systematically, may be explicable in part by extensions of this type of analysis. Genocides most often occur in tandem with high-magnitude warfare. Is it possible that such genocides also scale (Midlarsky forthcoming)? Future research on long-range patterns of warfare may reveal that distinct possibility.

*Theoretical analysis.* A variety of theoretical implications can be derived from equations (1) and (2), none of which can be addressed here due to space limitations. For example, different values of the fractal slope $b$ hold different implications for the self-similarity property, as could be demonstrated by calculating the wavelet transformations of each series in the COW or LORANOW data. Another direction for future theoretical research is the relationship between equivalent probabilistic and scaling treatments of the same class of high-magnitude wars. For example, the relationship between the power laws given by equations (1) and (2) and the corresponding set of hazard force equations is not intuitive, but such a link should exist and is important for a better understanding of the underlying dynamics of extreme events such as high-magnitude wars. This type of formal theoretical analysis can be especially fruitful and insightful when founded on empirically tested models, as is now increasingly the case for power laws of warfare.

*A driven-threshold-systems conjecture.* Cioffi-Revilla and Rundle (1999) have conjectured that wars and other large-scale events in a driven-threshold system (DTS), particularly high-magnitude wars, represent extreme events or coherent structures characteristic of a multiscale system in nonequilibrium conditions. Accordingly, a high-magnitude war, such as an event $\mu > 5.0$ in the COW data, is caused by a critical phase transition, which in turn results from the nucleation of a high-magnitude metastable state when the DTS enters a bifurcation set. Onset of the extreme event is caused by the growth of space-time correlations that can be observed in macroscopic COW data. Such a DTS theory would provide a new dynamic explanation for the occurrence of scaling in warfare.

*Computational modeling and simulated data.* Recent advances in agent-based simulation models of international processes (Cederman 1997, 2001; Hoffmann 2003; Min, Lebow, and Pollins 2003) will soon permit in-depth comparative analysis of similarities and differences between empirical data and synthetic or simulated data. Do agent-based simulations of international processes wherein warfare, conquests, dis-

26

integration, and other phenomena occur also give rise to power laws and scaling? If not, what would be required in terms of additional rules to observe the type of scaling behavior that we have demonstrated for warfare in the real world? If scaling does occur in such simulations, to what extent does it compare with the known features of empirical scaling patterns?

These and other puzzles in the research frontier of the scientific study of war await future investigation. No doubt the Correlates of War Project data, as well as many of its concepts, hypotheses, and methods, will continue to play a key role in advancing our understanding of the causes of war and the conditions for peace.

## SUMMARY

This study investigated the scaling and fractal properties of highest-magnitude warfare in the international system, as measured by the Correlates of War data files on international and civil wars. After describing the general characteristics of power laws and defining the relevant class of extreme events—wars in the top decile of the intensity distribution in terms of fatalities—we explained our empirical procedure for testing power laws on COW Project war data. Our findings demonstrated the strong presence of power laws across all types of high-magnitude wars (international wars, civil wars, and wars in general) for three different dimensions of warfare (onset, magnitude, and duration). Different parameters for the total set of wars, on the one hand, and highest-magnitude wars, on the other, reflect both the "democratization" and "finiteness" of war in the latter category and the evolution of warfare to virtually unsupportable levels. These findings therefore replicate Richardson's original discovery of magnitude scaling for "deadly quarrels" and extend that discovery to a more diverse set of conflicts and different dimensions of warfare, not just magnitude. The fact that warfare shows significant temporal-magnitude scaling holds not just intrinsic importance as a general covering law, in the sense of Hempel, but also has a set of implications on emergence, the so-called long peace phenomenon, and conflict management and mitigation policies.

# A NEURAL NETWORK ANALYSIS
# OF MILITARIZED DISPUTES, 1885–1992
## Temporal Stability and Causal Complexity

*Monica Lagazio and Bruce Russett*

Great progress has been made in predicting and explaining interstate conflict. Improved data, theory, and methods all deserve credit. Yet much remains to be done. First, whereas many variables (e.g., geographical proximity, relative power, alliances, political regime type, economic interdependence) have important effects, even the most successful multivariate analyses leave much of the variance in conflict behavior unaccounted for, due to inadequate data, specification, or theory, or simply random variation. Consequently, questions arise about the predictive power of such analyses. Can we identify, with enough accuracy for policy purposes, those relationships very likely or very unlikely to experience militarized disputes? Can we reduce the number of false negatives and false positives? Second, interstate conflicts are complex phenomena often displaying nonlinear and nonmonotonic patterns of interaction. Those complexities are hard to model. Finally, there are questions about whether causal or predictive relationships are stable across time and space. One such question is whether democracy reduced the risk of interstate conflict throughout the twentieth century (Thompson and Tucker 1997; Maoz 1998; Russett and Oneal 2001) or its effect was limited to the Cold War era (Gowa 1999) due to particular conditions like ideological rivalry, bipolarity, or nuclear weapons. Some early COW analyses (e.g., Singer and Small 1968a) also emphasized nineteenth- and twentieth-century systemic differences.

Recent innovations have employed neural network analysis, a mathematical technique especially suitable to the interactive, nonlinear, and contingent relations across the variables that may trigger militarized interstate disputes (Schrodt 1991; Beck, King, and Zeng 2000). As a descriptively predictive rather than overtly theoretical tool, neural network analysis does not require rigid a priori assumptions on the mathematical nature of such complex relationships as do commonly used multivariate statistical techniques (Garson 1991; Zeng 1999). Moreover, it provides a clear answer to questions about predictive accuracy, with measures of the percentage of correct predictions both for dyads that actually experienced disputes and those that did not. And it readily lends itself to analyses whereby one can inductively establish a pattern of regularities in a data set for one time period (e.g., the Cold War era) and then measure how accurately that empirically derived pattern of regularities postdicts to disputes, and their correlates or causes, in a data set for another period (e.g., the decades preceding the Cold War).

To assess the possibility of uncovering durable conflict dynamics with a complex model we develop and test a neural network model of Cold War interstate conflicts, then test its performance on data covering more than a century (1885–1992). Since predictive accuracy is a major criterion by which models are assessed, our exercise can reveal the extent to which the Cold War causal structure is representative of earlier historical contexts. Thus the first of our three goals for adding to existing neural network analyses of international conflict is to discover whether the process at work in determining interstate conflicts during the Cold War was a consequence of specific systemic conditions, such as East–West confrontation or U.S. hegemony, or whether some complex regularities at the dyadic level were characterizing conflict outcomes. We find, rather, that much the same regularities exist in the pre–Cold War era. Using many data sets originating in the COW Project, we can correctly predict 82 percent of militarized disputes and 72 percent of nondisputes in the Cold War era and nearly 65 percent of disputes and nondisputes in the pre–Cold War decades, with economic interdependence, democracy, and international organizations providing strong input to the predictions in both periods.

Another extension of previous work is to further develop the methods of neural network analysis for international conflict. Schrodt's (1991) and Garson's (1991) first efforts to use this technique in political science exposed two major drawbacks. One is that neural networks are not efficient classifiers of rare events, because they are biased toward the modal value (the most common value in the output). This can be a serious problem in large-$N$ conflict analysis as militarized disputes are indeed rare events, with 95 percent of observations usually coded as zero. In addition, it is hard to comprehend the causal model that the trained neural networks have internally constructed. To address the issue of rare events' prediction in neural models, we propose a sampling technique called *balanced training with cross-validation strategy*. It makes use of the advantages of selecting on the dependent variable, while avoiding selection bias.

Our third goal is to offer three measures as guides to interpreting the relative influence of different variables on conflict. The different information provided by each generates insights into the complex regularities discovered by the network. Since our analysis uses variables from both realist and liberal theories, interpreting the network model also provides a test for hypotheses from the two theoretical perspectives.

The first two sections of this chapter consider why a neural network model is suitable for studying international conflict and then discuss the model. Next we focus on the analytical issues of rare event prediction in neural networks and use of the balanced training with cross-validation strategy as a solution for the rare event bias in neural networks. The fourth section briefly discusses the data utilized, and the final sections summarize the results. Much of the discussion of the methodological innovations must be technical. We nonetheless think these innovations are important, and that the results are substantively and theoretically interesting.

## WHY NEURAL NETWORKS IN CONFLICT ANALYSIS?

The COW Project has ranged over several levels of analysis. J. David Singer (1961b) initially endorsed the systemic level as most promising and expressed skepticism about the power of the nation-state level of analysis—a position shared, ironically, by a very different kind of scholar (Waltz 1979). Subsequently, Small and Singer (1976) expressed doubt about the value of a middle level of analysis between the systemic and state levels; that is, on pairs of states, or dyads. Notably they questioned the democratic peace hypothesis, a position Henderson too quickly endorses in this volume.[1] (Geller and Singer 1998, 85–96, might suggest some subsequent mellowing on this point.) Nevertheless, Singer was centrally involved in the origin and development of the militarized international dispute data set, which has proven one of the great achievements of the COW project. His early influence is evident in conceptualizing (Leng and Singer 1977) MIDs as bilateral interactions and in a more recent report on use (Jones, Bremer, and Singer 1996). Much of COW use of MIDs in the early years was predominantly descriptive and inductive in mapping characteristics of the international system and had an implicit assumption that the important relationships would be more or less linear. Recently, however, other COW associates (Maoz and Abdolali 1989; Bremer 1992) have made major innovations in theoretically driven use of MIDs at the dyadic level. This chapter extends that development, working further in what is now called the Kantian peace research program that extends the scope of dyadic influences from democracy to economic interdependence and international organizations. In so doing it looks intently at the implications of using neural network analysis to relax the assumption that key relationships are fundamentally linear.

In light of the dominance of statistical methods in conflict research, we need to consider the benefits that can result when neural network methodologies are applied to conflict data. Statistically trained political scientists may ask, why neural networks? Wouldn't simpler and more established multivariate statistical techniques do better? Answers to these questions can be articulated both from the methodological and theoretical levels.

First, neural networks can provide a powerful method to develop nonlinear and interactive models of militarized disputes, redressing the restrictive linear and fixed effect assumptions that have dominated the field.[2] Recent development in the liberal peace literature seems to indicate that the causal processes at work in interstate conflicts result from complex interactions. In recognition of these complex dynamics, Russett and Oneal (2001, 39) express doubt that individual causal relationships can be considered well in isolation. Peace may result from multiple and overlapping liberal behaviors, shaped by democracy and interdependence, which interact with the opportunities offered by the realist variables. A synthesis of Kantian and realist effects emphasizes an interpretation of constraints on states' willingness and ability to resort to violence. Beck, King, and Zeng (2000) similarly interpret the realist variables as creating a pre-scenario of low or high ex ante probability of military conflict from which the influence of the liberal variables is plucked. Or the effects of relative power on dispute outcomes—strong between nondemocracies—may be much weaker when democracies settle their disputes (Gelpi and Griesdorf 2001). Other studies assume that a reciprocal relationship, or feedback loop, runs between democracy and interdependence. Democratic institutions may indirectly increase the weight of the economic constraints on militarized behavior by empowering economic interest groups in the state. Another link may run as interdependence in turn increases the number of international political constraints. High levels of dyadic trade often create a need for new institutions to manage and stabilize the existing commercial relations. These new institutions add more restraints on militarized behavior.

This interactive and nonlinear perspective can be fully embraced by neural network models. By superposing multiple nonlinear functions and avoiding a priori constraints on the functional nature of the data examined, multilayer networks can construct different causal structures in the same model and combine them together in a systematic way. Indeed, a wide variability of the inputs' effect is allowed, while avoiding the independence assumption of the random effect model (Beck, King, and Zeng 2000, 25).

Second, neural networks do not require independent observations, and thus they deal better with the suspected influences that militarized events exercise on each other (Sarle 1994). As Beck, Katz, and Tucker (1998) argue, the conflict history of a state can either positively or negatively affect the state's willingness to become involved in future conflict. To overcome this problem, they suggest that a control for the number of years that have elapsed from the most recent occurrence of a conflict should be used. However, that solution is problematic. While solving the independence problem, the year correction opens new issues. It rests on the assumption that the effect of the other explanatory variables and time can be separated. This seems very unlikely for some of the important variables in conflict analysis. For instance, liberal theory expects interdependence to fall with the outbreak of a conflict, but to rise over time after a conflict ends.

Finally, model formulation in neural networks is shaped not only by theoretical but also empirical considerations, making the neural methodology a middle-range approach between deductive and inductive model building. This characteristic of neural networks should not be regarded as a negative aspect. The increasing number of factors and reciprocal interactions that may characterize the causal structure of international conflicts makes the development of fully specified theories more difficult.[3] As result, some aspects of the causal interaction may remain undefined. What is left unexplained by the theory can be "discovered" by the neural networks themselves since their flexible methodology enables them to learn from the empirical data. Without deemphasizing model building based on first principles, neural modeling can strengthen theory building by supporting a constant interplay between theory and data.

### THE NEURAL NETWORK MODEL

Backpropagation multilayer networks implement a nonlinear mapping, or a function approximation, from a set of $n$ input, $x_1, x_2, \ldots, x_n$, to a set of $m$ outputs, $y_1, y_2, \ldots, y_m$. Although mapping is not new in quantitative studies, the way in which neural networks perform this input-output transformation represents an important development for mathematical models of complex input-output relations. In neural networks the complex relation between the inputs and outputs is modeled using a superposition of multiple nonlinear functions, represented by neurons. By increasing the number of functional transformations, the model can approximate any hypothetical relations between the selected explanatory and dependent variables. The key point is that the number of nonlinear functions, or neurons, need grow only as the complexity of the mapping itself grows (Hornik, Stinchcombe, and White 1990; Hornik and Stinchcombe 1992).

The major implication of using the flexible functional form provided by the superposition method is that the network functions become nonlinear functions of the network adaptive parameters, the weights $(w_j)$. Because of the complexity involved in the mathematical structure of the network, the procedure for determining the value of the parameters becomes a problem in nonlinear optimization, which requires finding efficient learning algorithms to reduce the network overall error function (Bishop 1996). Our network model utilizes the backpropagation algorithm to calculate the weight values. The backpropagation process is relatively simple in concept. The objective is to compare the *actual output* calculated by the network with the *target output,* given in the training set, each time the network is presented with a sample case. This comparison produces an error value in the output layer that is calculated as a function of the weights. Then the error is propagated backward to the previous layer and used to adjust the weight values in each nonlinear function in order to reduce the difference between the actual output and the target output.[4] Each time a new comparison is made, the error is further reduced.[5]

Besides selecting the learning algorithm, another issue in neural network modeling is how to determine the optimum network architecture. This mainly involves deciding the number and type of functional transformations needed. Selecting the appropriate network architecture is an important part of model building. A higher number of functions (neurons) will produce highly flexible networks, which may learn not only the data structure but also the underlying noise in the data. Too few neurons will produce networks that are unable to model complex relationships. In addition to deciding the number and type of activation function for the network, other parameters need also to be selected. Because of the number of parameters involved in the selection process, choosing the appropriate network architecture is a multicriterion search problem. To perform a global search through the space of possible combinations

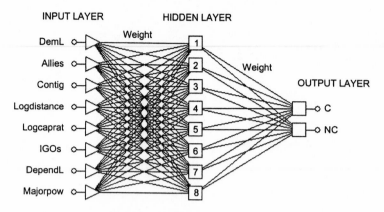

Fig. 1.   Diagram of the best neural network configuration

we adapt a genetic algorithm that uses a Darwinian model of evolution (Holland 1992; Davis 1991). The genetic algorithm was used to calculate the number of hidden layers and hidden neurons, best activation functions, and values of the learning rate, $\eta$, and momentum, $\alpha$.[6] The training patterns were entered in a shuffled order, and the training was repeated ten times to avoid bias.[7] The genetic algorithm found that the optimal configuration is a multilayer neural network with one input layer, one hidden layer, and one output layer. The input and hidden layers contain eight processing units each, with two in the output layer. The hidden units utilize the *tanh* function, whereas the output units adopt the logistic function.[8] Finally, the networks perform better using a learning rate and momentum equal to 0.7. Figure 1 provides a schematic representation of the optimal configuration. The appendix presents the genetic algorithm optimization process and its results.

### *Neural Network Models for Rare Events: A Balanced Training Set with Cross-Validation*

Interstate conflict data are often coded as binary dependent variables, with zero as by far the most common value. This implies that a data set of such events will be characterized by an unbalanced dependent variable, with important consequences for the analysis and prediction of interstate disputes with neural network models as with other multivariate models. In such rare event domains the estimated event probability may be so small as to make efficient event prediction very difficult (King and Zeng 2000). Unbalanced data sets also affect the perform-

34

ance of neural network models. The learning process that neurally based models use to update their weight estimates is biased toward commonly encountered (modal) values in the training sample (Garson 1998, 88). Consequently, practical strategies need to be developed, during the training phase, to improve the neural networks' prediction ability for rare events.

The neural network literature has given little attention to the rare event problem. Few attempts have been made to address it, and the results have not been very successful. Schrodt's (1991) experimental work on conflict data utilizes a replication strategy to increase the number of conflict cases in the training set. It does increase prediction in the training set, but at the cost of reducing the model's ability to correctly classify new cases. What is missing is a correction strategy to reduce the bias produced by intentionally selecting training cases on the dependent variable.

To develop a practical procedure that increases accuracy in the neural network classification of rare events, we extend a strategy suggested by King and Zeng (2000) for logistic regression models to the neural network approach. This solution focuses on selecting data on the basis of the dependent variable (endogenous stratified sampling) while at the same time using a statistical correction (prior correction) for the logistic estimates to avoid selection bias. In the neural network analysis, instead of directly correcting the estimates, as Beck, King, and Zeng (2000) suggest, the correction mechanism is provided indirectly by the cross-validation set. However, both corrections rely on the same principle, which is based on prior information about the incidence of the rare event in the population, $\tau$.

As with any form of data analysis, the meaningfulness of a neural network prediction depends heavily on the extent to which the relevant explanatory variables are selected and included among the network input. If important explanatory variables are omitted, the neural network models cannot produce meaningful predictions. Assuming that the important explanatory variables for the classification have been selected by the researcher and used as the network inputs, we can think of two reasons for poor performance by neural network classifiers that utilize unbalanced training sets: (1) the inadequate type of information that the unbalanced training set provides and (2) the way in which the learning algorithm, which is used during the backpropagation process, minimizes the prediction error and changes the weight values.

Regarding the first point, many political scientists (e.g., Maoz and Russett 1993, 627) suggest that most of the nonconflict cases provide the model with little information. The data on these dyads is often similar and repetitive, as many of the conditions allowing stability show little variation. More information lies where the action (conflict) is, since disputes are often preceded by changes in other patterns of international interaction. Moreover, since researchers commonly believe that conditions causing international conflicts are highly nonlinear and interactive, the effect of the explanatory variables (the neural network's inputs) may vary widely over the observations. Whereas the effect of many explanatory variables may be undetectable for most dyads—the nonconflict ones—it may be very substantial for the conflict cases.

Since the conflict observations display sensitive input-input and input-output effects, this sensitivity becomes key to understanding and predicting the likelihood of conflicts in the international context. Feeding the neural network with an unbalanced training set, heavily loaded with nonconflict dyads, runs the risk of overemphasizing a single output pattern (nonconflict). The network, in this case, is not exposed to all the possible input-output effects stored in the databases. As a result, the internal model constructed by the neural network during the training will be only partially representative of the much more complex "causal" model embedded in the data and so will be unable to generalize (Garson 1998, 87).

Another important contributor to poor classification performance in neural network models with unbalanced training sets derives from how the backpropagation algorithm works. As explained earlier, backpropagation is achieved in neural networks by an iterative process, as the network repeatedly tries to learn the correct output for each training pattern. During this learning phase, the weights are modified on the basis of error signals generated from the output learned by the network. Thus if the majority of the outputs used in the learning process belong to one class (nonconflict), the error minimization process will concentrate overwhelmingly on that class. The less frequent value of the output (dispute) will account for only minor changes in the network's weights. This negative process would be further strengthened by the fact that neural networks do not have a linear response to the input and are less sensitive to outliers (Schrodt 1991, 372). Indeed, the nonlinear functions used by the network to model the input-output relation have the effect of "squeezing" the values of the data in the training set, especially at the high and low ends of the data range, thus reducing the effect of outliers. Consequently, incidences of dispute, which are the outliers in the conflict data, will not produce dramatic change in the network's internal model even if the input-output effect that they reproduce is quite large.[9] Because few changes in the weight values are determined by the dispute output, and because of the nonlinear impact of the dispute dyads on the neural network's weights, the learning process in the backpropagation algorithm will be biased toward the modal values of the training set. Unless care is taken to construct training sets with a more balanced representation of the two output classes, the neural network models will be less useful in predicting rare events.

One obvious way to avoid an inadequate information flow to the network and an error minimization process that is biased toward the modal value is to adopt an endogenous stratified sampling for the training set, which is also known as choice-based or case-control design.[10] This sampling strategy focuses on selection within the range of the dependent variable. A predefined number of observations, for which the dependent variable is equal to one, is randomly selected. The same number of cases is also randomly chosen from all the observations with output equal to zero (the control), perfectly equalizing the two outputs in the training set. A perfectly balanced training set alone does not, however, provide the optimal solution. Selecting on the dependent variable is widely recognized as a possible source of biased conclusions.[11] A correction mechanism should be used, together with the balanced approach, so as to avoid biases that will produce the opposite effect of the unbalanced training set.

A way to integrate the equally important needs for a balanced training set and to correct against possible selection bias is to provide the network with prior knowledge of the actual distribution of classes' occurrence. This prior knowledge should be able to correct the weight estimates produced by the balanced training set without affecting the network's ability to learn equally from both classes. Unfortunately, it is hard to incorporate prior knowledge into neurally based classifiers (Barnard and Botha 1993). In neural networks, information about input-output relations is distributed across multiple weight values, making the direct correction of the weight with a priori probabilities of class membership nearly impossible.[12] Since it is so difficult to manipulate the weight values directly, we need new types of correction mechanisms that are both efficient and easy to apply. An alternative approach to incorporate prior knowledge is to use a cross-validation set reproducing the frequency of the rare event in the population, $\tau$.[13] This makes it possible to "correct" the value of all the weights in the network in a distributed way, while allowing the network to produce weight values that focus on both classes.

How does this cross-validation correction strategy work to intervene on the weight values calculated by the training set? The function of cross-validation is to stop the training when the prediction error in the cross-validation set, *MSE*, reaches a predefined local minimum.[14] Thus, when a balanced training set is used together with an unbalanced cross-validation set, a double divergent process on the error minimization calculation occurs. On the one hand, the error minimization process in the training will be shaped by both classes, since the training set is balanced. The network's search for the optimal weights would be executed on the basis of a minimal error that takes into consideration the correct prediction in both classes. On the other hand, an early stop in the training process is determined by the reduction of the error in the cross-validation sample. Since the more dominant class in the sample is the non-conflict class, training ends when the prediction in this class reaches its minimum error. The goal is to select the combination of weights that equally improves the prediction result on both classes but, at the same time, can offer the best prediction on the more dominant class of the population.[15]

By experimenting on the double levels of the error minimization process (one level supervising the weight change and the other determining the end of the training) the balanced training set with cross-validation correction strategy can solve some of the problems that rare event prediction, specifically conflict prediction, presents to neural network models.[16]

### VARIABLES AND ANALYSIS

The network inputs include MIDs as the dependent variable and eight dyadic independent variables. Our theoretical perspective is that of the Kantian research program, addressed to the system of directed and reciprocal relations among democracy, economic interdependence, international organizations, and militarized conflict or the lack thereof, as laid out in Russett and Oneal (2001). Consistent with the view that liberal states carry on relations with each other differently from their power-oriented relations with other states, the analysis includes five variables usually associated with realist analysis, and three Kantian variables. The realist variables include *Allies,* a binary measure coded 1 if the members of a dyad are linked by any form of military alliance. *Contig* is also binary, coded 1 if both states are geographically contiguous, and *Logdistance* is an interval measure of the distance between the two states' capitals. *Majorpow* is a binary variable coded 1 if either or both states in the dyad is a major power, and *Logcaprat* measures the dyadic balance of power on an interval scale. The first Kantian variable, *DemL,* is a 21-point scale for the level of democracy in the less democratic state in each dyad. *DependL* is a continuous variable measuring the level of economic interdependence (dyadic trade as a portion of a state's gross domestic product) of the less economically dependent state in the dyad. *IGO* measures the number of international organizations in which the two states share membership. Most of these measures (e.g., MIDs, alliances, contiguity, major power, capability, and IGOs) derive from conceptualizations of the COW project and are measured by COW. We lag all independent variables one year to make any inference of causation temporally plausible.[17]

Our data set is the population of politically relevant dyads for the pre–Cold War period (PCW), from 1885 to 1945, and the Cold War and immediate post–Cold War period (CW), from 1946 to 1992, as described extensively and used by Russett and Oneal (2001). For the first population, PCW, only the initial year of the two world wars, 1914 and 1939, is included in the data set. This restriction ensures that the analysis is not unduly influenced by World Wars I and II and by the absence of adequate trade data for the wartime and immediate postwar years.

We chose the politically relevant population (contiguous dyads plus all dyads containing a major power) because it sets a hard test for prediction. Omitting all distant dyads composed of weak states means we omit much of the influence that variables not very amenable to policy intervention (distance and national power) would exert in the full data set; by that omission we make our job harder by reducing the predictive power of such variables, but also make it more interesting. By applying the training and cross-validation sampling technique we show that a strong performance is achieved even when the analysis is restricted to the politically relevant group. By focusing only on dyads that either involve major powers or are contiguous, we test the discriminative power of the neural network on a difficult set of cases.[18] The neural network system is fed with only highly informative data since every dyad can be deemed to be at risk of incurring a dispute, yet it is harder for the network to discriminate between the two classes (dyad-years with disputes and those without disputes) because the politically relevant group is more homogeneous (e.g., closer, more interdependent) than the all-dyad data set. If the balanced training with cross-validation correction strategy outperforms the other techniques with these data, by providing models that can successfully generalize in different time frames, it should also be successful for researchers who wish to consider the entire population of dyads.[19]

The unit of analysis is the dyad-year. There are a total of 27,737 cases in the Cold War population, with 26,845 nondispute dyad-years and 892 dispute dyad-years. The pre–Cold War population comprises 11,686 cases, with 11,271 nondispute dyads and 415 dispute dyads. The dependent variable (*Dispute*), or network output, is 1 if a militarized interstate dispute (MID) was begun and 0 otherwise. Only dyads with no dispute or with only the initial year of the militarized conflict are included, since our concern is to predict the onset of a conflict rather than its continuation. Other investigations (e.g., Bennett and Stam 2000b; Russett and Oneal 2001) find substantial commonality between the influences on dispute initiation and dispute continuation, but it is best not to assume their similarity, so we limit ourselves to the former.

The CW data are used to generate three training sets (*Balanced Training, Balanced-Replicated Training,* and *Unbalanced Training*), five cross-validation sets (*CV prior correction I, CV prior correction II, CV no correction III, CV no correction IV,* and *CV no correction V*) and five testing sets (*CW Test I, CW Test II, CW Test III, CW Test IV,* and *CW Test V*) according to the different training strategies and their relative sampling rules. The size of these sets varies slightly for each training strategy, as more or fewer dyads are needed to satisfy sampling requirements. Another testing set, *PCW Test,* comprises the complete population of the pre–Cold War period. The training tests are used to fit the model through the backpropagation learning algorithm, the cross-validation tests determine the end of the training (fitting) process, and the error matrices of the testing sets measure the accuracy of each training strategy. Since one objective is to determine whether the pattern discovered by the neural networks for the Cold War period can also explain the pre–Cold War period, only CW data are used in the training and cross-validation set, while the PCW cases are used only as a testing set. The difference in accuracy between the CW and PCW testing sets, achieved by the different training strategies, gives us a measure of stability for the CW model. Similar accuracy for the two periods means that the relationships at work during the Cold War were already in place during the previous era.

The *Balanced Training* set contains a randomly predefined equal number of conflict and nonconflict cases. In the *Balanced-Replicated Training* set we replicated the number of conflict cases of the *Balanced Training* set once and then randomly selected an equal number of nonconflict cases to match the duplicated conflict observations.[20] Finally, the *Unbalanced Training* set comprises an uneven number of conflict and nonconflict cases randomly sampled from the CW population. This last training set is almost half of the entire CW population. By selecting such a large training sample we can show empirically that, quite differently from multivariate statistical techniques, in neural networks the rare event bias does not decrease in large samples.[21]

For the cross-validation phase we generated two sets (*CV prior correction I* and *CV prior correction II*) reproducing the class frequency in the CW population for use as prior correction for the two balanced training sets (*Balanced Training* and *Balanced-Replicated Training*). In this case, the nonconflict class represents 97 percent of the population, while the conflict class is only 3 percent. The remaining cross-validation sets (*CV no correction III, CV no correction IV,* and *CV no correction V*) provide no correction to the training since they equalize the two classes. These balanced cross-validation sets can test the performance of our correction strategy.

The CW testing sets contain the remaining dyads after the training and cross-validation sets were selected. There are no common cases in the training set, cross-validation set, and testing set, which are used together for each training strategy. Table 1 shows all the totals. To evaluate the performance of the three different training strategies, with and without the cross-validation correction, we compute the kappa and conditional kappa coefficients, $K_{hat}$ *statistic* and $K_{hatk}$ respectively (an estimate of kappa). Kappa analysis, a discrete multivariate technique, offers a comprehensive accuracy measurement for neural classifiers applied to

TABLE 1.   Summary of the Data Sets Used for the Neural
Network Simulations

| Data Set | C | NC | Total Cases |
|---|---|---|---|
| Balanced Training (Bal) | 564 | 564 | 1,128 |
| Balanced-Replicated Training (Rep) | 1,128 | 1,128 | 2,256 |
| Unbalanced Training (Unb) | 382 | 10,712 | 11,094 |
| | | | |
| CV prior correction I (used with the Balanced Training) | 10 | 312 | 322 |
| CV prior correction II (used with the Balanced-Replicated Training) | 19 | 625 | 644 |
| CV no correction III (used with the Unbalanced Training) | 92 | 2,682 | 2,774 |
| CV no correction IV (used with the Balanced Training) | 161 | 161 | 322 |
| CV no correction V (used with the Balanced-Replicated Training) | 322 | 322 | 644 |
| | | | |
| CW Test I (used with the Balanced Training with correction) | 318 | 25,969 | 26,287 |
| CW Test II (used with the Balanced Training without correction) | 167 | 26,120 | 26,287 |
| CW Test III (used with the Balanced-Replicated Training with correction) | 309 | 25,092 | 25,401 |
| CW Test IV (used with the Balanced-Replicated Training without correction) | 167 | 25,395 | 25,562 |
| CW Test V (used with the Unbalanced Training) | 418 | 13,451 | 13,869 |
| PCW Test | 415 | 11,271 | 11,686 |

rare event domains. While overall accuracy stresses the overall result of the classification by focusing only on the main diagonal of the classifier's error matrix, kappa analysis calculates how the accuracy is distributed across the individual classes. By considering both individual class accuracy and overall accuracy, kappa analysis does not bias accuracy evaluation toward the dominant class in the testing set as overall accuracy does.[22] Moreover, it is especially appropriate here because dispute data are not continuous and normally distributed (Jensen 1996, 250). Once the kappa and conditional kappa coefficient have been calculated, a pairwise test Z statistic is used to determine whether the prediction results of an error matrix are significantly better than a random result, as well as whether similar error matrices, which consist of identical classes but are the product of different classifiers, are significantly different.[23]

## RESULTS AND DISCUSSION

We initially discuss the results of the kappa analysis for all the training strategies, with and without the cross-validation correction, on the CW data set. We also show individual error matrices for each strategy to further support the kappa results.[24] Finally, we focus on the ability of the Cold War models, selected from the best training strategy, to postdict the pre–Cold War dyads. By comparing the accuracy between the CW and PCW testing sets, we test the hypothesis that the causal relationships triggering interstate conflicts have been stable over time.

Table 2 summarizes the results of the kappa analysis for the Cold War period, in the form of significance matrices.[25] Those matrices show all the Z values from comparing the kappa coefficients of the different

TABLE 2. Significance Matrix for Comparing the Training Strategies Using Kappa Analysis and the Cold War Testing Sets

| CW | CVBal | Bal | CVRep | Rep | Unb |
|---|---|---|---|---|---|
| KAPPA | 0.045 | 0.022 | −0.016 | −0.009 | 0 |
| VAR | 0.000009 | 0.000004 | 0.000002 | 0.000001 | 0 |
| CVBal | 15 | | | | |
| Bal | 6.38 | 11 | | | |
| CVRep | 18.39 | 15.51 | −11.31 | | |
| Rep | 17.08 | 13.86 | 4.04 | −9 | |
| Unb | 15 | 11 | 11.31 | 9 | 0 |

*Note:* The table also presents the Kappa coefficient and the variance for each training strategy. Bold Z values indicate a significant improvement in the performance of the training strategies at 95% confidence level (Z > 1.95). The bold values in the main diagonal indicate that the classification of the training strategy is worse than a random one at 95% confidence level (Z > 1.95).

training strategies (off-diagonal elements) two at a time, as well as the Z statistic that measures the significance of each individual classification (main diagonal elements). The tables also present the kappa coefficient and variance for each training strategy in the first two rows. If the Z value exceeds the critical value, $Z_{\alpha/2}$, then the classifications are significantly different, or, as with the Z values in the main diagonal, are worse than a random one. A better performance is given by the training strategy with the higher kappa coefficient.

The first two rows following the kappa coefficient and variance row show the result of the two balanced training techniques starting with the balanced training using the cross-validation prior correction (*CVBal*) and then the one without it (*Bal*). The balanced-replicated training follows, again initially utilizing the cross-validation prior correction (*CVRep*) and then without it (*Rep*). Finally, the result of the unbalanced training is shown (*Unb*). We use the acronyms C (conflict) and NC (nonconflict) in the conditional kappa matrices.

The importance of constructing a meaningful training set emerges clearly from the table 2 results. Three classifications, *CVRep, Rep*, and *Unb*, are statistically insignificant, since the Z values in the main diagonal are smaller than 1.95 (the critical value at $p < .05$), $Z = -11.31$, $Z = -9$, and $Z = 0$, respectively (significant values are in boldface). Only the two balanced training strategies (*CVBal, Bal*) are significantly better than a random classification. This underlines three important factors. First, balanced training is a key to produce robust classifications in backpropagation networks. Second, in backpropagation classifiers, rare event bias remains significant in large unbalanced samples. Finally, replication strategies are not efficient since they largely reduce the network's generalization ability. This is because the duplication of cases in the training sets leads the network to learn too well the training cases, so fitting data noise rather than data structure. And table 2 stresses another important result: *CVBal* performs statistically better than all the other training sets. Indeed *CVBal* also achieves better accuracy than *Bal* ($Z = 6.38$). This is empirical evidence that the cross-validation prior correction is effective in significantly reducing selection bias in balanced samples.

In table 3, the error matrix of the *CVBal* technique in the Cold War analysis shows that this training strategy achieves the highest individual class accuracy. It correctly predicts 82.4 percent of the militarized outcomes and 72.2 percent of the nonmilitarized outcomes during the Cold War period. Because it far less often fails to identify the politically costly and dangerous dispute dyads as nondisputes while still providing a high accuracy on the nondispute class, *CVBal* emerges as the best training strategy to adopt with rare event data in international relations.[26] Since

TABLE 3. Error Matrices of the Three Training Strategies with and without the Cross-Validation Prior Correction for the Cold War Testing Set

| CW/Method | CVBal | | Bal | | CVRep | | Rep | | Unb | |
|---|---|---|---|---|---|---|---|---|---|---|
| Output/Desired | C | NC | C | NC | C | NC | C | NC | C | NC |
| C | 262 | 7229 | 137 | 7778 | 73 | 18109 | 35 | 18172 | 0 | 0 |
| NC | 56 | 18740 | 30 | 18342 | 236 | 6983 | 132 | 7223 | 418 | 13451 |
| Class Accuracy | 82.39 | 72.16 | 82.03 | 70.22 | 23.62 | 27.83 | 20.96 | 28.44 | 0.00 | 100 |
| Overall Accuracy | 72.29 | | 70.30 | | 27.79 | | 28.39 | | 96.97 | |

these predictions are out-of-sample forecasting, they indicate that the interactive model developed by the neural network and the balanced with cross-validation correction strategy can extract much of the influences embedded in conflict data. Consequently, we believe that neural networks together with the balanced training with cross-validation correction constitutes a viable and efficient method to improve model forecasting ability in conflict analysis, especially analyses of pooled annual dyadic time-series data.

Finally, we address a key theoretical and substantive question: Are the patterns stable? The error matrices of *CVBal* for the PCW data set in table 4 show that the CW model provides a high level of accuracy for the pre–Cold War period too. As table 4 shows, postdiction of the pre–Cold War dyads is similar to the Cold War result (64.8 and 65.5 percent accuracy for the PCW dispute dyads compared with 82.4 and 72.2 percent for the CW ones). However, these results are deceptive since the PCW and CW testing sets are different in size. To prevent differences in sample size from influencing the result, we performed kappa and conditional kappa analysis together with a pairwise $Z$ test statistic on the *CVBal* result as a measure of normalized accuracy, thus making the PCW and CW error matrices directly comparable.

TABLE 4. Error Matrices of CVBal Strategy for the Pre–Cold War Testing Set

| PCW/Method | CVBal | |
|---|---|---|
| Output/Desired | C | NC |
| C | 269 | 3888 |
| NC | 146 | 7383 |
| Class Accuracy | 64.81 | 65.50 |
| Overall Accuracy | 65.48 | |

Table 5 summarizes the kappa and conditional kappa analysis results in the form of a significance matrix. Whereas the levels of accuracy for the two periods are similar, the overall performance of the CW model is *significantly better* on the pre–Cold War dyads ($Z = 2$), with the kappa coefficient for the PCW accuracy larger than for the CW (0.056 > 0.045). This is mainly because the class accuracy for the conflict dyads in the pre–Cold War years is substantially better than in the Cold War era ($Z = 2.21$) with the conditional kappa for the PCW being larger than the CW (0.03 > 0.023). However, while the model does substantially better in predicting disputes (avoiding false positives) in the pre–Cold War period, it loses some predictive ability regarding non-disputes (more false negatives). The accuracy for the CW nonconflict class is significantly better than for the PCW one, though the difference in performance is not as large as for the conflict dyads since, as mentioned before, PCW accuracy is better overall. In the case of the nondispute class $Z = 8.12$, this time the conditional kappa for CW nondisputes exceeds the PCW coefficient (0.454 < 0.754).

These findings lead to three important inferences. First, not only is the pattern of dyadic influence discovered by the networks for the Cold War disputes reasonably representative of the pre–Cold War context, those influences enabling conflicts were even stronger in the earlier period. Second, in relation to peace, the structure of influence was already in place in the pre–Cold War years, although showing slightly less strength. This slight difference in strength can be explained by the maturation of democratic institutions and the transformation of the economy from national to global in the twentieth century. Most likely, these two factors have increased the positive influence of democracy and economic interdependence, which was already coming into place late in the

**TABLE 5.** Significance Matrix for Comparing the CW and PCW Accuracy of the CVBal Training Strategy Using Kappa and Conditional Kappa Analysis

| CW/PCW | CW | PCW | CW_(C) | PCW_(C) | CW_(NC) | PCW_(NC) |
|---|---|---|---|---|---|---|
| KAPPA | 0.045 | 0.056 | 0.023 | 0.03 | 0.754 | 0.454 |
| VAR | 0.000009 | 0.000027 | 0.000002 | 0.000008 | 0.000888 | 0.001287 |
| CW | 15 | | | | | |
| PCW | 2 | 10.78 | | | | |
| CW_(C) | • | • | 14.67 | | | |
| PCW_(C) | • | • | **2.21** | 10.83 | | |
| CW_(NC) | • | • | • | • | 25.29 | |
| PCW_(NC) | • | • | • | • | **8.12** | 12.65 |

*Note:* The table also presents the Kappa coefficient and the variance for each training strategy. Bold $Z$ values indicate a significant improvement in the accuracy at 95% confidence level ($Z > 1.95$).

nineteenth century, in the subsequent years (Russett and Oneal 2001; Sachs 1998).

Finally, since the reduction in influence on peace does not match the increase in influence on disputes, the overall pattern fits the pre–Cold War years even better than it does the Cold War ones. As some differences do emerge in the strength of the effect, we next turn to the relative performance of individual predictor variables and whether they underline stability or difference.

## MODEL INTERPRETATION

We now interpret the causal model that the neural networks using the balanced with correction strategy developed during the training. Although valid indications about the causal structure can be offered by the following analysis, our task is difficult and, at this stage, should be regarded as tentative. Interpretation of the causal hypotheses represented by a trained neural network is a complex exercise for several reasons. First, neural network models encode their knowledge across hundreds or thousands of parameters (weights) in a distributed manner. These parameters embed the relationships between the input variables and the dependent output. The sheer number of parameters and their distributed structure make the task of extracting the network knowledge not an easy one. Second, the weight parameters of a multilayer network usually represent nonlinear and nonmonotonic relationships across the variables, making it difficult to understand both the relative contributions of each single variable and their dependencies. Thus, to extract a causal model developed by the trained network we utilize three different approaches. By doing so we can interpret the network model from single variable and dependency perspectives. We calculated three measures of input influence: a relative evaluation of the general influence of each input variable, the specific influence of the individual input variables on the network output, and the input relation factor of each input.

### General Influence of Inputs

The general influence measure, *GI*, provides an estimate of the relative overall influence exerted by each input variable on the output. It relies on the absolute value of the weight of the trained network. Inputs connected to the hidden and output units by weights of large absolute magnitude will have more relative influence than those inputs with smaller magnitudes. Since *GI* focuses on single input variables in isolation without taking their dependencies into account, it should be regarded as an approximate measurement. Following Howes and Crook (1999):

$$GI(x_i, net) = \frac{\sum_{j=1}^{h} \left|\left(w_{ji} \div \sum_{k=0}^{n} |w_{jk}|\right)v_j\right|}{\sum_{j=0}^{h} |v_j|} \tag{1}$$

with $x_i$ being the $i$ input variable, *net* referring to the network architecture, $w_{ji}$ being the weight from the $i$th input node to the $j$th hidden node, and $v_j$ giving the weight from the $j$th hidden node to the output node.[27] Because our network presents two output nodes, we compute two separate $GI$ values for each input node.

Table 6 reports the general influence results for the balanced with cross-validation correction network. Economic interdependence and democracy exert the greatest general influence on both the conflict and nonconflict outcomes (*DependL* = 0.173 for dispute and 0.213 for nondispute, *DemL* = 0.160 and 0.197, respectively). This supports the liberal thesis that the state with the lower level of interdependence and democracy in the dyad has the major impact on dyadic relationships. Another Kantian variable, *IGOs*, also has a high general influence value (0.154 for the conflict output and 0.188 for the nonconflict one), indicating that international organizations can constrain interstate behavior. Other variables that matter are *Logdistance* (0.142 for C and 0.174 for NC), *Allies* (0.136 for C and 0.167 for NC), and *Logcaprat* (0.131 for C and 0.161 for NC). Thus proximity, alliance, and power also play a part in providing opportunities and incentives for interstate action. Overall, the result supports theories first of the democratic peace, then the liberal peace of both democracy and economic interdependence, and finally the Kantian peace of democracy, trade, and IGOs. However, three realist variables, *Logdistance, Allies,* and *Logcaprat,* cannot be ignored. The relationship of democracy and interdependence and interstate conflicts is to some extent mediated by both the dyadic balance of power and geographical proximity. This supports Russett and Oneal's (2001) and Beck, King and Zeng's (2000) syntheses of liberal and realist in-

TABLE 6.  General Influence of the Network's Input Variables

| GI | DemL | Allies | Contig | Logdistance | Logcaprat | IGOs | DependL | Majorpower |
|----|------|--------|--------|-------------|-----------|------|---------|------------|
| C  | 0.160 | 0.136 | 0.066 | 0.142 | 0.131 | 0.154 | 0.173 | 0.038 |
| NC | 0.197 | 0.167 | 0.081 | 0.174 | 0.161 | 0.188 | 0.213 | 0.047 |

fluences. For example, proximity is positively related to both trade and the probability of disputes, so a failure to control for distance can readily produce the erroneous impression that trade causes conflict.

## Specific Influence of Inputs

The specific influence of inputs, *SI,* measures the degree to which each input variable contributes to the dependent output. Instead of relying on the weight value, *SI* compares the output of the network with the network's new output produced by a modified form of the input pattern. Using an approach similar to Saito and Nakano's (1998), we iteratively increase the value of one input variable in the training set by a small amount (initially 0.1 of a standard deviation from the mean, to keep the increases comparable across variables, then 0.3, and finally 0.5), while keeping all the other inputs unchanged.[28] Then we reinterrogate the network, record the difference in the output values as percentages, and then present the overall result as the average. Those input variables producing a large percentage change on the dependent output contribute significantly to the network's prediction. The measurement nevertheless should be regarded as an estimate, since the interdependence across variables means that no scheme of single ratings per input can reflect all the subtleties of the full situation.

Table 7 shows the *SI* of the eight input variables for the conflict and nonconflict outcome. In both cases, the input variables identified by the *GI* as the most significant are still the ones having the greatest general influence on the output. In addition, this time, *DependL* (*SI* = 23.77 and 25.65) and *DemL* (*SI* = 21.31 and 20.55) have the strongest *SI* value, for both the conflict and nonconflict outcomes. This means that small increases in values for the state with the lower economic dependence or democratic score move the conflict output toward the nonconflict outcome and make the nonconflict value more evident. Again this underlines that the degree of democracy and economic interdependence in the less constrained state in the dyad has a strong influence on the probability of conflict. *Logdistance* (15.55 and 15.50) and *IGOs* (12.83 and 12.57) follow, both for conflict and nonconflict dyadic outcomes. Greater geographical distance between states or a larger num-

TABLE 7. Specific Influence of the Network's Input Variables

| SI | DemL | Allies | Contig | Logdistance | Logcaprat | IGOs | DependL | Majorpower |
|----|------|--------|--------|-------------|-----------|------|---------|------------|
| C | 21.31 | 8.58 | 6.94 | 15.55 | 12.42 | 12.83 | 23.77 | 3.79 |
| NC | 20.55 | 8.46 | 6.84 | 15.50 | 11.21 | 12.57 | 25.65 | 3.70 |

ber of shared memberships in international organizations cuts the probability of conflict by nearly 16 percent and almost 13 percent, respectively. Conversely, the nonconflict probability increases almost exactly the same amount. Finally, another variable, *Logcaprat*, is also important from the *SI* perspective (12.41 and 11.21). Increases in the dyadic power ratio reduce the probability of conflict while increasing the chance of a peaceful outcome.

The *SI* measurements once more stress the influence of increasing economic interdependence and democracy on reducing the incidence of interstate disputes. The results also show the importance of two key realist variables: geographical proximity and power ratio. And as in the case of *GI*, the *SI* values indicate the need to hypothesize complex causal patterns of interaction across the variables deemed to trigger interstate disputes.

### Input Relation Factor

The input relation factor (*RF*) tries to uncover the dependencies across the input variables. An input variable may have a low *GI* and *SI* but a high *RF*. This means that input variable would not likely trigger the outcome, but it is important in enabling the other explanatory variables to do so. In other words, *RF* measures the degree to which an input variable is *necessary* for producing the network output, although it alone may not be *sufficient* to determine it. To calculate the *RF* of our eight input variables we developed a heuristic procedure, switching off one variable at a time in the Cold War and pre–Cold War testing sets by replacing its values with zero. We then calculated the deterioration in modeling performance by comparing the change in class accuracy between the test with all the active input variables and the ones with one input variable switched off.[29] Since the network learned the causal structure taking in consideration all the relationships across all the variables, the deterioration in accuracy indicates the enabling power of the switched-off input variable.

The *RF* values for the eight variables produced by the CW and PCW tests in tables 8 and 9 identify the same variables as the main ones, although the model deterioration for the PCW period is higher. This

TABLE 8. Input Relation Factors for the Cold War Years

| CW | All | DemL | Allies | Contig | Logdistance | Logcaprat | IGOs | DependL | Majorpower |
|----|-----|------|--------|--------|-------------|-----------|------|---------|------------|
| C | 82.39 | 6.50 | 62.58 | 88.05 | 41.82 | 52.51 | 66.99 | 0 | 73.90 |
| NC | 72.16 | 94.66 | 80.88 | 54.56 | 86.42 | 86.81 | 75.66 | 100 | 75.84 |

shows that the *interactive* pattern in the two periods is similar, but with stronger effects for several variables in the pre–Cold War period. The liberal variables make the most difference on the conflict outcome. *DependL* has the greatest *RF* (low *RF* values indicate high impact). When this input variable is switched off, the model's performance drops hugely, from the original 82.4 percent and 64.8 percent for Cold War and pre–Cold War years respectively, to *0 percent* in both periods. *DemL* follows with a very significant *RF* value for the conflict outcome (6.5 percent for the CW set and 4 percent for the PCW data). As previously indicated, *Logdistance* (41.82 percent *RF* value for the Cold War dispute cases and 25.54 percent for the pre–Cold War disputes) and *Logcaprat* (52.51 percent for CW conflicts and 40.72 percent for the PCW conflicts) also have substantial enabling power. Finally, *Allies* (62.58 percent for CW and 42.62 percent for PCW) and *IGOs* (62.58 percent for CW and 43.61 percent for PCW) to a lesser degree influence the effect of the other variables on disputes in both periods. In addition, for *IGOs*, the model deterioration is higher in the PCW years. From these results, not only do we reject the hypothesis that low democracy and shared participation in international organizations had weaker dispute-enabling effects in the pre–Cold War era, we support the opposite hypothesis: that they had *even stronger effects earlier.* Furthermore, low economic interdependence appears to be the most important necessary condition for conflict in both periods.

These results once again show the power of interdependence, democracy, and distance. Since these variables have high values by each test— *GI*, *SI*, and *RF*—they emerge as key variables. They affect war directly and enhance other variables' influence on dispute initiation. This supports Beck, King, and Zeng's (2000) conclusion that the effect of the input variables varies significantly across dyads as a consequence of input-to-input interactions as well as a feedback loop between democracy and economic interdependence (Papayoanou 1997; Burkhart and Lewis-Beck 1994; Weede 1996; Przeworski and Limongi 1997).

In predicting nondispute outcomes, the only input variable with a significant *RF*, both for the CW and PCW test, is *Contig* (54.56 percent for the Cold War data and 40.28 percent for the pre–Cold War years).[30] (Not surprisingly, contiguity was more important in the pre–

TABLE 9. Input Relation Factors for the Pre–Cold War Years

| PCW | All | DemL | Allies | Contig | Logdistance | Logcaprat | IGOs | DependL | Majorpower |
|-----|------|-------|--------|--------|-------------|-----------|-------|---------|------------|
| C   | 64.81 | 4.00 | 42.63 | 82.89 | 25.54 | 40.72 | 43.61 | 0 | 59.52 |
| NC  | 66.50 | 98.00 | 80.97 | 40.28 | 90.83 | 80.37 | 78.54 | 100 | 62.89 |

Cold War years of less effective military technology to exert force at a distance.) Contiguity makes *DemL, DependL, IGOs, Logdistance,* and *Logcaprat*—the variables with significant *GI* or *SI* values—more important in reducing disputes. Again the close *RF* value for the Cold War and pre–Cold War period stresses a stable structure of influence over time at the interaction effect level.

The difference between the predictions of disputes and nondisputes means that the interaction between the explanatory variables is also nonlinear. Although low levels of economic interdependence, democracy, distance, power imbalance, and shared membership in international organizations and alliances interact to create multiplicative effects that enhance the likelihood of a dispute, high levels of those variables do not have the same multiplicative effect on peace. Low values produce strong interaction effects, while high values display more of an additive relationship in which they complement each other more than they interact with each other. If two states are geographically close, low levels of interdependence and democracy, a relatively equal balance of power, and low level of participation in international organizations and alliances interact with each other and with proximity to substantially raise the risk that a dispute will occur. But for more distant states (not contiguous), each variable makes a substantial contribution to keeping the peace even in the absence of much help from others.

Disputes can be quite effectively explained as deriving from low levels of democracy and interdependence, geographical proximity, a relatively equal balance of power, and low shared membership in international organizations and alliances within the dyad. That is, "unhappy" relationships stem from the lack of one or more of the constraints that interdependence, democracy, distance, an imbalance of power, and international organizations could provide. These are the conditions under which the anarchic Hobbesian world of each against all identified by the realists applies. By contrast, "happy" relationships are a mixture of those dyads where one or more of the constraints do apply, and of those states that are not contiguous and so lack the immediate set of opportunities and capabilities which contiguity provides as inducements to disputes among states not otherwise constrained. For the former, "happiness" derives more from the liberal attributes that suppress violent conflict, whereas for the latter it derives more from their separation (Kinsella and Russett 2002).

The causal interpretation provided by the three measures of input influence does not uncover the full model developed by the neural network. However, it does offer interesting findings with which to refine theories on peace and war. Relationships across the variables do appear to be nonlinear, contingent, and nonmonotonic. Also, the liberal variables—economic interdependence, democracy, and international organizations—play important direct as well as indirect roles in producing war and maintaining peace. Their influence is strengthened both by some interaction between them and by their interactions with the realist variables of geographical proximity, contiguity, balance of power, and alliances.

## CONCLUSION

The interstate dispute model we developed, using backpropagation multilayer neural networks, a balanced training with cross-validation strategy, and Cold War data, improves on the dispute prediction capability of the initial pioneering efforts utilizing neural network methodologies.[31] Our preferred model correctly categorizes 82.4 percent of the Cold War dispute dyads and 64.8 percent of the pre–Cold War ones. For the nondispute cases the accuracy is high: 72.2 percent for the Cold War years and 65.5 percent for the pre–Cold War. But when we compare these postdiction results using kappa and conditional kappa analysis— which is necessary because of the different sizes between the pre–Cold War and Cold War testing sets—we find that the overall accuracy of the model for the pre–Cold War period is significantly better than for the Cold War years. These results over both periods indicate an underlying stability of the network structure, both overall and in the consistent strong effect of economic interdependence, democracy, and to some extent international organizations, on the conflict outcome. Indeed, the somewhat better accuracy on disputes for the pre–Cold War period underlines that the pattern of interactions leading to conflict remains highly representative across time and space, not one vulnerable to changes in systemic or state-level characteristics. Although nonlinear and nonmonotonic relationships often characterize the interaction across the variables, our findings indicate that this complex interaction was fully in place during the pre–Cold War era.

In relation to peace (nondisputes), the results are different. Although the Cold War model for nondisputes does well in the pre–Cold War period, it has less predictive power. While interdependence, democracy, distance, difference in power ratio, and shared participation in international organizations and alliances all were important variables for maintaining peace in the previous period, their influence was slightly weaker than in the Cold War context.

The final analysis, of dependencies across the eight input variables for the Cold War and pre–Cold War period, provides additional evidence that the relationships producing interstate disputes are structurally similar but stronger for the pre–Cold War context. Furthermore, analysis of the peaceful interactions shows how similar the dependence structure was in the two periods. While the variables display a slightly weaker influence on peace in the pre–Cold War years, the interactive effect leading to peace is stable over time. Interdependence and democracy consistently emerge as key variables, together with proximity, power ratio, international organizations, alliances, and contiguity. All this extends and deepens earlier indications (Russett and Oneal 2001) that the same fundamental pattern of influences applied for more than a century. In doing so it gives a stronger basis to believe that it will continue to apply in the twenty-first century—under conditions when democracy, interdependence, and international organizations are deeper and more widespread than ever before.

Our analysis indicates, moreover, that the pattern of relationships affecting disputes often is not linear, and that interactions are common. For example, instead of exerting a constant effect, economic interdependence and democracy may vary their influence as they are either enabled or not by interaction effects between themselves and with the realist influences. Russett and Oneal (2001) suggested some of these interactions, but they are more apparent with the new neural network model used here. This analysis, however, only begins to understand what those relationships may be. It represents a challenge to theorists and methodologists to carry on the task of understanding the complexity, even in terms of the limited number of variables employed here, of the international system in which we try to live in security and peace.

## APPENDIX

A genetic algorithm solves optimization problems by creating a population or group of possible solutions to the problem at hand. In our case this method starts when a large random population of network configurations is constructed following the number of input and output variables and the general neural structure required. Each configuration is then expressed as a string of values, a "chromosome," in which each value, a "gene," represents a network parameter. Then each network in the population is trained and a fitness score assigned to it on the basis of a fitness function. The fitness function may incorporate many criteria in evaluating the network quality. Here, the accuracy of the network, the complexity of the configuration, and the ability to learn rapidly are of importance. Indeed, the genetic algorithm process aims to

TABLE 10.   Output of the Genetic Algorithm Optimizing the Network Configuration

| Rating | Fitness | Genetic String | 1 Hidden Layer Neurons | 2 Hidden Layer Layer | Learning Rate | Momentum | Output Neurons |
|---|---|---|---|---|---|---|---|
| 1 | 0.8320 | 1111111100000000110000001101000011010 | 8 Tanh | none | 0.7 | 0.7 | 2 Logistic |
| 2 | 0.8314 | 1111111100000000100000110111110001111 | 17 Tanh | none | 0.7 | 0.7 | 2 Logistic |
| 3 | 0.8297 | 1111111100000000110100001100010111111 | 2 Logistic 31 Tanh 2 Linear | none | 0.7 | 0.7 | 2 Logistic |
| 4 | 0.8292 | 1111111100000001000000100000111111111 | 3 Logistic 58 Tanh 3 Linear | none | 0.7 | 0.7 | 2 Logistic |
| 5 | 0.8291 | 1111111100000001011000010100111111010 | 2 Logistic 45 Tanh 2 Linear | none | 0.7 | 0.7 | 2 Logistic |
| 6 | 0.8289 | 1111111100000001100000011010000011010 | 2 Logistic 36 Tanh 2 Linear | none | 0.7 | 0.7 | 2 Logistic |
| 7 | 0.8289 | 1111111100000001001000100010001001011 | 3 Logistic 51 Tanh 3 Linear | none | 0.7 | 0.7 | 2 Logistic |
| 8 | 0.8283 | 1111111100000000010100011111001111011 | 2 Logistic 39 Tanh 3 Linear | none | 0.7 | 0.7 | 2 Logistic |
| 9 | 0.8282 | 1111111100000000000001101111001010 | 17 Tanh 2 Linear | none | 0.7 | 0.7 | 2 Logistic |
| 10 | 0.8280 | 1111111100000000010000010010001111111 | 27 Tanh 2 Logistic | none | 0.7 | 0.7 | 2 Logistic |

minimize the network's training and cross-validation errors, complexity, and learning time. Furthermore, each criterion is normalized and weighted according to its importance.

On the basis of the assigned fitness score, the best network configurations are selected. These networks go through a process of genetic manipulation, which involves crossover of genetic material (mating of genes) and mutation (randomizing of genes). The crossover mechanism allows us to recombine the fittest network parameters while narrowing down the genetic algorithm's search space. Instead, mutation encourages extension of the search space and is useful if the population has converged on a local suboptimum solution.

The genetically modified network configurations are then retrained, their fitness calculated and compared with previous values. If the resulting networks offer higher fitness scores than previous attempts, then they are used as parents for the next generation. In this way, the genes, which represent the network parameters of the fittest networks, are maintained during the evolution process. This sequence of training, replication, crossover, and mutation continues either until a prespecified number of generations has been reached or until a desired fitness value has been achieved.

Table 10 shows the final result after twenty generations of optimization of the neural network configuration. Only the top ten performing networks with their calculated fitness values and genetic string are shown. The combination of neural activation functions within the hidden and output layers is also illustrated, as well as the network's learning rate and momentum. As can be seen from the table, the optimal configuration selected by the genetic algorithm is the one described previously in figure 1.

### NOTES

*Authors' Note:* We thank the Carnegie Corporation of New York, the Ford Foundation, the National Science Foundation, the Weatherhead Initiative on Military Conflict as a Public Health Problem, the Economic and Social Research Council, and the Foreign and Commonwealth office for financial support, and Richard Aldrich, Neal Beck, Scott Boorman, Evan Govender, Gary King, John Oneal, Carlos Vieira, and Langche Zeng for helpful comments. We gave an earlier version of this chapter at the annual meeting of the Peace Science Society (International), New Haven, October 2000. Our data, from Russett and Oneal (2001), are at www.yale.edu/unsy/democ/democ1.htm.

1. Henderson is provocative but mistaken. His major effort is to run many additive and multiplicative combinations of regime scores to show the insignificance of the democratic peace in the presence of political distance. But there

are better ways to test this. The simplest is in Oneal and Russett (1997), which is the source of Henderson's data: Instead of combining the lower and higher regime scores of a dyad in any way, just include each in the regression model. This shows clearly that political distance does matter, in what we call the cats and dogs effect—but there is also a democratic peace. Democratic dyads are most peaceful, autocratic dyads less so, and mixed dyads least peaceful. Also see Peceny and Beer (2002), who show that even when autocracies are divided into dyads of similar types, democratic dyads still are more peaceful.

Alternatively, create an indicator that identifies truly democratic pairs (both states above +6), and one that gives political distance (*DemH* minus *DemL*). Enter both. Both are significant. This test also shows that the effect of regimes is best captured by truly democratic dyads (above +6) and truly autocratic dyads (below −6). There—with coherent regimes—the democratic peace is clearest. Neural networks analysis is well suited to find such unanticipated non-linearities.

2. Related concerns drove the debate over whether fixed-effects models are useful in analyses of disputes, with the consensus in the negative. See Green, Kim, and Yoon (2001) with rebuttals by Beck and Katz (2001), Oneal and Russett (2001), and King (2001); also see Bennett and Stam (2000b). Neural networks analysis addresses some of the problems Green et al. identify.

3. As Weinberg (1975, 18–25) underlines in his conceptualization of scientific inquiry, social behavior belongs to the realm of organized complexity and, as such, may be too complex for analytical treatment.

4. The weight change, $\Delta W$, at the time $t$ for all the weights' value in the network is

$$\Delta W_{(t)} = \eta \delta X + M \Delta W_{(t-1)} \tag{2}$$

where $\eta$ is a small positive constant called learning rate, usually between 0 and 1, $\delta$ is the local error gradient for the neuron considered, $X$ is the input of the neuron, $M$ is a constant called the momentum coefficient ranging between 0 and 1, and $\Delta W_{(t-1)}$ is the change in error in the weight value in the previous time period, $t - 1$. Ripley (1994) describes the backpropagation algorithm.

5. However, the backpropagation algorithm is not guaranteed to find the global minimum. The error surface that is the geometrical representation of the error function is multidimensional, displaying not only a global minimum but also multiple local minima. In its search for the optimal solution, the backpropagation algorithm can easily get trapped in these local minima. To avoid this, a momentum term, $\alpha$, is added to the backpropagation formula. Another strategy in avoiding local minima is to run the training process numerous times starting from randomly selected initial values—that is, from different ordering of the training data and/or different initial random weights (Garson 1998, 50–54). Early stopping, which adopts a cross-validation set during the training, may also reduce the danger of settling in a local minimum (Sarle 1995).

6. For genetic algorithms applied to neural network optimization see Miller, Todd, and Hegde (1989), Yao (1999), and Blanco, Delgato, and Pegalajar (2000).

7. The order in which the training patterns are presented to the network can also affect performance. If the data are grouped in the same manner, rather than being randomly organized, the system may "remember" the last group better than the previous ones, with the obvious consequence that the system's predictive result would be biased toward the information contained in this last grouping. To avoid this problem, the neural analysis should be repeated multiple times using differently ordered data and different initial weight values, both randomly chosen. Moreover, in order to further reduce the possibility of local mimima, the network training was repeated ten times, and the lowest accuracy (training and cross-validation errors) was selected to be used in the fitness function (Bengio 1996, 31).

8. On the *tanh* function see Abramowitz and Stegun (1966, 83).

9. As mentioned before, because of the unusual character of dispute events, the dispute dyads often contain information on large input-output effects.

10. The term *choice-based sampling* is used in econometrics, while *case-control design* is more common in epidemiology. For further discussion see Breslow (1996).

11. As King and Zeng (2000, 7) stress, "Designs that select on Y [the dependent variable] can be consistent and efficient but only with the appropriate statistical correction." This is because a sample selected on the values of the dependent variable can increase the effect of the input on the output and the estimated probability of conflict events for all dyads (note that this bias is exactly opposite to the one produced by an unbalanced training set).

12. Prior correction in conventional statistical classifiers involves estimating the coefficients using the sample selected on the dependent variable and then correcting the estimates with a priori probability of class membership. This a priori probability takes into account the ratio of the classes in the population and in the sample. For examples of a priori correction see King and Zeng (2000, 5–6), McKay and Campbell (1982), and Strahler (1980).

13. The importance of class size as a means to provide the network with prior knowledge of class allocation in the population is discussed in the neural network literature. On incorporating prior knowledge into neural network classifiers see Foody (1995) and Foody, McCulloch, and Yates (1995).

14. The MSE for the cross-validation set is

$$MSE = \frac{1}{n}\sum_{p=1}^{n}(t_p - y_p)^2 \tag{3}$$

where $t_p$ is the target output of each cross-validation sample, $y_p$ is the actual output calculated by the network, and $n$ is the number of cases in the cross-validation set.

15. In the literature, cross-validation has mainly been used to improve the generalization ability of the network model. Instead of stopping the training process when the MSE on the training set reaches the minimum, the MSE of the cross-validation set is used for early stopping. By doing this we avoid possible

overfitting of the data, which refers to the extent to which the network has gone beyond learning the optimal pattern from the training data to also learning the idiosyncratic noise particular to that specific training set (Mosteller and Tukey 1977, 36–41). However, while performing this function, the cross-validation can also be used to provide additional information to the network. Without moving away from the traditional use of cross-validation, we suggest extending the cross-validation method to encompass prior knowledge functionality. Consequently, we use cross-validation both for early stopping during training and to provide the network with prior knowledge on class distribution.

16. Some analytical solutions suggested in the literature directly correct the probabilistic output produced by the neural network or, in the case of a network with a logit output function, the constant term in the hidden neuron to output layer (see King and Zeng 2000, 24). Though these efforts are valid and theoretically well grounded, any estimation errors in the network parameters could be aggravated by the analytical correction, making the final corrected result less accurate than the uncorrected one. Thus the cross-validation correction strategy we employ still provides, in this case, a better solution for producing more accurate results.

17. When attributing cause in reducing conflict we follow the theoretical reasoning of Russett and Oneal (2001), supported by the lag. Oneal, Russett, and Berbaum (2003) use distributed lag models to validate that reasoning more persuasively, finding that trade and peace constitute a feedback loop of mutual reinforcement, and that IGOs increase trade. Other known causal links (Russett and Oneal 2001, chap. 6) include from peace, democracy, and trade to IGOs, and democracy to trade. Pevehouse (2002) reports a link from IGOs to democratization. Kant saw such influences as creating what is now called a dynamic feedback system.

18. This restriction may provide another theoretically relevant advantage. By dropping the non-PRDs, characterized by great distance and weakness, we eliminate many dyads for which such constraints on dispute initiation as democracy and trade may have a lesser role to play in preventing disputes that are highly unlikely to arise anyway. Of the relatively few disputes falling outside of the politically relevant dyads, many are multistate disputes with small powers being drawn into disputes between major powers (Lemke and Reed 2001b). Expected utility calculations seem less informative with nonrelevant dyads; see Bennett and Stam (2000c).

19. Like logistic regression and many other multivariate models, network analysis does not readily identify such historical dynamics as contagion, diffusion, and imitation.

20. We designed the replication strategy so as to increase the size of the training set. The need to keep a balanced ratio of the two classes in the training set reduces the size of the training sets, since the number of conflict cases that can be utilized is limited. To assess whether bigger balanced training sets produce better results we replicate the conflict cases in the training set.

21. King and Zeng (2000, 17–19) show that in logit analysis the rare event

bias becomes minimal in large samples, since increase in sample size improves efficiency. In backpropagation networks the opposite seems to happen. The larger the sample (so the larger the class unbalance) the less robust the network. Indeed, large unbalanced training samples dramatically reduce the ability of the network to discriminate between the modal and rare class, to the extent that no conflict case is correctly predicted. Again, we believe this situation is caused by the error minimization process adopted by the backpropagation algorithm. With large samples, the weight parameters are mainly determined by the non-conflict class, since the large difference between the two classes significantly increases the proportion of changes in error in the weight value, $\Delta w$, calculated on the basis of the nonconflict class. In conclusion, it appears that in backpropagation neural networks a significant loss of efficiency is associated with increase in class unbalance (rare event bias), which large samples imply. This plays a bigger role in comparison to the parallel increase in efficiency that the larger sample size provides.

22. Schrodt (1991, 370), one of the first political scientists to suggest an alternative accuracy method to overall accuracy, stresses the inadequacy of overall accuracy as the measure for conflict prediction models. His solution is to use an entropy ratio (ER), which is equal to model entropy (ME) divided by the dependent variable entropy (DE).

23. Comprehensive reviews of the calculation involved in kappa analysis and the test Z statistics can be found in Goodman and Kruskal (1963) and Congalton and Green (1999, 43–57).

24. Kappa analysis was implemented by the software FUNCPOW.C, authored by Carlos Vieira of the School of Geography, University of Nottingham. The software was developed in standard C language and on the Unix platform.

25. The term *significance matrix* is relatively new. It has been adopted in the remote sensing literature by researchers dealing with classifiers' performance (Vieira and Mather 1999).

26. The difference in accuracy across training strategies becomes more evident when focusing on the other results. *Unb* cannot discriminate between the dispute and the nondispute class. Indeed, the unbalanced training set correctly predicts no dispute dyad, although it predicts 100 percent of nonconflict outcomes. However, as stressed by Beck, King, and Zeng (2000, 29), "This is not great success, of course, since the optimistic claim that conflict will never occur is correct 96 percent [in our case 97 percent] of the time." This result again shows how rare-event bias can preserve and even increase its negative influence in large heavily unbalanced samples. Also, the two balanced-replicated training strategies, *CVRep* and *Rep,* do not offer high accuracy on either class. Their accurate prediction on both dispute and nondispute dyads is less than 30 percent.

27. The denominator in (1) operates as a normalizing factor, which avoids the negative effect of the network activation function squeezing the weight value into a smaller range.

28. In order to increase variable comparability we also normalized the network's inputs so as to achieve means of zero for all input variables.

29. Here we can directly compare class accuracy since the testing sets have the same size.

30. Conditional kappa analysis and a pairwise test $Z$ statistic were performed between the model with all the active inputs and those with one input switched off. The result indicates a significant deterioration, at least in one class accuracy, when *DependL, DemL, Logdistance, Logcaprat* are switched off.

31. Beck, King, and Zeng (2000, 29) say that their model, developed on the 1947–85 period, predicts 99.4 percent of the nondispute cases in 1986–89, but only 16.7 percent of disputes.

# PART II  NATIONAL AND SUBNATIONAL FACTORS

# STATESMEN, POPULAR WISDOM, AND EMPIRICAL REALITIES IN THE STUDY OF CONFLICT AND WAR
## Extending the "Predictors of War in History and in the State of the World Message"

*Zeev Maoz*

In 1974, J. David Singer and Melvin Small published "Foreign Policy Indicators: Predictors of War in History and in the State of the World Message," in *Policy Sciences*. Like many other pathbreaking studies by these two authors, the pioneering nature of this study was largely overlooked. For example, since its publication this article was cited only twenty-three times. It was reprinted in Coplin and Kegley (1975) and has probably appeared in a few reading lists in various graduate courses.

However, even now, thirty years after its publication, the innovative ideas underlying this study, on the one hand, and its elegance and simplicity, on the other, are still compelling. The basic idea of this article was to examine the fit between the beliefs that world leaders have about the causes (or predictors) of war and the empirical evidence. Using Richard Nixon's 1972 State of the World Message, as a source representing this "conventional wisdom," Singer and Small extracted hypotheses about war and peace in international affairs. They subjected some of these ideas to fairly simple empirical tests, showing that many of them have little or no empirical foundation.

The wish to be relevant for policymakers, or to "bridge the gap" between theory and policy (George 1997), has always been a goal of international relations researchers. However, it seems that only a few political leaders have adapted ideas and facts that emerged out of empirical research on international politics. In most cases, political leaders have developed ideas of their own about international affairs. These ideas have become the source of knowledge that in many cases is either detached from or opposite to the knowledge obtained through scientific investigations of various aspects of world politics. This message comes out loud and clear in Singer and Small's study, which ends on a somber note: "We conclude with an emphasis . . . on the need for a very different kind of 'education for world affairs.' In the primary and secondary schools, in colleges and graduate schools, and, perhaps more critically, in the public and private discussions of public policy questions, it is essential that we move out of the Neanderthal Era."

Even when politicians cite actual academic research, they typically demonstrate a superficial understanding of the scholarly ideas and empirical results entailed in such research. Worse, in many cases, politicians deliberately reframe and manipulate these findings. An example concerns the use of the democratic peace proposition by political leaders. The notion that democracies do not fight each other—which had received considerable support at the dyadic level of analysis—has often been extended by political leaders to the systemic or monadic level of analysis, where this proposition either does not apply at all or applies under specific conditions (Maoz 2001). Furthermore, the democratic peace proposition specifies a *sufficient but not necessary* condition for peace. This means that whenever two states are democratic, they will avoid fights with each other. It does not mean that peace cannot exist between democratic and nondemocratic states. However, politicians have often used it as a *necessary but not sufficient* condition, arguing that if a given state does not convert to democracy, it is unwise to make peace with it, because any agreement is bound to be violated (Maoz 1998).

In light of the apparent discrepancy between political leaders' notions about war and peace and the available evidence, it may be instructive to examine if the pessimistic conclusions entailed in the Singer and Small (1974) study withstood the test of time. It is also useful to examine whether a new generation of leaders of different states had new and improved notions about empirical reality and whether the fit between the leaders' notions and the data is better than in the original Singer and Small study.

My aim in the present study is threefold. First, I wish to replicate Singer and Small's (1974) study by reexamining some of the issues raised by the authors. This replication is meaningful given the availability of new or updated data, as well as more complex estimation procedures. Second, I attempt to extend this study by deriving a more up-to-date version of statesmen's "conventional wisdom about war and peace." I use the statements of leaders during the UN Millennium Summit of September 6–8, 2000, as the source for these notions. I extract a number of statements made at that summit about war and peace and rephrase them as testable hypotheses. Third, I evaluate these statements by pitting them against the historical record. On the basis of these analyses, I reassess Singer and Small's sad conclusion.

This chapter is organized as follows. First I outline a number of propositions that have been extracted from national leaders' statements at the UN Millennium Summit. I derive testable hypotheses from these statements. The following section discusses the research design of the study. Then I replicate the original Singer and Small's article, using more recent data and more elaborate estimation procedures. Next, I test the hypotheses derived from the Millennium Summit and conclude by discussing the implications of these findings for theory and policy in world politics.

## PROPOSITIONS ABOUT WAR AND PEACE: THE UN MILLENNIUM SUMMIT

Singer and Small's focus on leaders' intuitive notions about war and peace is important not only from the didactic point of view, as they have suggested in their conclusion. It is significant from a policy point of view as well. Leaders' beliefs about the sources, courses, and consequences of conflict serve as the foundations of international security policy. To the extent that the belief-policy nexus is indeed valid, it is instructive to broaden the scope of this exercise of fitting leaders' beliefs to empirical reality. First, the "causal" beliefs about war and peace that Singer and Small extracted from Nixon's State of the World Message were couched in a realist conception, with the notion of "war begets war" driving the logic. This may have been a common conception in a bipolar world wherein the superpowers were engaged in a cold war, yet searching for ways to coexist despite their differences and the competition between them. Second, Nixon's beliefs may have been representative of the realist conception of world politics; they may have even been representative of a broader American conception of the world. Yet, it is unclear that Nixon's ideas were representative of the beliefs of leaders in other states at the time. It makes sense therefore to broaden the scope of the people who express their beliefs about war and peace in the international system. Third, a long time has passed since Nixon's State of the World Message. The world has experienced revolutionary change on almost every dimension of the human experience. It is therefore important to examine whether and how these changes are reflected in leaders' beliefs about war and peace in the international system.

On September 6, 2000, political leaders from over 150 nations gathered in New York for the UN Millennium Summit, convened under the title "The Role of the UN in the Twenty-first Century." In the course of this conference, all leaders made statements concerning their own nation's policies as well as about the state of the world.[1] I have selected a number of statements made by various leaders that suggest notions about the causes of conflict and the conditions of peace.

To choose the statements, each was examined for the keywords *conflict, war, peace,* and related terms (e.g., *conflict-ridden, peaceful, warlike, war-prone*). Once a phrase containing the keyword was found, I examined its context. I excluded any statement about the causes and consequences of conflict that was not couched in general terms. In many cases, leaders referred to a specific conflict or war, or to a specific state or group of states.[2] These statements were excluded. Also, I have excluded statements about the causes and consequences of war for which I could not develop testable hypotheses (e.g., that shared beliefs about the unity of mankind and our responsibility to future generations would enhance the prospects of global peace). Finally I have excluded testable hypotheses for which I could not find appropriate data for an empirical test (e.g., a large number of statements about the effect of peacekeeping operations on peace, or on relationships between conflict and environmental issues).

The following statements are neither exhaustive nor representative of the entire spectrum of views and conceptions represented at the Millennium Summit; in fact, the number of exclusions is vastly larger than the number of statements included here. However, these statements do reflect what we can consider as "conventional policy wisdom" about these issues. There were hints to similar ideas in other statements, but if they were not sufficiently explicit, they were not included in the sample.[3] I present these notions verbatim. I provide my interpretations to each of these statements and convert them into testable hypotheses.

A fair number of leaders addressed internal and ethnic conflict, mostly in specific states or regions. This suggests a growing concern with non-interstate wars, a concern that is reflected in a general trend in modern warfare (Levy, Walker, and Edwards 2001). Some have also hinted to a relationship between external and internal conflicts. I start out with what is probably the clearest statement in this regard, a hypothesis about the impact of external intervention on the duration of internal wars.

1. *Afghanistan* (Burhanudin Rabanni). The Islamic State of Afghanistan wishes to emphasize that in most of conflicts termed *internal,* external politicoeconomic and strategic inter-

ests and interventions play a primordial role in sustaining that conflict.

This statement suggests that local or internal conflicts are better left to themselves if they are to be resolved quickly. International intervention in such conflicts serves only to prolong them. The implication is spelled out in the interventionism hypothesis.

**A. INTERVENTIONISM HYPOTHESIS:** **External interventions in a domestic conflict prolong the conflict. Domestic conflicts involving intervention by states external to the conflict last longer than conflicts without such intervention.**

One of the most important trends in the scientific analysis of world politics in the last two decades is the decline in the number and impact of system-level analyses of international relations. This is also reflected in the prominent absence of system-level statements—at least of the realpolitik variety—in most statements in the Millennium Summit. Yet, some leaders still have beliefs about the relationships between structure and stability in international politics. Here is the clearest statement on this issue.

> 2. *China* (Xiang Zemin). To build common security is the prerequisite to the prevention of conflicts and wars. To promote a multipolar international configuration is required by the progress of our times, conforms to the interests of the people of all countries, and also contributes to world peace and security. A multipolar configuration differs from the old one in which big powers contended for hegemony and carved up spheres of influence as seen in history. All countries should be independent. Mutual cooperation and partnership of various forms between countries should not be targeted at any third party. The big countries have an important responsibility for the maintenance of world and regional peace. The big countries should respect the small ones, the strong should support the weak, and the rich help the poor.

It is probably a bit of a stretch, given the latter part of the statement, but it may seem that Xiang Zemin was in fact suggesting the stability of a multipolar world, to paraphrase another important contribution by J. David Singer (Deutsch and Singer 1964). Therefore, we will keep this proposition.

B. MULTIPOLARITY HYPOTHESIS: A multipolar international system is more stable than other types of system.

More in line with recent trends in the scientific literature are statements linking domestic structures and processes to international relations and international processes. One of the more prevalent ideas in the scientific literature is the diversionary war hypothesis (e.g., Levy 1989) that focuses on the relationship between domestic conflict and international conflict. In contrast, some of the most interesting beliefs of political leaders stress the relationships between external penetration and control of states and their level of development.

> 3. *Cuba* (Fidel Castro). The poverty and underdevelopment prevailing in most nations as well as the inequality in the distribution of wealth and knowledge in the world are basically at the source of the present conflicts. It cannot be overlooked that current underdevelopment and poverty have resulted from conquest, colonization, slavery, and plundering in most countries of the planet by the colonial powers and from the emergence of imperialism and the bloody wars motivated by new distributions of the world.

Castro seems to suggest that most conflicts in the modern international system result from poverty, underdevelopment, and unequal distribution of wealth across states. It is also suggested that colonization and conquest indirectly affect conflict propensity through underdevelopment.

Curiously, the president of the United States, Bill Clinton, concurred with these statements.

> 4. *United States* (Bill Clinton). We must also work with just as much passion and persistence to *prevent* conflict, recognizing the iron link between [economic] deprivation and war. (Emphasis in original)

The representatives of Norway and of Pakistan made the complementary argument, namely, that development promotes peace.

> 5. *Norway* (King Harald V). The elimination of poverty is not only a bridge to peace and development, not only a bridge to human rights and individual dignity, but also a bridge to the preservation of the environment for future generations.

6. *Pakistan* (Gen. Pervez Musharraf). The best assurance for the consolidation of global peace lies in the economic development and prosperity of all regions and all peoples.

Accordingly, the following hypotheses are derived.

C.1. POVERTY AND CONFLICT HYPOTHESIS: The greater the extent of world poverty, the more conflict does the world experience.
C.2. INEQUALITY BREEDS CONFLICT HYPOTHESIS: The higher the economic inequality in the international system, the more conflict the system experiences.[4]

Castro and Clinton did not specify whether the rich attack the poor, the poor attack the rich, the rich attack each other, or the poor attack each other. Thus, we have some ambiguity regarding the dyadic and monadic version of these beliefs. Hence, I develop several subhypotheses from this proposition regarding dyadic and monadic implications.

C.2.1. INEQUALITY AND DYADIC CONFLICT: Conflict between economically unequal states is more/less likely than between economically equal states.
C.2.2. INEQUALITY AND MONADIC CONFLICT: Poor states are more/less likely to get involved in conflict than rich states.

In contrast to these notions that treat poverty, underdevelopment, and inequality as *predictors* or *causes* of conflict, the following statement treats development as a possible *outcome* of peace.

7. *India* (Shri Atal Bihar Vajpayee). We cannot have true development without peace between nations and democracy within them. Indeed, democracy and peace continue to remain the best guarantors for unhindered development; each secures the other.

The implication here is that conflict in one period inversely affects development in subsequent periods. The same applies to the effect of democracy on development, but this is an issue to which I turn later. Here, however, I reverse the hypotheses regarding development and conflict stated earlier.

D.1. The higher the rate of conflict during a given period in history, the slower the rate of development in the subsequent period.

**D.2. The higher the rate of democratization in one period, the higher the rate of development in another period.**

As in the case of ideas about the relationship between economic development and conflict, which are probably characteristic of the beliefs of leaders in the post–Cold War era, another favorite topic in the Millennium Summit was some version of the democratic peace hypothesis. Consider the following quotes.

8. *Germany* (Gerhard Schroeder). For effective protection of human rights is an important prerequisite for peace and stability.
9. *France* (Jacques Chirac). Democracy, because democracy alone ensures respect for human rights and human dignity, because it is the surest path to stability, development, and progress for all. Because it is also the surest way to guarantee peace.

We interpret these statements to be in line with the monadic and systemic version of the democratic peace notion. Specifically:

**E.1. Democratic states that protect their citizen's right experience less conflict and war than nondemocratic states.**
**E.2. As the proportion of system members that protect human right increases, the level of peace and stability in the system also increases.**

An inverse idea suggests that democracy is the victim of (possibly external) conflict.

10. *Jordan* (King Abdullah II). Peace, stability, and prosperity still elude many countries at the turn of the century, sacrificing the noble principles of justice, equality, and democracy, and widening the digital divide that separates them from the developed world.

This statement suggests that conflict involvement of states in one period prohibits democratization in those as well as in subsequent periods. This statement can also be converted into a systemic version of this logic. Specifically:

**F.1. The greater the level of conflict involvement of a state, the less democratic it is likely to be in subsequent periods.**
**F.2. The higher the level of conflict in the international system,**

the lower the proportion of democratic states in the system during the same or subsequent periods.

These hypotheses seem to be consistent with the argument that it is peace that promotes democracy, not democracy that promotes peace. The system-level version of this hypothesis is particularly consistent with this argument (Thompson 1996).

As noted, this is a small and probably unrepresentative sample of political leaders' beliefs about the "laws" that guide international politics. What is interesting about these statements, however, is their shift from power-based issues to issues of democracy, economic development, and their effect on peace. Judging from this sample of statements, one can argue that leaders' beliefs in the post–Cold War era are embedded more in liberal notions of world politics than in realpolitik ones. The remainder of this essay attempts to test these statements against available empirical data.

## METHOD

### Spatial and Temporal Domain

I use both the war and MID data set which determine the temporal domain as the 1816–1992 period. To minimize selection bias, a feature that probably was a problem in the Singer and Small article, we rely on all states that existed in the interstate system during that era. For the dyadic analyses we employ the Maoz and Russett (1993) definition of politically relevant dyads (also Maoz 1996) to delimit our analyses only to those dyads that have a meaningful a priori probability of conflict and war involvement. As noted by Lemke and Reed (2001b), this definition does not lead to any significant level of selection bias in relation to the study of conflict as a dependent variable.

### Data

In general, since most of the focus in our analyses is on conflict and war as dependent variables, we employ the Dyadic MID (Maoz 1999b) data set as the principal source for measuring these dependent variables. In addition, we employ COW military capability data (Singer 1991) to measure economic development and military capability. To measure economic indices over the 1950–90 period we use the Penn World Table (Heston, Summers, and Aten 2002). Finally, we employ the Polity VI data set to code regime attributes.

## Variables

Rather than providing a list and a set of operational definitions for all variables used herein, we define the specific variables and indicators as we do the hypothesis testing, much in the spirit of the Singer and Small article. At that point we also mention the sources used to derive the specific measures employed.

## Statistical Techniques

Singer and Small's strategy was to test the variables derived from the State of the World Message against the dependent variable in a series of bivariate tests. We follow this approach but also employ multivariate estimation methods employing other control variables commonly used in the empirical literature of recent years. The specific estimation procedure used to test a given hypothesis is spelled out along with the discussion of this hypothesis.

### FINDINGS

### *Reanalyzing Singer and Small's (1974) Findings*

Singer and Small's first extraction from the State of the World Message was the notion that "war begets war."
This proposition was also repeated in the UN Millennium Summit.

*Georgia* (Edward Shevarnadze). The unsettled conflicts of today—both between and within states—could flare up into horrific conflagration tomorrow.

Singer and Small tested this proposition by examining whether the outbreak of war at a given time affected the frequency of war outbreak in a subsequent year. I start by simply replicating this result, using a temporal domain that is twenty-eight years longer than that of Singer and Small. I then extend this test to examine the "MID begets MID" notion, looking at MID outbreaks. Here, however, I examine whether highly disputatious years (with number of dispute dyads above the average) are followed by conflictual years. I employ a number of estimation methods, starting with simple bivariate contingency table tests and going on to more sophisticated multivariate tests. The type of test is specified in table 1.
The findings reported here largely corroborate Singer and Small's

conclusions about this issue, but the extensions of test types and data suggest that other conclusions may be possible. For example, we see a statistically significant effect of MIDs on subsequent MIDs. We also observe significant effects of past MIDs on present wars. Thus, Singer and Small's conclusion that "the prediction is not solidly based" is corroborated only in the confines of the kind of analysis they had conducted. If we expand the analysis to examine the impact of MID outbreak on future MID outbreak, or the impact of MID outbreak on subsequent wars, then the notion of "conflict begets conflict" receives significant support in the last two centuries.

Another set of tests of the "conflict begets conflict" hypothesis that

**TABLE 1.** Tests of the "Conflict Begets Conflict" Hypothesis

| Dependent Variable | Independent Variable | Stratum | Type of Estimation Procedure | Test Statistic | Value of Statistic | PRE Statistic | N |
|---|---|---|---|---|---|---|---|
| War year 0 no 1 yes | Lagged war year (1 yr. Lag) | None | Crosstab | Chi-square | 1.744 | 0.100 | 176 |
| | | 19th C. | Crosstab | Chi-square | 0.005 | −0.008 | 83 |
| | | 20th C. | Crosstab | Chi-square | 0.724 | 0.088 | 93 |
| MID freq. 0 low 1 high | Lagged MID freq (1 yr. Lag) | None | Crosstab | Chi-square | 131.56** | 0.865 | 176 |
| | | 19th C. | Crosstab | Chi-square | 5.300** | 0.253 | 83 |
| | | 20th C. | Crosstab | Chi-square | 64.413** | 0.832 | 93 |
| War year | Lagged no wars (1 yr. Lag) | None | Logit | Parameter estimate | 0.089* | 0.022+ | 176 |
| | | 19th C. | Logit | Parameter estimate | 0.172 | 0.028+ | 83 |
| | | 20th C. | Logit | Parameter estimate | 0.053 | 0.012+ | 93 |
| War frequency | Lagged war freq (1 yr. Lag) | None | TS-regression | Parameter estimate | 0.209 | 0.044ˣ | 176 |
| | | 19th C. | TS-regression | Parameter estimate | 0.049 | 0.003ˣ | 82 |
| | | 20th C. | TS-regression | Parameter estimate | 0.102 | 0.010ˣ | 95 |
| MID frequency | Lagged MID freq (1 yr. Lag) | None | TS-regression | Parameter estimate | 0.859* | 0.737ˣ | 176 |
| | | 19th C. | TS-regression | Parameter estimate | 0.549** | 0.305 | 82 |
| | | 20th C. | TS-regression | Parameter estimate | 0.747** | 0.546 | 95 |

\* $p < .05$    \*\* $p < .01$
+ Pseudo = $R^2$    ˣ $R^2$

73

Singer and Small conducted entailed introducing various controls into this relationship. Specifically, using the wars themselves as units of analysis, they tested for each war whether it was preceded by a previous war as well as whether (1) the target was allied, and (2) the initiator of the previous war won. Rather than repeat their limited control contingency table analysis, I conduct a more conventional proportional-hazard estimation with a number of control variables. In order to explicate the nature of this test, we start out by spelling out the unit of analysis.

*Method*

It is important to note that this data set was prepared for a study replicating Maoz (1984) on the impact of prior dispute outcomes on the outbreak of subsequent disputes, a topic much related to the notion of "war begets war" that is our focus here. This data set is based on the Dyadic MID data set. It is in organized as a dyad-by-year unit, but—for each dyad—it is left-censored, starting with the first dispute between dyad members. From that point on, each dyad-year is recorded.

The key variables used for this analysis include the duration of peace, defined as the number of days that have elapsed between disputes. This is the time variable in the proportional-hazard estimation model. The outbreak of a dispute is considered a failure and the time variable is again set to 1 the day after the termination of the dispute. So what we are estimating is the duration of peace between disputes or wars. Rather than test for the outbreak of a militarized dispute within a fixed time interval as a function of a prior conflict, we examine how long it would take to two states to engage in another conflict given that they engaged in 1, 2, . . . , *k* conflicts in the past.

The independent variable is the number of past MIDs between the states. Control variables include the following.

1. The number of allies of each state, weighted by the type of alliance and the status (minor or major power) of each ally (Maoz 1996, 169–70). The minimum of both dyads' allies is used, based on the weak link notion established in the democratic peace literature (Maoz 1998).
2. The existence of a formal alliances between members of the dyad.
3. The outcome of the previous dispute, coded as −1 (initiator lost), 0 (the previous dispute ended in a draw), or +1 (initiator won).

4. Joint democracy, coded as 1 (both states were democracies) or 0 (otherwise) (Maoz 1996, 53–54).
5. Capability ratio (ratio of military capability of strongest member of dyad to weakest) (Maoz and Russett 1993).

Table 2 provides the results of this test. We focus only on militarized interstate disputes because there appeared to be no significant effects of past wars on the duration of peace between wars. Table 2 suggests indeed that the number of past disputes between members of the dyad significantly affects the duration of peace between successive disputes. Like Singer and Small, we find that having third-party allies has no significant effect on the duration of peace between disputes. Also, an alliance between dyad members has no significant effect on the duration of peace between disputes. However, in contrast to Singer and Small, we find that if the initiator won the previous dispute, this tends to increase the peacetime between disputes. Likewise, in contrast to Singer and Small, the relationship between past disputes and current disputes is stable across the two centuries. Other variables show significant effect on the duration of peace between disputes. Joint democracy and high capability disparity significantly increase the duration of peace between disputes.

It seems that quite a few of Singer and Small's findings withstand the

TABLE 2. Cox Proportional-Hazard Estimation of the Duration of Peace (1816–1992) between Dyad Members, as a Function of Prior Conflict and Control Variables

| Independent/Control Variable | Parameter Estimate (SE) | Change in Probability of Conflict[a] |
|---|---|---|
| No. of past MIDs between dyad members | 0.090** (0.003) | 0.043 |
| Alliance between members of dyad | −0.074 (0.069) | −0.001 |
| Joint democracy | −0.660** (0.141) | −0.318 |
| Weighted allies of dyad members | 0.015 (0.010) | 0.001 |
| Initiator's outcome in previous dispute | −0.232** (0.079) | −0.115 |
| Capability ratio in dyad | −0.001** (0.000) | 0.002 |

*Note:* Number of observations, dyads, and MIDs refer only to politically relevant dyads (Maoz 1996) with at least two disputes. First dispute between each dyad is omitted from observation.

[a] Negative probabilities indicate reduction in the hazard rate of MID outbreaks.

* $p < .05$    ** $p < .01$

75

test of time. However, moving from wars to disputes changes things quite a bit. Specifically, the notion of "MID begets MID" appears to hold rather strongly. This brings us to the test of the other hypotheses derived from the Millennium Summit speeches.

### Testing the Interventionist Hypothesis

In order to test the hypothesis that external intervention in internal conflicts prolongs the conflict, I employ a simple test of war duration by intervention. The data used are the COW intrastate war data set (Sarkees 2000).[5] Table 3 provides the results of this analysis. This very simple test tends to support the hypothesis. External intervention tends to prolong civil war. However, this effect is present only in the twentieth century, and it does not hold for the nineteenth century. The small number of cases of external interventions in civil wars in the earlier century prohibits a definite rejection of the hypothesis for this century. All in all, the proposition that civil wars involving outside third parties tend to last longer than those that are fought only between indigenous groups seems to have some empirical foundation, at least in the twentieth century.

As we have done in the previous analyses, we want to examine whether the proposition connecting external intervention to the duration of civil wars holds when controls are introduced. But before we do that, we wish to provide an alternative measure of outside intervention. This alternative measure is simply the number of outside states that intervened in the civil war. This number ranges from 0 (no outside intervention) to 5 (in the Russian civil war of 1917–21). This measure could be connected indirectly to the Afghani president's statement. If external intervention prolongs the duration of civil wars, then the more states intervene, the longer is the civil war expected to last.

We introduce four control variables.

TABLE 3.   The Effect of International Intervention on the Duration of Civil Wars, 1816–1997: Analysis of Variance

| Period | Intervention? | Mean Duration in days (SD) | No. of Wars | F-Statistic |
|---|---|---|---|---|
| 1816–1997 | No | 905.18 (1,337.93) | 164 | 14.19** |
|  | Yes | 1,867.68 (1,890.44) | 41 |  |
| 1816–99 | No | 862.76 (1,027.20) | 63 | 0.00 |
|  | Yes | 862.63 (881.56) | 8 |  |
| 1900–1997 | No | 931.64 (1,418.58) | 101 | 13.90** |
|  | Yes | 2,111.33 (1,995.86) | 33 |  |

* $p < .05$    ** $p < .01$

1. *Regional Locus of the War.* We wish to test regional differences in civil war duration. Thus we used a series of dummy variables for the five regions (Western Hemisphere, Europe, Africa, Middle East, Asia).[6]
2. *History of Statehood and Instability.* The degree of past political stability in the focal state may affect the duration of civil war. We measure the number of years that have elapsed from the previous regime change in the state to the year of civil war outbreak.
3. *Democratic Involvement in the War.* Democratic states are typically assumed to have low tolerance for long-fought wars. Thus if a democracy is involved in a civil war (either as an indigenous participant or as a third-party intervener), this might shorten the duration of the civil war. We code this variable as 1 if a democratic state was involved in the war and 0 otherwise.[7]
4. *Ethnic Diversity of the Focal State.* States with a more heterogeneous population in terms of ethnic composition are more likely to get entangled in longer civil wars than countries that are more homogeneous in nature. We code this variable as the number of ethnic groups that amounted to 10 percent or more of the state's population in the decade prior to the outbreak of the civil war.[8]

Since the duration of civil war is a discrete count variable, we ran a Poisson regression of the duration of the civil war in days on the number of intervening states and the various control variables. The clear message, shown in table 4, is that external intervention in civil wars has a significant impact on its duration. This is so even when we control for a number of potentially confounding variables. The observation of the Afghani president—who should know this from personal experience—appears in this case to be right on the mark.

### Testing the "Multipolarity Breeds Stability" Hypothesis

Several measures of polarity have been offered in the literature (Wayman and Morgan 1990). It was noted that there are some logical and empirical problems in these measures in terms of their relationship to war and peace. Here, however, we use a simple measure of the number of major powers in the system in any given year and their alliance relationships. The major power list is given by Small and Singer (1982). To measure polarity we used the following procedure. First, for any given number of major powers *m,* we compute the maximum polarization index. This maximum occurs when the major powers are split into two blocs, nearly equal in size. We calculate the number of possible alliance dyads in each of these (near) halves, then sum across the two blocs.[9] Next, we count the number of dyadic alliances between major powers and divide it by the maximum polarity score. We term this variable *polarity*. Since we conduct a more comprehensive analysis of system conflict in connection with the next hypothesis, the results for the "multipolarity breeds stability" hypothesis are given in table 5.

In general, multipolarity appears to be associated with peace. The higher the polarity (the more bipolarized the system), the more disputes and the more war exists. However, for MIDs this association holds for the entire period and for the nineteenth century, but not for the twentieth century. In the case of wars, the relationship appears to be consis-

TABLE 4. The Duration of Civil Wars Regressed on the Number of Intervening States and Control Variables

| Independent/Control Variable | Entire Period, 1816–1997 | 19th Century | 20th Century |
|---|---|---|---|
| No. of intervening states | 0.364** | 0.158** | 0.413** |
| | (0.003) | (0.008) | (0.003) |
| Western Hemisphere | 5.644** | −1.160** | 5.867** |
| | (0.577) | (0.014) | (0.577) |
| Europe | 5.112** | −1.220** | 4.665** |
| | (0.577) | (0.014) | (0.577) |
| Africa | 6.066** | NA | 6.021** |
| | (0.577) | | (0.577) |
| Middle East | 5.863** | −2.299** | 5.950** |
| | (0.577) | (0.014) | (0.577) |
| Asia | 6.350** | NA | 6.234** |
| | (0.577) | | (0.577) |
| Years of previous regime | −0.0001 | −0.015** | 0.005** |
| | (−0.001) | (0.004) | (0.001) |
| Democracy involved | −0.148** | −0.420** | −0.121** |
| | (0.006) | (0.015) | (0.008) |
| No. of distinct ethnic groups of 10% and above | 0.022** | −0.046** | 0.028** |
| | (0.001) | (0.002) | (0.001) |
| Constant | 1.033 | 8.157** | 0.950 |
| | (0.577) | (0.008) | (0.577) |
| Model statistics | $\chi^2 = 60,517.06$** | $\chi^2 = 24,766.29$** | $\chi^2 = 43,918.30$** |
| | Pseudo-$R^2 = 0.187$ | Pseudo-$R^2 = 0.331$ | Pseudo-$R^2 = 0.186$ |
| | $N = 194$ | $N = 69$ | $N = 125$ |

*Note:* Standard errors in parentheses.
* $p < .05$    ** $p < .01$

78

tent over time. In terms of this fairly simple measure of polarity, then, it appears that Xiang Zemin of China can find some empirical support in the history of the last two centuries.

### Testing the "Inequality and Poverty Breed Conflict" Hypothesis

This hypothesis can be tested at various levels of analysis, but the system level appears to best capture Fidel Castro's and King Harald's statements. To measure these variables we use two measures from the Correlates of War Material Capabilities Dataset (COW2).

1. *Inequality in the Distribution of Economic Wealth.* This is simply the Gini index of a mean measure of the proportion of energy consumption and iron and steel production of states in a given year.

2. *Proportion of States below the "Poverty Line."* For each year a "poverty line" was calculated using the following index. First, I calculated the average energy consumption score over all states for a given year. Second, I draw the poverty line for each year as 50 percent of the average energy consumption level for that year. Finally, I created an index of energy poverty, by assigning a state a score of 1 if its actual share of energy consumption was less than 50 percent of the mean level of energy consumption (and 0 otherwise). I repeated this set of operations for iron and steel consumption. Now I ranked states for each year as follows.

$$POVERTY = \begin{cases} 0 & if\ ENCONPOV = 0\ and\ IRNSTLPOV = 0 \\ 1 & if\ ENCONPOV = 1\ or\ IRNSTLPOV = 1 \\ 2 & if\ ENCONPOV = 1\ and\ IRNSTLPOV = 1 \end{cases} \quad (1.1)$$

where poverty level 1 is quite poor and poverty level 2 is very poor. Now for each year I summed across the number of quite poor and very poor states and divided the number of poor and very poor states by the number of states in the system, to get the proportion of states below the "poverty line."

The dependent variables in this test are the number of dyadic militarized interstate disputes and the number of dyadic wars in the system in a given year. The independent variables are the degree of economic

TABLE 5. Economic Inequality, Poverty, Polarity, Control Variables, and Conflict in the International System, 1816–1992: A Poisson Autoregressive Model

| Independent/Control Variable | Entire Period, 1816–1992 | 19th Century | 20th Century |
|---|---|---|---|
| | **No. of MIDs** | | |
| Constant | 0.274 | −0.871 | −9.727* |
| | (0.279) | (0.892) | (4.504) |
| Proportion of states in | 11.644** | 20.810** | 8.729** |
| alliances | (2.398) | (5.975) | (1.629) |
| Proportion of jointly | −57.315** | −56.026 | −41.929** |
| democratic dyads | (8.323) | (37.946) | (8.673) |
| Polarity of major power | −0.732* | −2.096** | −0.410 |
| system | (0.333) | (0.746) | (0.340) |
| Gini index of economic | −0.001 | −0.001 | 12.792** |
| inequality | (0.001) | (0.001) | (4.758) |
| Proportion of states below | 6.474** | 6.187** | 3.009** |
| poverty line | (0.510) | (1.822) | (0.818) |
| AR(1) | 0.807** | 0.154 | 0.788** |
| | (0.049) | (0.122) | (0.067) |
| Model Statistics | $F = 109.86$** | $F = 7.33$** | $F = 33.71$** |
| | Pseudo-$R^2$ = 0.794 | Pseudo-$R^2$ = 0.319 | Pseudo-$R^2$ = 0.693 |
| | $N = 171$ | $N = 82$ | $N = 88$ |
| | **No. of Wars** | | |
| Constant | −0.995 | −3.987 | −49.908** |
| | (0.706) | (2.130) | (14.800) |
| Proportion of states in | 27.839** | 33.760 | 16.981** |
| alliances | (3.489) | (19.827) | (4.640) |
| Proportion of jointly | −85.150** | −225.119* | −44.815* |
| democratic dyads | (22.974) | (93.561) | (24.068) |
| Polarity of major power | −2.979** | −5.328* | −1.710* |
| system | (0.718) | (2.594) | (0.991) |
| Gini index of economic | −0.002 | −0.005* | 58.389** |
| inequality | (0.003) | (0.002) | (15.473) |
| Proportion of states below | 4.526** | 10.461* | −0.601 |
| poverty line | (1.420) | (4.369) | (2.541) |
| AR(1) | 0.791** | 0.327** | 0.474** |
| | (0.052) | (0.103) | (0.085) |
| Model Statistics | $F = 53.50$** | $F = 4.43$** | $F = 15.66$** |
| | Pseudo-$R^2$ = 0.650 | Pseudo-$R^2$ = 0.203 | Pseudo-$R^2$ = 0.500 |
| | $N = 171$ | $N = 82$ | $N = 89$ |

Note: Standard errors in parentheses.
* $p < .05$    ** $p < .01$

inequality in the system and the share of states below the poverty line. As was the case in previous analyses, I use a number of control variables to prevent confounding effects in the relationship.

The control variables include the following:

1. Proportion of states in formal alliance networks (Maoz 2001).
2. Proportion of states in democratic networks (Maoz 2001).[10]
3. Proportion of major powers in the system that are in dyadic alliances with each other (discussed previously).

All independent/control variables are lagged one year back. We use Poisson regression allowing for autocorrelation and overdispersion (the ARPOIS function in Stata 7).[11] Table 5 provides the results of this analysis.

The results of this analysis provide mixed support for the hypotheses. With regard to MIDs, the Gini index of economic inequality does not appear to be related to the amount of conflict in the system in the general population and in the nineteenth century, but it does positively affect the number of MIDs in the twentieth century. On the other hand, the proportion of states below the poverty line does show a significant relationship to the number of MIDs in general and in both centuries.

The Gini index of economic inequality is significantly related to the number of wars in the twentieth century. The proportion of states below the poverty line is also significantly related to wars in the nineteenth century, but not in the general population and in the twentieth century.[12] All in all, the findings suggest that there is some empirical basis to the inequality and poverty hypotheses, but the evidence is not as definitive as Castro and Harald IV would have us believe.

Moving to the dyadic and national level, we use the dyad-year and nation-year unit to test this hypothesis, as well as the following measures to represent economic inequality and poverty. For the nation level I use the state's percentile in the distribution of economic wealth (consisting of an average of its percentile on the energy consumption and iron and steel production distributions, respectively). The control variables for the national analyses are applied from a number of studies on national conflict behavior (Maoz 1997b, 2000b, 2001), specifically, the following six variables.

1. Number of states in the focal state's politically relevant international environment (PRIE) (see Maoz 1996 for a discussion of this concept).
2. Capability ratio of the state's military capability to the sum of military capability scores of members of its PRIE.

3. Weighted number of allies of the state (Maoz 1996).
4. Average number of MIDs the state was involved in over the three-year period preceding the current year (Maoz 1997b).
5. Regime change in the state in the four years preceding the current year (coded 0 for no regime change and 1 for regime change).
6. Regime score of the state multiplied by the average regime score of its PRIE.[13]

For the dyadic level analysis I use the two variables mentioned by the statesmen. First I employ the minimum and maximum (high/low) economic wealth percentiles of the members of the dyad to examine how the dyad members are ranked in terms of wealth, relative to all nations in the system. Second, I use a wealth ratio, which is the ratio of the richest-to-poorest members of the dyad. Control variables are the typical variables used in the other analyses. Estimation procedures are cross-sectional time-series regressions, with *AR1* corrections for autocorrelation. Table 6 provides results of the nation-level test, and table 7 provides the results of the dyadic-level test.

As table 6 shows, the impact of economic inequality on national conflict involvement is statistically significant, but the evidence suggests the opposite of what is implied in the leaders' statements. In general, it is the rich who are the more conflict-prone states. Specifically, as the percentile of economic wealth of a state goes up, the amount of conflict involvement (both MID involvement and war involvement) goes up as well. Here, too, the results are not robust. For example, in the nineteenth century, economic wealth has a nonsignificant effect on MID involvement and a significant, but negative, effect on war involvement. The results for the entire period and for the twentieth century are in line with the proposition that rich states are typically more conflict prone than poor states (Maoz 2000a).

The results in table 7 suggest that, just as in the case of the nation-level analysis, as the minimum level of economic wealth of the dyad increases, the more likely is that dyad to engage in conflict. However, the more equal the economic wealth of dyad members (measured by the ratio of the richest member to the poorest), the less likely is the dyad to get entangled in conflict. These results hold for the entire period and for the twentieth century, but not for the nineteenth century.

On the whole, the economic inequality and poverty hypotheses received some support, but this empirical support is neither simple nor extremely robust. First, on the system level, there is some support to the notion that the greater the number of states living in relative poverty,

**TABLE 6.** Economic Status and Conflict Involvement of Nations, 1816–1992: Poisson Cross-Sectional Time-Series Analysis

| Independent/Control Variable | Entire Period, 1816–1992 | 19th Century | 20th Century |
|---|---|---|---|
| No. of dyadic MID involvements of a state | | | |
| No. of states in PRIE | 0.010** | 0.032* | 0.007* |
| | (0.003) | (0.017) | (0.003) |
| Capability ratio state-to-PRIE | 2.207** | 2.566* | 3.123* |
| | (0.736) | (1.356) | (1.423) |
| Weighted no. of allies of the state | −0.005 | −0.095** | −0.010* |
| | (0.006) | (0.018) | (0.005) |
| No. MIDs state was involved in past three years | 0.044** | −0.056 | 0.045** |
| | (0.014) | (0.067) | (0.011) |
| Regime score*regime score of PRIE | −0.012** | −0.009 | −0.011** |
| | (0.005) | (0.022) | (0.004) |
| Regime change in last four years? | 0.138 | 0.523* | 0.045 |
| | (0.139) | (0.209) | (0.146) |
| Percentile economic wealth of state | 1.057** | 0.432 | 1.025** |
| | (0.310) | (0.712) | (0.338) |
| Model's statistics | $N = 7,663$ | $N = 2,358$ | $N = 5,305$ |
| | States = 154 | States = 47 | States = 136 |
| | $\chi^2 = 215.38$** | $\chi^2 = 236.21$** | $\chi^2 = 182.19$** |
| No. of dyadic war involvements of states | | | |
| No. of states in PRIE | 0.006 | 0.068** | 0.003 |
| | (0.005) | (0.021) | (0.005) |
| Capability ratio state-to-PRIE | 1.271** | 2.388** | 1.453* |
| | (0.399) | (0.758) | (0.770) |
| Weighted no. of allies of the state | −0.052** | 0.028 | −0.061** |
| | (0.021) | (0.020) | (0.024) |
| No. MIDs state was involved in past 3 years | 0.082** | 0.036 | 0.076** |
| | (0.017) | (0.219) | (0.019) |
| Regime score*regime score of PRIE | −0.014* | −0.014 | −0.014* |
| | (0.008) | (0.033) | (0.007) |
| Regime change in last four years? | 0.410** | 0.729* | 0.338* |
| | (0.151) | (0.325) | (0.175) |
| Percentile economic wealth of state | 1.783** | −1.191* | 2.314** |
| | (0.423) | (1.014) | (0.637) |
| Model's statistics | $N = 7,663$ | $N = 2,358$ | $N = 6,580$ |
| | States = 154 | States = 47 | States = 145 |
| | $\chi^2 = 458.30$** | $\chi^2 = 33.13$** | $\chi^2 = 137.89$** |

*Note:* Standard errors in parentheses.
* $p < .05$    ** $p < .01$

the more conflict the system experiences. However, the expectation that increased economic inequality breeds conflict is only partially supported. When we get down to the monadic and dyadic levels, we observe that there is a consistent set of links between economic wealth and conflict. Richer states are more likely to engage in conflict than poorer ones, but economically equal dyads are less likely to engage in

TABLE 7.  Economic Status, Economic Inequality, and Dyadic Conflict, 1816–1992: Probit Cross-Sectional Time-Series Analysis (Politically Relevant Dyads)

| Independent/Control Variable | Entire Period, 1816–1992 | 19th Century | 20th Century |
|---|---|---|---|
| **No. of dyadic MID involvements of a state** | | | |
| Minimum regime score | −0.003** | 0.003* | −0.005* |
| | (0.001) | (0.001) | (0.001) |
| Capability ratio | −0.0002** | −0.002* | −0.001* |
| | (0.000) | (0.001) | (0.000) |
| Alliance | −0.294** | −0.196 | −0.368** |
| | (0.063) | (0.131) | (0.072) |
| Contiguity | 0.128** | 0.073** | 0.143** |
| | (0.013) | (0.023) | (0.019) |
| Minimum percentile wealth | 0.811** | 0.423 | 0.894** |
| of dyad members | (0.046) | (0.302) | (0.148) |
| Wealth ratio | −0.154** | −0.172* | −0.161** |
| | (0.049) | (0.089) | (0.053) |
| Model's statistics | $N = 57{,}047$ | $N = 11{,}316$ | $N = 45{,}697$ |
| | Dyads = 1,136 | Dyads = 260 | Dyads = 1,065 |
| | $\chi^2 = 188.74^{**}$ | $\chi^2 = 33.26^{**}$ | $\chi^2 = 214.20^{**}$ |
| **No. of dyadic war involvements of states** | | | |
| Minimum regime score | −0.005** | −0.001 | −0.006** |
| | (0.001) | (0.003) | (0.001) |
| Capability ratio | −0.002** | −0.010** | −0.002* |
| | (0.001) | (0.004) | (0.001) |
| Alliance | −0.480** | −0.039 | −0.572** |
| | (0.120) | (0.205) | (0.136) |
| Contiguity | 0.046* | 0.082** | 0.036 |
| | (0.019) | (0.031) | (0.022) |
| Minimum percentile wealth | 0.534** | −0.249 | 0.647** |
| of dyad members | (0.209) | (0.350) | (0.246) |
| Wealth ratio | −0.065** | −0.164 | −0.064 |
| | (0.064) | (0.121) | (0.078) |
| Model's statistics | $N = 57{,}047$ | $N = 11{,}316$ | $N = 45{,}697$ |
| | Dyads = 1,136 | Dyads = 260 | Dyads = 1,065 |
| | $\chi^2 = 101.09^{**}$ | $\chi^2 = 21.88^{**}$ | $\chi^2 = 108.89^{**}$ |

*Note:* Standard errors in parentheses.
* $p < .05$     ** $p < .01$

conflict than economically unequal dyads. Conflict between rich and poor states is more common than between rich states only or between poor states only.

## Testing the Effect of Conflict and Democratization on Development

This hypothesis can be tested on different levels of analysis, but it seems that, in order to be loyal to the spirit of the statement from which it had been extracted, the systemic level is the most appropriate level to analyze it. I used three indices to measure the level of world's economic development. The first two measures are the world's per-capita energy consumption and iron-steel production levels per year. These measures cover the entire 1816–1992 period. Second, for the post-1950 period, I used the world's per-capita GDP in real (1980) prices. Third, I used yearly percentage rates of change on these indices to measure the effects of democratization and conflict on change.

The independent variables for these analyses are the proportion of democracies in the system and the number of MIDs and wars in the system, lagged one year back. Results are shown in table 8. We list only a subset of the analyses on the various dependent variables. The results of the other analyses are fundamentally similar to those reported herein. This analysis suggests, again, that there is some—albeit weak—evidence in support of the hypothesis that conflict impedes the world's economic growth. The evidence that democratization facilitates economic growth on a global scale is more consistent; yet, it is not sufficiently robust to suggest an unequivocal confirmation of these hypotheses. The impact of conflict and democratization on development and economic growth depends on the measure of economic growth used and on the time-horizon. In general, the results for the twentieth century give more support to these hypotheses than do the results for the nineteenth century. This suggests that the linkages between politics—domestic and international—and economics have been more apparent in the twentieth century than in the nineteenth century.

### Testing the Democratic Peace Proposition

The democratic peace proposition was arguably the single most tested proposition by the scholarly international relations community in the last decade and a half. Thus, we will not delve too much into the test of Schroeder's notions derived from this proposition. However, since democracy—or more broadly defined regime type—was used as a control in most of the analyses of the other hypotheses, we can address this hypothesis quite simply.

The test of hypothesis E.1, which suggests that democratic states that protect their citizens' rights experience less conflict than those states that do not, is presented in table 6. The results of this table cor-

TABLE 8. The Effect of Conflict and Democratization on the World's Economic Development: A Time-Series Analysis, 1816(1950)–1992

| Dependent Variable | Independent Variable | Entire Period | 19th Century | 20th Century |
|---|---|---|---|---|
| Per-capita energy | Proportion of democratic | 105.397** | 23.958 | 93.528* |
| consumption | dyads | (37.386) | (30.390) | (54.284) |
| | Lagged no. of MIDs | −0.042** | 0.010 | −0.052* |
| | | (0.017) | (0.006) | (0.025) |
| | Constant | −26.664 | 168.999* | −884.113** |
| | | (17.488) | (65.649) | (200.030) |
| Model's statistics | | $N = 175$ | $N = 82$ | $N = 92$ |
| | | $F = 8.49^{**}$ | $F = 1.44$ | $F = 4.37^{**}$ |
| | | $\bar{R}^2 = 0.079$ | $\bar{R}^2 = 0.011$ | $\bar{R}^2 = 0.069$ |
| | | D-W = 1.90 | D-W = 2.57 | D-W = 1.83 |
| Rate of change in | Proportion of democratic | 2.552** | −0.762 | 3.666** |
| per-capita iron and | dyads | (0.552) | (0.880) | (0.905) |
| steel consumption | | | | |
| | Lagged no. of MIDs | −0.000 | −0.000 | 0.001 |
| | | (0.003) | (0.001) | (0.001) |
| | Constant | −0.022 | 0.057** | 0.184* |
| | | (0.029) | (0.017) | (0.085) |
| Model's statistics | | $N = 175$ | $N = 82$ | $N = 92$ |
| | | $F = 10.27^{**}$ | $F = 1.24$ | $F = 8.33^{**}$ |
| | | $\bar{R}^2 = 0.096$ | $\bar{R}^2 = 0.006$ | $\bar{R}^2 = 0.139$ |
| | | D-W = 1.90 | D-W = 2.57 | D-W = 1.83 |
| Percent change in | Proportion of democratic | 1.337* | NA | NA |
| world's per-capita | dyads | (0.448) | | |
| GDP (1950–92) | | | | |
| | Lagged no. of MIDs | 0.000 | NA | NA |
| | | (0.000) | | |
| | Constant | −0.062 | NA | NA |
| | | (0.041) | | |
| Model's statistics | | $N = 41$ | | |
| | | $F = 4.69^{**}$ | | |
| | | $\bar{R}^2 = 0.156$ | | |
| | | D-W = 1.99 | | |

*Note:* Standard errors in parentheses.
* $p < .05$     ** $p < .01$

86

roborate Maoz's (2001a) findings. Generally speaking, if Schroeder's notion about the impact of the preservation of human rights within a state on its international conflict involvement ignored the kind of environment the state lived in, then this notion has no empirical support. However, if we do take into account the fact that a spillover effect from domestic practices to international practices can occur only in environments where the preservation of human rights is a general norm, then Schroeder's notion has fairly robust empirical support. This is true especially for the twentieth century. But it appears to apply both to the impact of democracy on MID behavior and to the impact of democracy on war behavior. We can thus suggest that there is a solid foundation in international history, at least in the twentieth century, for a modified version of the belief regarding the idea that domestic protection of human rights has a dampening impact on conflict behavior.

The results for the systemic version of this hypothesis (E.2) are given in table 5. If we control for other systemic factors that may confound the relationship between democratization and peace, then the proportion of democratic dyads has a dampening impact on conflict, but this impact appears to be characteristic only of the history of the twentieth century, but not earlier. This is probably because the networking between democracies in the twentieth century was much more prevalent—thus generating more pronounced spillover effects—than in the nineteenth century. We can thus state cautiously that Schroeder's version of the democratic peace proposition rests upon fairly solid empirical foundations.

### Testing the Effect of Conflict on Democracy

Following King Abdullah's proposition, we now examine whether conflict affects democratization. The tests are conducted on the national and systemic levels of analysis. On the national level, I test the effect of conflict involvement on democratization using a cross-sectional time-series regression of regime score (Maoz and Russett 1993). I use two sets of analyses. One is based on a nation-year unit, wherein a state's regime is regressed on a set of independent variables lagged one year back. The other analysis employs the nation-half-decade unit. In this analysis, a nation's average regime score during a given five-year period (starting with its first five years of independence and continuing in five-year intervals) is regressed on a set of independent variables lagged one five-year period back.[14] This kind of analysis is based on the supposition that the effects of conflict on regime structure take more time to materialize.

The independent variables in the analyses include the number of

TABLE 9.   The Effect of Conflict on Democracy and on Development of States, 1950–1992: Time-Series, Cross-Sectional Regression

| Independent Variable | Entire Period 1816–1992 | Unit of Analysis Nineteenth Century 1816–1899 | Twentieth Century 1900–1992 |
|---|---|---|---|
| **Nation-Year Unit of Analysis** | | | |
| Constant | 0.377 | 1.439* | 0.348 |
| | (0.336) | (0.624) | (0.407) |
| Avg. democracy score of PRIE | 0.061** | 0.055* | 0.051** |
| | (0.014) | (0.023) | (0.018) |
| Past level of democracy | 0.901** | 0.942** | 0.891* |
| | (0.012) | (0.016) | (0.014) |
| Lagged no. of MID involvement | 0.049 | −0.081 | 0.040 |
| | (0.107) | (0.190) | (0.117) |
| Lagged economic wealth | 0.119* | 0.079 | 0.133* |
| | (0.061) | (0.086) | (0.064) |
| Model statistics | $N = 10,062$ | $N = 2,484$ | $N = 7,577$ |
| | States = 158 | States = 48 | States = 149 |
| | $\chi^2 = 10,898**$ | $\chi^2 = 8,605**$ | $\chi^2 = 5,730**$ |
| **Nation-Five-Year Unit of Analysis** | | | |
| Constant | −11.463** | 0.654 | 2.367** |
| | (1.824) | (0.731) | (0.649) |
| Avg. democracy score of PRIE | 0.163** | 0.025 | 0.022 |
| | (0.049) | (0.021) | (0.027) |
| Past level of democracy | 0.818** | 0.949** | 0.781** |
| | (0.015) | (0.017) | (0.017) |
| Lagged no. of MID involvement | 0.167** | −0.093 | 0.158* |
| | (0.066) | (0.140) | (0.070) |
| Lagged economic wealth | 0.257* | 0.393* | 0.301** |
| | (0.115) | (0.195) | (0.116) |
| Model statistics | $N = 2,158$ | $N = 540$ | $N = 1,617$ |
| | States = 179 | States = 52 | States = 166 |
| | $\chi^2 = 4,121**$ | $\chi^2 = 5,626**$ | $\chi^2 = 2,546**$ |
| **System-Year** | | | |
| Constant | −0.007 | −0.0001 | 0.012 |
| | (0.017) | (0.020) | (0.030) |
| Capability concentration | 0.025 | −0.008 | 0.059 |
| | (0.036) | (0.047) | (0.055) |
| Lagged no. of MIDs | 0.001** | 0.0002* | 0.000 |
| | (0.000) | (0.001) | (0.000) |
| Lagged proportion of poor states | 0.015 | −0.003 | −0.009 |
| | (0.021) | (0.036) | (0.036) |
| Lagged proportion democracies | 0.925** | 0.964** | 0.882** |
| | (0.032) | (0.059) | (0.049) |

TABLE 9—*Continued*

| Independent Variable | Entire Period 1816–1992 | Unit of Analysis Nineteenth Century 1816–1899 | Twentieth Century 1900–1992 |
|---|---|---|---|
| Model statistics | $N = 175$ | $N = 82$ | $N = 92$ |
| | $F = 1,148.30**$ | $F = 363.48**$ | $F = 126.08**$ |
| | $\bar{R}^2 = 0.964$ | $\bar{R}^2 = 0.947$ | $\bar{R}^2 = 0.846$ |
| | D-W = 2.012 | D-W = 1.977 | D-W = 2.039 |
| | **System Five-Year** | | |
| Constant | −0.164 | NA | NA |
| | (0.137) | | |
| Capability concentration | 0.153 | NA | NA |
| | (0.138) | | |
| Lagged no. of MIDs | 0.001** | NA | NA |
| | (0.000) | | |
| Lagged proportion of poor states | 0.215 | NA | NA |
| | (0.166) | | |
| Lagged proportion democracies | 0.670** | NA | NA |
| | (0.091) | | |
| | $N = 34$ | | |
| | $F = 28.37**$ | | |
| | $\bar{R}^2 = 0.768$ | | |
| | D-W = 1.931 | | |

*Note:* Standard errors in parentheses.
$* p < .05$    $** p < .01$

MIDs (or wars) the state was involved in during the last year or five-year period, the state's level of economic development, and the average regime score in the state's politically relevant environment. Table 9 provides the results of this analysis. Table 9 suggests that conflict involvement does have an impact on democratization at both the monadic and systemic level, but (1) the impact is, by and large, positive, as opposed to the negative impact that was expected by King Abdullah and by Thompson (1996), and (2) it is not especially robust. Thus it appears that conflict may be an excuse for avoiding democratization, but it is empirically related to greater rather than lower rates of democratization.

## CONCLUSION

Where do we stand now compared to the exercise that Singer and Small (1974) attempted over thirty years ago? Before we perform this comparison, we must keep in mind several caveats. First, the Singer and Small article was principally a didactic exercise. They called for a re-education of the world's leaders to include more pertinent empirical knowledge on the issues they were dealing with, in general, and on war-and peace-related issues, in particular. The empirical analyses contained in that article were of a primarily heuristic value. Second, the evidence that we have today on these matters is based on a considerably richer database than that available to Singer and Small in the early 1970s. Third, the statistical and programming tools available today are almost incomparable to the ones available to scholars of international conflict at that time. Clearly J. David Singer's contributions were invaluable in terms of the upgrading of the level of data and the quantum improvement in the quality and sophistication of quantitative research on war and peace that characterizes current scholarship. In light of these improvements, the comparison of our findings to Singer and Small's is like comparing the speed and quality of computing and programming using a 1940s von Neumann computing machine to that of a supercomputer in the twenty-first century.

With these caveats in mind, we can say that our effort to examine the empirical foundations of leaders' beliefs about international affairs leads to more encouraging conclusions than those of Singer and Small thirty years ago. First, we corroborated some of Singer and Small's findings regarding the "war begets war" hypothesis and some of the control variables' effects on this notion. However, when we expanded this hypothesis to the "conflict begets conflict" version, we found that leaders' notions about this fact have substantial empirical support. More important, the history of the twentieth century adds considerable credence to the "conflict begets conflict" notion.

Second, with respect to the statements extracted from leaders' speeches at the UN Millennium Summit, we emerged more hopeful regarding the correspondence between leaders' beliefs and the empirical record. Admittedly, our sample of leaders' beliefs is quite small and probably unrepresentative of the whole. But on the basis of what we did examine, we can say that most of the hypotheses derived from these statements receive at least some degree of empirical support. One can also say—this may be more true with respect to some of the hypotheses than others—that leaders of the early twenty-first century are more attuned to what scientists find out than they have been in the past.

Let us now summarize what we have found when we compared leaders' notions about international conflict to the actual empirical record.

1. *The "Conflict Begets Conflict" Hypothesis.* This hypothesis appears to be strongly supported for short-of-war militarized interstate disputes, but not with respect to war. Specifically, it is fair to say that "MIDs beget MIDs" but "wars do not beget

wars." What we did discover (see, e.g., the bottom part of table 6) is that "MIDs beget war."

2. *Intervention and the Duration of Civil Wars.* This hypothesis appears to be clearly supported by the empirical record, at least in the twentieth century. This is true both as to the question of whether or not outside intervention occurs in the course of a civil war and also with respect to the question of how many outside states have intervened in a civil war. This notion holds even when we control for other factors that may affect civil war duration. This hypothesis has not—to the best of our knowledge—been examined by previous research. The support for this hypothesis provides a number of interesting policy-relevant suggestions.

3. *Multipolarity Affects Peace.* This proposition appears to have some support. It must be noted, however, that the general record of tests of the relationships between multipolarity and peace is mixed at best (e.g., Bueno de Mesquita and Lalman 1988). We need, therefore to take this support as very qualified and tentative.

4. *Inequality, Poverty, and Conflict.* There is some empirical support to the notion that economic inequality and poverty breed conflict. This is true at the systemic level where in some cases the level of inequality in the system and the proportion of states below the poverty line is significantly related to the number of MIDs and wars in the system. However, it is typical that richer states are more conflict prone than those that are poor, and the higher the level of economic equality between states, the more likely they are to engage in conflict. This corroborates a more structural analysis of conflict-proneness and pacifism (Maoz 2000a).

5. *Democratic Peace, Democratization, and Economic Growth.* It does seem that conflict has an adverse impact on economic growth as measured by energy consumption, but this does not apply to other—some more commonly used—measures of wealth. Here, too, there is some empirical evidence that leaders' beliefs are grounded in reality, but the evidence is far from clear and unequivocal.

The question is whether the glass is half-full or half-empty. The good news is that there is some evidence that supports leaders' beliefs. However, the bad news is that the evidence is neither sufficiently strong nor sufficiently robust to justify the level of conviction that comes out of these statements. There still is a need to educate leaders not only to use more cautious language when it comes to identifying the causes of conflict and the conditions for peace, but also probably to place some of their beliefs in a more tentative mode. It is fair to advise them to be more cautious about those issues prior to making policy based on such beliefs.

## NOTES

1. For texts of these statements see http://www.un.org/millennium/sum mit.htm.

2. A vast majority of the leaders' speeches were of that nature, i.e., dealing with their own states' or regions' specific disputes and the conditions for their resolution.

3. Finally, I have only reviewed statements that had an English version. There were quite a few statements that were not given in English, and no English version was available for them. Those were omitted.

4. Note that, following the Norwegian and Pakistani statements, the complementary proposition is also raised, namely, that economic development and prosperity breeds peace.

5. The data can be downloaded from the COW2 website at http://cow2 .la.psu.edu/cow2dslist.htm.

6. There is a regional coding for Oceania, but no civil war observations for this region.

7. Data for the last two variables is obtained from the Polity IV data set.

8. Ethnic composition data set can be obtained in the COW2 Project website.

9. The formula is $\frac{m}{2}(\frac{m}{2} - 1)$ for even $m$ and

$$\frac{(\frac{m-1}{2})(\frac{m-1}{2} - 1)}{2} + \frac{(\frac{m+1}{2})(\frac{m+1}{2} - 1)}{2}$$

for odd $m$.

10. Maoz (2001) discusses the notions of networks in the context of testing the democratic peace proposition across different levels of analysis. He defines a network as a set of at least three states that (1) are politically relevant to each other and (2) share a common property or are linked by some trait. Accordingly, an alliance network is a set of at least three states that are politically relevant and allied with each other. This is what network analysis calls *cliques* (Wasserman and Faust 1994, 253–57). A democratic network is a set of at least three states that are politically relevant to each other and are democratic. The proportion of states in alliance nets is the set of states in alliance nets divided by the number of the politically relevant dyads. For a more general discussion of these concepts see Maoz et al. (2002).

11. This program can be downloaded from Stata's website (STB-46). See www.stata.com.

12. I ran a similar analysis on the number of civil wars in the system and found both the Gini index of economic inequality and the proportion of states below the poverty line to be significantly related to the dependent variable in both the entire period and in the twentieth century. I do not report this in detail because it is not directly derived from the leaders' statements. But it is a fact worth noting.

13. Based on the finding by Maoz (2001) that the monadic version of the democratic peace works (that is, democracies are *generally* less conflict prone) if we take into account not only the regime of the state, but also the regimes of other states in its politically relevant environment. This specific version of the regime measure is also relevant for testing the E.1 hypothesis (discussed later).

14. The values of independent variables are also averaged over the preceding five-year period.

# THE NATIONAL INTEREST VERSUS
# INDIVIDUAL POLITICAL AMBITION

## Democracy, Autocracy, and the Reciprocation of Force
## and Violence in Militarized Interstate Disputes

*Bruce Bueno de Mesquita and James Lee Ray*

Some time ago, J. David Singer (1980b, xxxvi–xxxvii) observed, "Every national security decision will reflect . . . the pluralistic distribution of power within that society, be it near the autocratic or democratic end of the spectrum. From this it follows that a central and continuing preoccupation of the decisional elite is to remain in office." In so doing, Singer focused on what is arguably a fundamental division within every society. "There are two classes, those with authoritative roles and those without, and these classes define opposing attitudes (i.e., a particular structure of conflict). . . . *This is the main one manifested in societal and collective conflict and political struggle*" (Rummel 1977, 104; emphasis added).

Singer himself never did explore in any great detail the possible implications of his statement regarding the priority that "decisional elites" give to remaining in power. He and many others in the field were much more enamored at the time with "structural" explanations focusing on the impact of various systemic factors on the war-proneness of the entire international system (Deutsch and Singer 1964; Singer, Bremer, and Stuckey 1972). Nevertheless, he and a coauthor were among the first to evaluate what can now be viewed, for reasons we will discuss later, as one of the more important implications of this assumption about the priorities of leaders of states when he analyzed the relationship between regime type and interstate conflict in "The War-Proneness of Democratic Regimes, 1816–1965" (Small and Singer 1976). In this essay, we are going to discuss briefly some recent developments using the assumption that leaders give priority to maintaining themselves in power as a starting point for the analysis of foreign policies and international politics. We will then address issues regarding the impact of regime type on interstate conflict; more specifically we will focus on whether joint democracy, or regime similarity in general, has the greater pacifying impact on interstate relations. The theoretical approach discussed here will lead us to the conclusion that democratic states should be less conflict prone in general in their relationships with each other than undemocratic or autocratic states. We will evaluate this idea with analyses of data on militarized interstate disputes occurring between 1816 and 1992, in which we will focus in particular on the tendency of states in those disputes to reciprocate the use of force and violence. We will conclude with a discussion of the implications of our findings for the debate about the relative importance of the pacifying effects of joint democracy, on the one hand, and the more general political similarity, on the other.

## THE RELATIONSHIP BETWEEN DOMESTIC AND INTERNATIONAL POLITICS

Decades ago, the evolution and consolidation of the bipolar international system encouraged a focus on the impact of system structure on interstate politics (e.g., Kaplan 1957; Rosecrance 1963; Waltz 1967), while realism (Morgenthau 1948) and neorealism (Waltz 1979) have long encouraged the conceptualization of states as unitary rational actors (Keohane 1983). Both of these important theoretical proclivities share a tendency to deemphasize the impact and importance of factors internal to the states whose policies and interactions are being analyzed.

Bueno de Mesquita's (1981) original model of interstate interaction dealt exclusively with the capabilities of states and international factors in its attempt to account for interstate war initiations. However, Bueno de Mesquita and Lalman (1992) compare a realpolitik model of interstate interactions to a domestic variant that differs most importantly on one out of seven basic assumptions. The realpolitik variant is based on an assumption that a state's foreign policy decision makers are "without regard for the wishes and objectives of domestic political constituencies." In contrast, the domestic variant stipulates that the foreign policy decision-making process in every state is "determined by internal political rules, procedures, norms, and considerations and may or may not be attuned to foreign policy considerations" (Bueno de Mesquita and Lalman 1992, 41). A systematic empirical evaluation of both models reveals a preponderance of evidence in favor of the domestic variant.

Bueno de Mesquita and Siverson (1995, 842–43) argue that "political leaders are intent on maintaining themselves in power," and that "our view differs from the realist approach in that the selection of policy options . . . may be seen as endogenous to domestic political concerns rather than just to the international system's structure." Influenced by an earlier version of this argument (i.e., Bueno de Mesquita and Siverson 1993), Ray (1995, 39) emphasizes the potential relevance of such a basic assumption to the democratic peace proposition.[1] He concludes that "this version of the theoretical base for the democratic peace proposition would assert that leaders in democracies might avoid wars against other democratic states . . . because they feel that fighting such wars might be harmful to their chances of staying in power" (40).

Bueno de Mesquita and Siverson (1996, 2) develop a "domestic theory of international politics" relying in a fundamental way on the assumption that "foreign policy leaders . . . choose actions with an eye to staying in power." It focuses on the impact of different sizes of the "selectorate" (the subset of a state's population that participates in the selection of political leadership) and the winning coalition (the subset of the electorate that controls the minimum amount of resources necessary to maintain the governing coalition in power).[2] Roughly speaking, "democratic" regimes are those based on political systems with large selectorates and large winning coalitions, and "autocratic" regimes are marked by large selectorates and small winning coalitions. Ray (1995) argues that an approach emphasizing the basic assumption that leaders desire to stay in power constitutes a relatively modest modification of realist theory but later (Ray 1999) concludes that moving beyond such axioms as states seek power (Morgenthau 1948) or states seek security (Waltz 1979) toward a model featuring the assumption that political leaders give the highest priority to maintaining themselves in power is potentially a paradigmatic shift of substantial importance. Such an innovation makes it possible to integrate domestic and international "games" (Putnam 1988) played by leaders in autocratic as well as democratic regimes in a theoretically coherent, axiomatically based manner. Of special interest in the context of this essay, Bueno Mesquita, Morrow, Siverson, and Smith (1999) explain how a model based on the assumption that leaders give priority to keeping themselves in power can account for seven important empirical regularities regarding the relationship between regime type and interstate conflict, in addition to the democratic peace proposition that democratic states do not fight interstate wars against each other.

The extent to which such an approach contrasts with current predominant theoretical competitors is reflected in a recent review of theoretical developments in the field of international politics. Legro and Moravcsik (1999, 21) discuss realist, liberal, epistemic, and institutionalist theoretical arguments. They conclude that "nearly all concur . . . that governments generally place a high, perhaps superordinate value on national security, territorial integrity, and political independence." In short, realist as well as many prominent contemporary competitive approaches rely on assumptions such as "states seek power" or "states seek security." An axiomatic basis emphasizing that state leaders are instead primarily interested in their own political fortunes and fates constitutes a distinctive point of departure in the analysis of interstate politics. Bueno de Mesquita et al. (1999, 2003) demonstrate theoretically and provide empirical evidence in support of the idea that even national defeat in war can be *preferred* and *chosen* over pursuit of victory in interstate conflicts as a means to maximize survival in office, given the right domestic political considerations. This is a possibility directly at odds with the view that all regimes place the highest value on national security and territorial integrity.

In short, we will argue, as J. David Singer emphasized over two decades ago, that "a central . . . preoccupation of the decisional elite is to remain in office." We will argue further that it is possible to analyze international politics in a manner that focuses on the division in every society between the rulers and the ruled, and that such an approach has important potential to improve our understanding of international politics. Perhaps most important, it can significantly expand our ability to comprehend the interrelationships between domestic and interstate politics. We will deal most intensively here with a current controversy regarding the relationship between regime type and interstate conflict suggested by our theoretical approach, and in a manner that will generate evidence important to the evaluation of competing arguments on both sides of this controversy. Let us turn now to the specifics of this debate.

## JOINT DEMOCRACY, POLITICAL SIMILARITY, AND INTERSTATE CONFLICT

Both Bueno de Mesquita et al. (1999, 802) and Ray (2001) divide states, for purposes of discussion, theoretical analyses, and empirical analyses, into the categories of "democratic" (or large selectorate, large winning coalition) and "autocratic" (or large selectorate, small winning coalition). We understand that sorting states into such dichotomous categories is not logically necessary and may well ultimately be undesirable. States do not "naturally" fall into such simple categories. The process of drawing the line of demarcation between such categories somewhere is

97

inescapably arbitrary, and assigning states to one side of that line or the other often involves "throwing away" information.

However, theorizing necessarily involves at least pruning information, and for some purposes at this early stage in the process of developing a theoretical approach that interests us, it may be useful to sort states into simple categories. Vasquez (1993), for example, assumes that wars between states relatively equal in military-industrial capabilities are fundamentally different in important ways from wars between states highly unequal in military capabilities, even though it is obvious that pairs of states cannot be sorted into neat, dichotomous categories such as "equal" and "unequal." Similarly, Waltz (1979) categorizes political systems as "hierarchical" and "anarchical," while being fully aware that "two simple categories of anarchy and hierarchy do not seem to accommodate the infinite variety our senses record."

Having sorted states into dichotomous categories of political regimes, Bueno de Mesquita and Ray have also both advocated *directed* dyadic analyses that keep track of "who does what to whom." Such a focus on directed dyads leads logically to the formulation of four basic categories of conflicts between states, namely: conflicts initiated by (1) democratic states against democratic states, (2) autocratic states against democratic states, (3) democratic states against autocratic states, and (4) autocratic states against autocratic states. Ray (2001) points out that categorizing conflicts in this fashion creates the basis for six fundamental hypotheses on the directed dyadic level of analysis about these conflicts: (1) Democratic states are less likely than autocratic states to initiate conflicts against other democratic states; (2) Democratic states are less likely to initiate conflicts against other democratic states than to initiate conflicts against autocratic states; (3) Democratic states are less likely to initiate conflicts against other democratic states than are autocratic states to initiate conflicts against other autocratic states; (4) Democratic states are less likely to initiate conflicts against autocratic states than are autocratic states to initiate conflicts against democratic states; (5) Autocratic states are less likely to initiate conflicts against democratic states than they are to initiate conflicts against other autocratic states, and (6) Democratic states are less likely than autocratic states to initiate conflicts against autocratic states.

One of us has suggested with respect to hypothesis 4 that democratic states are, under rarely achieved ceteris paribus conditions, more likely to initiate interstate wars against autocratic states than vice versa (see Bueno de Mesquita et al. 1999, 791; Bueno de Mesquita and Morrow 1999, 61–62). However, when all else is not equal, it is apparent from the selectorate theory that we should expect the propensity of democratic states to initiate wars against autocratic states to be about equal to the probability that autocratic states will initiate wars against democratic states.

In this essay, we will focus on a variant of hypothesis 3, having to do with the relative propensities for conflict among democratic states, on the one hand, and among autocratic states, on the other. This hypothesis is of particular interest in part because of its vivid contrast with an alternative notion that there is an "autocratic peace" as well as a "democratic peace." Furthermore, in this alternative view, the democratic peace hypothesis is merely a more particular example of the more general and therefore more interesting idea that it is political similarity that has the more important pacifying impact on relationships among states. Malin (1997, 375) for example, argues that "autocratic states can create and enjoy a stable peace, based on shared principles." Similarly, Elman (1997, 497–98) asserts in her concluding review of case studies relevant to issues regarding the democratic peace that "several contributors to this book find that nondemocracies . . . can share a peace based on normative consensus." One prominent critic of research on the democratic peace argues that "on the basis of the empirical evidence alone, it seems to make as much sense to differentiate between autocratic and other dyads as to distinguish between democratic and other pairs," and that "substantial evidence of an autocratic peace across time exists" (Gowa 1999, 107–8). Suzanne Werner (2000, 369) asserts that since "politically similar states are systematically less likely to disagree, we should anticipate that dyads comprised of politically similar states will generally experience fewer disputes." She concludes that for the time period from 1816 to 1985 "the empirical results are consistent with this conjecture." That finding reinforces the notion that states with similar interests or "political affinity" are less likely to become involved in interstate conflicts with each other. Gartzke (1998, 11) claims, for example, that "the argument that joint democracy may lead to similar preferences is theoretically plausible, but the argument is applicable to any type of regime. . . . If similar regime type leads to similar preferences, then we have not a democratic peace' so much as a regime type similarity peace'" (see also Lemke and Reed 1996).

Even many advocates of the democratic peace thesis agree that political similarity is a potentially important pacifying factor. Indeed, in their landmark article, Maoz and Russett (1993) devise their index of joint democracy in such a way that it reflects in important part not only how democratic a pair of states might be, but also how similar the two regimes are to each other.[3] And Oneal and Ray (1997, 768) acknowledge that "our results show, the probability of a dispute is not only a function of the average level of democracy in a dyad but also the political distance separating the states along the democracy-autocracy continuum."

Carried to its logical extreme, at least, the argument regarding the pacifying impact of political similarity between democracies as well as autocracies has the potential to subsume entirely the hypothesis that democracy has any independent pacifying effect. Joint democracies, according to this notion, are merely a subset of politically similar states (as are joint autocracies), and it is the similarity of regimes within pairs of states, rather than democracy per se, that exerts the important pacifying impact on relationships among states.

## JOINT DEMOCRACY VERSUS POLITICAL SIMILARITY: A THEORETICAL ARGUMENT

However, our analysis of the impact of the size of selectorates and winning coalitions on policy decisions by leaders of states intent on remaining in power leads us to conclude that regime similarity is not pacifying. We anticipate that there is not an autocratic peace and that the democratic peace is not primarily a product of shared values. Rather, it is the product of the interaction of specific domestic institutional constraints that shape the incentives of leaders involved in disputes. We sketch the logic behind this conclusion here.[4]

For the sake of brevity, we will discuss the logic of our claim that there is no autocratic peace in terms familiar to analysts as well as critics of research on democratic peace. That is, we will in this argument rely on the terms *democracy* and *autocracy*, and skim over some details regarding the linkage between the size of winning coalitions, selectorate size, and categories of regime types. To make the linkage clear, we note here that while *democracy* and *autocracy* are not defined comprehensively or with precision by the size of winning coalitions or selectorates, these institutional factors are a crucial component distinguishing between regime types in the minds of most analysts and researchers, even if they do not think about these matters in such terms. Leaders in states typically thought of as democracies usually rely on large winning coalitions drawn from large selectorates; indeed, in democratic states the selectorates are virtually the entire adult citizenry of the state. To be sure, the proportion of selectorates included in winning coalitions varies across democracies. In systems where the presidents are directly elected, and in states where voters are presented national lists of candidates for parliament from competing political parties, for instance, the leadership must evoke the support of approximately half of the selectorate to form a winning coalition. In single-member district, first-past-the-post parliamentary systems, in contrast, a victorious prime minister may need support from only about one-quarter of the selectorate. This is so because roughly 50 percent of the vote in each district suffices to secure victory for a member of parliament, and the prime minister requires the support of only about half of all members of parliament. Therefore, a total of only about 25 percent of all voters are required to provide the prime minister with a majority in parliament. And in a multimember district proportional representation parliamentary system—in which there are typically more than two parties competing for office—the winning coalition can be substantially smaller than 25 percent.

In contrast, rigged election autocracies typically have winning coalitions that consist of 5 percent or less—sometimes much less—of the selectorate. In other words, "modern" autocracies tend to have small winning coalitions and large selectorates.[5] Other aspects of democracy or autocracy, such as the degree of corruption, public goods production, individual wealth, oppression, and so forth, can be shown to be endogenous products of the size of and the ratio of winning coalitions to selectorates (Bueno de Mesquita et al. 2003).

We assume that every leader wants to keep her position of power, and that every polity produces challengers who would like to depose the incumbent and replace her. Leaders maintain support for the regimes they head by providing a mix of public goods—goods that benefit everyone in the society—and private goods—rewards that go only to members of the winning coalition—with at least as much going to coalition members as the mix of valued goods that can credibly be offered by a political rival. Challengers have a disadvantage in that they cannot guarantee the continued payment of private goods to those who help bring them to power because it is obviously possible, even likely, that when the challenger rises to power, he will shake up his winning coalition. He will, for example, be likely to purge those he learns are less likely to be loyal in the future.

In fact, it turns out that in equilibrium the probability of any member of the selectorate making it into the winning coalition beyond the initial transition period is equal to the ratio of the size of the winning coalition ($W$) to the size of the selectorate ($S$). The smaller this ratio ($W/S$), the greater the loyalty that winning coalition members will have to their leader (beyond personal affinity, usually a minor factor), because if the winning coalition is small, relative to the size of the selectorate, then the probability that political defections will lead to the loss of privileged access to private goods is high. In other words, if winning coalitions in any political system are small relative to the size of the selectorate, the chance

that a defector will be sufficiently fortunate to be included in any suc-
ceeding winning coalition is accordingly reduced. In addition, the loyalty
of supporters of autocratic leaders is maximized by the fact that members
of such smaller winning coalitions receive larger proportions of private
goods, these being benefits that are dispensed to each coalition member,
since there are fewer members among whom those goods must be shared.
In short, supporters of autocratic rulers tend to be more loyal than are
the backers of democratic leaders because defection from the relatively
small coalitions in support of autocratic leaders is riskier and less promising, and because the support provided to autocratic leaders produces
larger individual payoffs to members of the relatively small coalitions
that maintain such leaders in power.

In contrast, in democratic systems the probability that defectors will
be included in successful, challenging winning coalitions is fairly high,
because the number of spots available in such coalitions is relatively
high (the $W/S$ ratio is relatively large). Members of such large, democratic coalitions tend be only weakly loyal to the incumbent both because coalition members have a high probability of making it into a successor coalition ($W/S$) and because the advantages of coalition
membership are relatively small. This is so because the members of large
coalitions each receive relatively small amounts of private goods, these
goods having to be spread across many coalition members. Indeed, as
coalitions get larger, the modest value of private goods to members leads
incumbents to shift their emphasis from providing private goods to producing public goods, including national security. These latter goods benefit everyone in society so that they do not confer an advantage on
those in the winning coalition. In autocracies, since private goods are
shared among smaller groups, and defectors are less likely to become
part of a successor coalition, the leaders tend to emphasize the provision
of private goods to their cronies rather than public goods, implying a
diminution of the attentiveness of autocrats to national security concerns. At the same time, autocratic leaders need to spend less to assure
the support of their winning coalitions because the structure of the autocratic systems tends to produce strong loyalty to the incumbent; this
means in turn that there will be more resources left over for leaders to
expropriate for their own personal use.

Victory in international disputes, especially interstate wars, is a public good. Victory protects the state's territorial integrity and helps ensure national security. Of course, all leaders prefer victory to defeat in
disputes, but leaders in different types of political systems have very different incentives for allocating resources to achieve victory. Democratic
leaders tend to be deposed or retained primarily in response to their

performance in producing public goods, the type of good on which the absolute size of their winning coalitions, as well as the large size of those coalitions relative to the selectorates in such systems, leads them to focus. Autocratic leaders are retained or deposed, in contrast, primarily on the basis of their provision of private goods that are able to purchase the loyalty of their winning coalitions, which are relatively small both in absolute terms and relative to the size of selectorates.

The structural differences between democratic (or large winning coalition and large selectorate) systems and autocratic (or small winning coalition and large selectorate) systems have direct implications for relationships among states. They lead us, to cite an example most relevant to our concerns here, to expect distinct differences in relationships between democratic systems, on the one hand, and between autocratic regimes, on the other, when they become involved in disputes with each other. Especially when leaders become involved in potentially violent interstate disputes, they must choose between shifting more resources into efforts to win those disputes, and so depleting those resources that are available as private goods that could be distributed to members of the governing coalition, or allocating those resources as private goods to ensure the loyalty of members of the winning coalition, thus depriving those resources from the effort to improve the prospects of victory in the dispute. Bueno de Mesquita et al. (1999, 2001) and Morrow et al. (2001) have shown that this argument is both theoretically valid (or logically implied by a few simple assumptions), as well as supported by empirical evidence. That is, democratic leaders try harder to win interstate disputes than do autocratic leaders.

It has also been shown theoretically (Bueno de Mesquita et al. 1999) that democratic leaders are willing to use force in interstate disputes only if they believe that they are virtually certain to win those disputes, while autocrats are willing to fight even when their prospects of victory are not so great. The greater the value a leader attaches to being in office, the starker this difference becomes between the risks autocrats and democrats are willing to take by using force. So when officeholding is very valuable to the incumbent—as we assume it always is—then democrats are inclined to negotiate their way out of disputes except when they believe they are nearly certain of victory. Under the same officeholding conditions, autocrats are inclined to fight rather than negotiate under a broader set of circumstances, including conditions under which their prospects of victory are relatively low. This is so theoretically because autocratic leaders are not judged by members of their winning coalition primarily by whether or not they are victorious in interstate disputes. Instead, autocrats are evaluated by their winning coalitions according to how well they provide private goods. This tendency is dramatically illustrated by the fate of Saddam Hussein's regime in Iraq during its last decade or so. Hussein led his state into one military disaster after another. However, he retained the loyalty of his winning coalition because he managed to provide the members of that group with generous allocations of private goods.

Thus, when two democratic regimes confront one another in a dispute, the leaders of each of those regimes must believe the probability that they can be victorious in that dispute is close to 1 in order to make a decision to fight an interstate war. Especially in light of the fact that both democratic regimes in such confrontations will be inclined to try very hard to achieve a victory if they fight, wars between two democracies are unlikely. If one democracy believes that it has an excellent chance of victory (or that its rival does not believe in its own good chances of victory), it may initiate the use of force anticipating that the rival democracy will back down, negotiating a settlement without responding with force. That is, democratic states may in fact opt to initiate the use of force in a dispute with a democratic target. But democratic targets are more likely to capitulate than are autocratic targets simply because they will not use force unless they believe they have an excellent prospect of victory. It is extremely unlikely that both parties to a dispute believe that their own chances of victory are close to a certainty.

Autocratic leaders, in contrast, do not require such excellent prospects of victory in order to retaliate against the use of force with force of their own (Bueno de Mesquita et al. 1999). Autocratic states make relatively attractive targets for disputes because it is understood by their potential rivals that autocratic leaders will not try very hard to win such disputes except under extreme circumstances—such as a world war—in which they recognize that defeat means loss of their political control over the leadership selection process. Striving hard for victory means, for autocratic leaders, sacrificing resources that would otherwise be available to ensure support from their relatively small winning coalitions. The sacrifice of such resources puts the autocrat's political survival at risk. Furthermore, autocratic leaders are relatively willing to use force even when their chances of victory are not exceptional. While they prefer winning to losing, their hold on their office is not put in as much risk by defeat as it is by the failure to allocate sufficient resources to keep members of their winning coalitions happy (Bueno de Mesquita and Siverson 1995; Bueno de Mesquita et al. 2003, chap. 6). Consequently, autocratic leaders are with some regularity inclined to initiate the use of force in disputes, and to respond to such uses of force with force of their own if they are targets in such disputes.

These considerations imply that autocratic states are more likely to initiate disputes against other autocratic states, rather than democratic states, all else being equal (especially the ex ante prospect of victory). Nevertheless, autocratic leaders are also more likely to respond to violent attacks by fighting back than are democracies because they are more risk acceptant in such situations; they do not require as high a probability of victory to respond forcefully to the use of force against them. Consequently, autocratic states should be more likely to fight other autocratic states than democratic states are to fight other democratic states. Democratic states will less frequently engage other democratic states in violent or forceful disputes, and will almost never be wrong in anticipating that targeted democratic states will back down if a democratic initiator does choose to use force against a democratic rival. In other words, initiating democratic states will have calculated correctly, in most cases, that a targeted democracy will back down, since both the democratic initiator as well as the democratic target will realize that the target almost certainly does not have a high enough prospect of victory to choose to retaliate with force. In sum, the use of force, and/or violence and interstate wars, should be significantly less likely between democratic rivals in disputes than between autocratic rivals in disputes. This in turn implies that there is not an autocratic peace, at least not a peace that is equivalent to that which is expected among democratic states.

### ANALYZING RELEVANT DATA

In order to evaluate these ideas about the relative peacefulness of relationships among democratic states, on the one hand, and among autocratic states, on the other, we analyze data regarding militarized interstate disputes occurring between 1816 and 1992 as identified by the Correlates of War Project (Jones, Bremer, and Singer 1996). More specifically, we utilize these Correlates of War data as provided by EUGene, a program that generates (as one option) data in directed dyadic form, along with data on several other related and theoretically relevant variables (Bennett and Stam 2000a).[6] The data on which we focus particular attention is in a directed dyadic form generated by Maoz (1999). We also concentrate only on the original protagonists in these disputes; in other words we do not include data on third, fourth, or fifth parties that sometimes join these disputes. In this data set, the "initiator" is that state that first engaged in militarized behavior, that is, at least explicitly threatened the use of force. According to these data, there were 2,222 cases of such dispute initiation in the years from 1816 to 1992.[7]

We are especially interested in two types of information regarding these militarized disputes. One has to do with the level of hostility reached by the states involved in the militarized disputes. In the MID data set, these levels are measured on an ordinal scale ranging from 1 through 5, with 1 corresponding to "no militarized action," 2 to "threat to use force," 3 to "display of force," 4 to "use of force," and 5 to war. Theoretical considerations lead us to be particularly interested in those occasions when decision makers opt at least for a "use of force." On occasion, when decision makers select such a policy option (which in the MID data set corresponds to such actions as blockades, occupation of territory, or limited, tentative military attacks), war is the ultimate result. But at least some times, on such occasions, the target of such "uses of force" may capitulate, and so war is avoided. In short, since decision makers cannot know ex ante when they decide to "use force" whether or not an interstate war will occur, we want to focus on choices to use force whether or not they result in war. Accordingly, in the analyses here, we dichotomize this hostility level variable in the MID data set, making it equal to 1 when the states in question reach *either* 4 or 5 on the hostility level scale, and 0 otherwise.

A crucial aspect of this particular dependent variable, for reasons to be emphasized later, involves its focus on *both* states in the dyad. In other words, our dependent variable equals 1 only if *both* states "use force" during the dispute in question. In some respects, the hypothesis on which we have chosen to focus here, namely, "Once in a dispute with each other, democratic states will be less likely to use force (or go to war) against each other than states that are not democratic," tends to obscure the directed dyadic character of the analyses we will perform.[8] This has the benefit in this case of reducing substantially the importance of identifying which of the states in question actually initiated the dispute or the use of force. We know, as long as both states reached at least level 4 in a given dispute, the regime type of the initiator of the dispute or the use of force, which is what we need to know in order to evaluate our hypothesis. Nevertheless, our analyses take place on the directed dyadic level of analysis, focusing as they do on the behavior of *both* states in the dyad toward *each other,* and on their roles as initiators and targets, with consequences to be discussed.

Our intent in focusing on the initiation *as well as* the reciprocation of force in this manner is to isolate decisions that involve a certain substantial amount of risk for the leaders who make those decisions. However, it is not entirely clear that the "use of force" in the MID data set is ideal for this purpose. The use of force by the disputants upon whom we focus in the years from 1816 to 1992, for example, did not often entail substantial violence in the form of significant numbers of deaths by the military forces involved. The "use of force" was quite common. At least one state escalated to the "use of force" in MID terms in 67 percent of the disputes we analyze. And yet both sides experienced as many as 100 battle deaths in only 2 percent of those disputes. Therefore, in order to analyze a set of disputes in which the decision makers in question made choices with (at least ex post, and perhaps ex ante) risks apparently more substantial than were often involved in decisions to "use force," in the following analyses we also take into account those decisions within disputes leading to at least 100 battle deaths for the initiator and the target. This means that for these analyses, the hypothesis is that democratic states are less likely to initiate and reciprocate violence (i.e., military action leading to at least 100 battle deaths) against each other than are states that are not democratic.

For the purpose of categorizing the states we analyze according to regime type, we utilize the Polity III data set (Jaggers and Gurr 1995) as modified to be more time-specific by McLaughlin et al. (1998). For our analyses here, we take into account each state's autocracy score in Polity IIID, on a scale from 0 to 10 (with 10 corresponding to the highest level of autocracy) and subtract that score from the democracy score for that same state (also on a scale from 0 to 10, with 10 representing "most democratic"). Any state with a resulting score of 6 or higher on this "democracy minus autocracy" index is categorized as "democratic."

Perhaps the first point that ought to be made about our analyses of state behavior within these disputes from 1816 to 1992 involves the inconsistency with which states choose to reciprocate levels of hostility exhibited by their counterparts. Reciprocation in interstate behaviors is quite prevalent in the international system, in general as well as during crises, as Leng (1993, 70–71) demonstrates. Nevertheless, our data show that in response to the first state's hostile action in a militarized interstate dispute, the second state responds with militarized hostile behavior only a little more than 50 percent (51.98 percent, to be exact) of the time. And, as table 1 shows, when the initiator of one of these disputes elects to "use force" against the target, the target responds with the use of force only a little more than 45 percent of the time.

This distribution of values on one of our main dependent variables is fortunate from our theoretical point of view. Our theory does not lead us to hypothesize that democratic states in general will be so much less likely to "use force" in the course of disputes in which they may become engaged. On the contrary, we anticipate that democratic states are *at least* as likely to use force as autocratic states, so long as the perceived risks involved in such actions are low. In other words, we expect democratic states to "use force" with regularity in situations where it could be anticipated with some confidence that the target of the force is likely to capitulate, or at least not respond in a vigorous, determined fashion. And we also anticipate that democratic targets in these disputes are disproportionately unlikely to respond in such a vigorous, determined fashion. Democratic initiators will be particularly good at seeking out low-risk targets, in other words, and those low-risk targets are quite likely to be democratic states that will make estimates regarding their likelihood of success in these disputes of a type similar to that made by the initiator of the disputes in the first place. Democratic states, then, should be significantly less likely to *reciprocate* when they are faced with dispute initiators that have chosen to use force against them, especially if the initiator is also democratic.

Therefore, it is interesting and reassuring to us to note that there are quite apparent differences in the rate at which democratic targets respond to the use of force by democratic initiators compared to the rate at which autocratic or undemocratic targets respond to autocratic initiators that choose to use force. If we restrict our focus to states that fail to qualify as "democratic" and dichotomize the hostility level variable so that it equals 1 when states reach 4 or 5 on this scale, and set it equal to 0 otherwise, there is a strong relationship between the level of hostility reached by the initiator and that reached by the target. Yule's $Q$ is .74, and it is clearly statistically significant. But if we focus instead only on democratic states and do the same simple tabular analysis of the relationship between the level of hostility reached by the initiator and the level reached by the target in response, Yule's $Q$ is only .42, and it is not statistically significant.

It is also consistent with our theoretical expectations that when democratic initiators face democratic targets, a militarized dispute is marginally *more* likely to escalate to the use of force than if neither the ini-

TABLE 1.   Relationship between the Use of Force by Dispute Initiator and the Use of Force by Dispute Target in Militarized Interstate Disputes, 1816–1992

| Target responded with use of force? | Initiator did not use force | Initiator used force |
| --- | --- | --- |
| No | 644 | 818 |
| | 89.44% | 54.46% |
| Yes | 76 | 684 |
| | 10.56% | 45.54% |

*Note:* All states, original disputants only.
$\chi^2 = 264.7$; $p < 0.0000$; $N = 2,222$.

tiator nor the target is democratic. This pattern is consistent with Paul Senese's (1997) finding that when democratic states face each other in disputes, force is more, rather than less likely to be used. But it is also entirely in line with our expectations that relationships between democratic states will be more "peaceful" than those between autocratic states, in a manner we will discuss later.

We take a somewhat more nuanced look at these data in terms of the logit analysis reported in table 2. Perhaps the first point that ought to be made about this analysis is that it focuses on the behavior of both the initiator and the target involved in the set of disputes occurring from 1816 to 1992. That is, the dichotomous dependent variable in this analysis equals 1 if and only if the state that initiated the dispute uses force, and if the target also uses force. (Which state actually initiated the use of force, as opposed to the dispute in question, and which reciprocated is virtually impossible to tell in most disputes, given the way the data set is constructed. To repeat, fortunately for our purpose of evaluating this particular hypothesis, it does not really matter which state initiated and which state reciprocated the use of force.) To the extent that it pays attention to "who does what to whom" in this way, it is a directed dyadic level analysis. And it also shows that two democracies involved in a dispute with each other are "significantly" less likely to initiate *and* reciprocate the use of force. It also suggests that two autocratic states are significantly *more* likely to engage, in the context of these disputes, in the reciprocal use of force.

The analysis in table 2 involves two binary independent variables. The first, called ONEDEM, is coded as 1 if and only if just one member of a disputing pair was democratic; otherwise it is coded as 0. TWODEM is coded as a 1 if and only if both members of the disputing pair were democratic; otherwise it is coded as 0. The CONSTANT term in the logit analysis, then, by itself assesses whether force is reciprocated

TABLE 2.    Relationship between Regime Type of Directed Dyads and the Initiation/Reciprocation of the Use of Force in Militarized Interstate Disputes, 1816–1992

| Variables | Coefficients | Standard Error | Z-Score | $P > |Z|$ |
|---|---|---|---|---|
| ONEDEM[a] | −.2773 | .0994 | −2.79 | 0.003 |
| TWODEM[b] | −.5365 | .2630 | −2.04 | 0.021 |
| Constant | −.6872 | .0668 | −10.29 | 0.000 |
| $\chi^2 = 10.47$ | P of $\chi^2 < .003$ | log likelihood $= -1,233.4$ | Number of dyads $= 2,019$ | |

*Note:* All states, original disputants only.

[a]One democracy present in the directed dyad.

[b]Two democracies present in the directed dyad.

when both parties to the dispute are autocrats (so that ONEDEM and TWODEM both equal 0). To evaluate the likelihood of the use of reciprocated force when both parties to a dispute are democrats, we care about the sum of the coefficients for TWODEM and the CONSTANT. (ONEDEM in this case equals 0, so that its coefficient has no impact on the likelihood of reciprocated force when both parties are democratic.) To evaluate the likelihood of reciprocated force when *at least* one democratic state is involved we must sum the coefficients for ONEDEM, TWODEM, and the CONSTANT. ONEDEM plus the CONSTANT reveals the likelihood of reciprocated force when the disputing dyad includes one democracy and one autocracy (TWODEM, of course, equals 0 in this case). Thus, the analysis in table 2 allows us to evaluate the likelihood of reciprocated violence for any possible mix of disputing pairs.

Table 2 shows that the likelihood of reciprocated violence, though low, is highest when two autocrats are in a dispute with each other. It is lowest when two democrats are in a dispute with each other. Asymmetric disputing dyads (i.e., one democrat and one autocrat) are more likely than two democratic states, but less likely than two autocratic states, to engage in reciprocated violence. The differences in the probabilities across the combinations of regime types are themselves statistically significant. Table 2 contradicts the idea of an autocratic peace, at least when the focus is on reciprocated use of force.

Table 3 reports an analysis that is structured in a way that is different from that in table 2 in a rather subtle manner that nevertheless produces a significant difference in the results. This is a more standard dyadic level analysis, focusing on the simpler question of whether one state, or the other, or both "used force" in the course of the dispute. It pays no attention, in other words, to "who did what to whom." The dichotomous dependent variable equals 1 whether the initiator only, the target only, or both the initiator and the target resorted to the use

TABLE 3. Relationship between Presence of Joint Democracy in a Dyadic Dispute and the Use of Force in That Dispute, 1816–1992

| Variables | Coefficients | Standard Error | Z-Score | $P > |Z|$ |
|---|---|---|---|---|
| ONEDEM[a] | −.1004 | .1007 | −1.00 | 0.159 |
| TWODEM[b] | .0217 | .2495 | 0.09 | 0.466 |
| Constant | .9591 | .0704 | 13.62 | 0.000 |
| $\chi^2 = 1.08$ | P of $\chi^2 < 0.2916$ | log likelihood $= -1,208.41$ | Number of dyads $= 2,019$ | |

*Note:* All states, original disputants only.
[a]One democracy present in the dyad.
[b]Two democracies present in the dyad.

of force during the dispute. In this case, switching levels of analysis in this way, even though the transition is quite subtle, produces very different results. Most specifically, while in the directed dyadic level analysis a democratic initiator and a democratic target are shown to be less likely to initiate and retaliate with force, this general, standard dyadic level analysis shows that there is no statistically meaningful relationship between the presence of joint democracies in disputes and the use of force. (A tabular analysis shows that disputes between pairs of democratic states have been slightly more likely to escalate to use force than disputes between mixed or jointly autocratic pairs.)

The probability of force (though not necessarily reciprocated force) being used in a dispute is shown in table 3 to be no different whether the disputing dyad is made up only of autocracies (the CONSTANT alone, which is significantly negative, indicating a low probability of any use of force in a dispute), is made up of an autocracy and a democracy (the CONSTANT + ONEDEM, which is significantly negative and not significantly different from the CONSTANT alone), is made up of two democracies (the CONSTANT + TWODEM, which is signifi cantly negative and not significantly different from the CONSTANT alone), or is made up of at least one democracy (the CONSTANT + ONEDEM + TWODEM, which is significantly negative and not significantly different from the CONSTANT alone). It is reasonable to infer that this analysis is structured in a way that is analogous to that used by Senese (1997) where he reports that disputes involving two democratic states are more likely to escalate to the use of force.[9] Our results produce a positive, though not statistically significant, coefficient for TWODEM. The analysis in table 3 thus exemplifies the dangers, pointed out by J. David Singer (1961b) in one of his most cited works, of attempting to infer the character of relationships on one level of analysis from knowledge about relationships on another. The difference in the results from the two analyses on different levels conforms encouragingly to our theoretically based expectations.

At this point (or even before), what has become a standard operating procedure among quantitatively oriented scholars of international politics would call for the introduction of several control variables (often a rather large number) into the analyses. We feel that the impact of this particular standard procedure is, more often than not, deleterious. As J. David Singer (1980b, xxiv) has pointed out: "It is well known that if we incorporate enough variables in a model, we can get closer and closer to accounting for all of the variance in the outcome. We do so, however, at the cost not only of parsimony and elegance, but, more importantly, the ability to make theoretical sense of the results." In at least some cases, such a confusing variety of potentially confounding variables, intervening variables, and alternative causes of the outcome variable are added to models that it is difficult, at best, to interpret the results of multivariate analyses.

There certainly is a long list of control variables that might conceivably be added to the analyses we have presented. For example, Hensel and Diehl (1994) report that targets much weaker in military-industrial capabilities than initiators are significantly less likely to respond to military threats or actions by initiators in the course of militarized interstate disputes. A result of such obvious relevance to our concerns here might seem to call for the introduction of military capability ratios into our analyses. However, from our point of view, the ratio of the target's military capabilities to the initiator's military capabilities is endogenous to our model. Democratic initiators, in other words, are more likely to pick targets for force or violence that are unlikely to reciprocate with force or violence; such targets are, according to our theoretical expectations, disproportionately likely to be democratic and/or considerably less powerful. This means that power ratios would be a kind of intervening variable in the process leading from regime type to reciprocated force or violence, which means in turn that controlling for power ratios might in fact eliminate the statistically significant relationship between regime type and reciprocated violence. But it would certainly be misleading to interpret such a result as evidence tending to disconfirm our hypothesis given that such a result is consistent with our theoretically derived expectations regarding selection effects.

For this reason, we are not inclined to proceed at this point with the introduction of what has become recognized as the standard list of control variables in analyses such as this one, because we feel that the results could be more confusing than helpful. We are not arguing, of course, that it is always a mistake to move beyond bivariate analyses (in fact, most of our analyses so far are already multivariate). In recognition of the potential value of multivariate analyses, we will take note of an argument made by Small and Singer (1976, 67) in their analysis of the absence of interstate wars between democratic states. Their view at that time was that "if war is most likely between neighbors, and if bourgeois democracies have rarely been neighbors, this may well explain why they have rarely fought against one another."

Since then, several analysts (e.g., Bremer 1992; Maoz and Russett 1992; Gleditsch 1995) have evaluated this argument by including contiguity as a control variable in analyses of the relationship between regime type and interstate war, and have found repeatedly that that relationship is not in fact eliminated by a control for geographic proximity.[10] Nevertheless, for two reasons we think it is potentially useful to include the geographic distance between the states involved in the militarized disputes we analyze as a control variable in our model. First, our dependent variable is sufficiently different from those in previous analyses that there is some question as to whether a control for geographic proximity might eliminate the relationship of major interest here between regime type and conflict. More important, we want to point out what may be an undervalued role for control variables in multivariate analyses. In general, the motivation for their addition seems to be to subject the relationship of major interest to their potentially confounding power in order to evaluate the validity of the hypothesis of greatest interest. But another reason for adding control variables is that they may allow the relationship of greatest interest to stand out in greater clarity. If there are factors other than the explanatory variable of central concern that also have an impact on the outcome variable, *and* these other factors are unrelated statistically or theoretically to that explanatory variable, then including such control variables in an analysis may relieve the initial explanatory variable of the burden of explaining variance in the outcome variable to which it has no relationship. In such cases, the addition of a control variable may lead the original statistical relationship of interest to be stronger, rather than to disappear as it might if a confounding variable is included in the analysis. So, for both of these reasons we have added the geographic distance, in miles, between the states in the disputes we analyze as a control variable; the results are shown in table 4.

Those results suggest, first, that controlling for geographic proximity does not eliminate the relationship between regime type and reciprocated uses of force; in other words, there is no evidence in table 4 that

TABLE 4.  Relationship between Regime Type of Directed Dyads and the Initiation/Reciprocation of the Use of Force in Militarized Interstate Disputes, Controlling for Geographic Distance, 1816–1992

| Variables | Coefficients | Standard Error | Z-Score | $P > |Z|$ |
|---|---|---|---|---|
| ONEDEM[a] | −.1771 | .1017 | −1.74 | 0.041 |
| TWODEM[b] | −.5496 | .2653 | −2.07 | 0.019 |
| DISTANCE[c] | −.0002 | .0000 | −7.32 | 0.000 |
| Constant | −.4753 | .0717 | −6.63 | 0.000 |
| $\chi^2 = 74.38$ | P of $\chi^2 < .0000$ | log likelihood = −1,201.434 | Number of dyads = 2,019 | |

*Note:* All states, original disputants only.
[a]One democracy present in the directed dyad.
[b]Two democracies present in the directed dyad.
[c]Geographic distance between the disputants, in miles.

the relationship on which we focus, between regime type and conflict, is spurious. On the contrary, the coefficient, the $z$-score, and the corresponding level of significance regarding the relationship between joint democracy (i.e., TWODEM) and reciprocated uses of force are all marginally increased in magnitude. We are not inclined to argue that these increases are substantively significant. They do serve, however, to exemplify the methodological point that introducing control variables into an analysis can emphasize or highlight, as well as diminish, the significance or strength of the relationship of major interest. That example, in turn, reinforces our main methodological point here. Control variables can have a variety of contrasting impacts on relationships between explanatory and outcome variables. They may confound such relationships, exert an intervening impact, or strengthen them. That every control variable can exert such different contrasting impacts, each with very different implications for the relationship of major interest, is just one of the reasons that multivariate analyses with more than a strictly limited number of control variables are extremely difficult to interpret. In fact, in a statement we are happy to endorse here, Christopher Achen (2002, 446), asserts that "a statistical specification with more than three explanatory variables is meaningless."[11]

Even though our results up to this point are suggestive and supportive of the theoretical framework on which this essay is based, we acknowledge that the relationships reported in tables 2 and 4, for example, between the regime type of dyads and the reciprocal use of force are less than striking. As we mentioned earlier, there are convincing indications in the MID data that the "use of force" by states involved in these disputes was not consistently a policy choice fraught with high degrees of risk. As we reported, the use of force in these disputes only rarely resulted in "significant" (i.e., over 100) battle deaths for the participants in the disputes. Therefore, the tendency for democratic disputants to be risk averse, especially in their interrelationships with each other, might well come into play only in a modest manner.

In order to construct what we believe is a superior test of our hypothesis, one focused on disputes in which both sides made apparently more risky policy choices, we concentrate now on those disputes where both disputants experienced at least 100 battle deaths. In other words, the dichotomous dependent variable in this analysis equals 1 if and only if both the initiator and the target in the dispute experienced at least 100 battle deaths. We attempted to conduct a logit analysis with this as the dependent variable, constructed in the same way as those depicted in tables 2 and 4. However, this proved not to be possible.

The reason for the failure to achieve an estimation for this model is revealed in table 5, where the regime type of the directed dyads analyzed is cross-tabulated with the occurrence of 100 battle deaths for both states in the militarized interstate disputes taking place from 1816 to 1992. That table shows that there were *no* militarized disputes between democratic states leading to as many as 100 battle deaths for both states during that time period. So, when these data are subjected to logit analysis, joint democracy predicts "failure" perfectly, and it is therefore dropped from the analysis. As King (2001, 503) points out, "although it might seem that perfect prediction is one of those problems that political scientists would love to deal with, it wreaks havoc with the logit model."

Admittedly, in part because of the relatively small numbers of disputes between jointly democratic pairs of states, and because of the relatively small numbers of disputes resulting even in as few as 100 battle deaths on both sides in this data set, even the perfect relationship shown in table 5 is not statistically significant according to traditional standards. However, Ray (2001) reports that, in an analysis of interstate war initiations occurring between 1816 and 1994 (with multilateral interstate wars disaggregated to identify war initiations occurring in the context of such wars), democratic states never initiated an interstate war against each other during that time period, while autocratic states initiated interstate wars against each other 70 times. (Furthermore, in this admittedly simple tabular analysis, the difference in the rate of war initiations by democratic states against other democratic states and that for autocratic states against other autocratic states is statistically significant.)[12] In our view, then, there is a substantial amount of evidence supporting the conclusion that democratic states are unlikely to select quite risky policy options, especially in conflicts with each other, while the leaders of autocratic states, especially in their confrontations with each other, exhibit such reluctance in a distinctively less consistent manner. In other words, while the preponderance of evidence provided and

TABLE 5. Relationship between Regime Type and Reciprocated Violence (100 Battle Deaths) in Militarized Interstate Disputes, 1816–1992

| Both States Experienced at Least 100 Battle Deaths | Both States Undemocratic | Both States Democratic |
|---|---|---|
| No | 1736 | 81 |
| | 97.7% | 100.0% |
| Yes | 41 | 0 |
| | 2.31% | 0.00% |

*Note:* All states, original disputants only.
$\chi^2 = 1.91$; $p < .084$; Yule's $Q = 1.00$; $N = 1,858$.

discussed here supports the notion of a "democratic peace," most of that evidence tends to undermine the idea that there is anything like an equivalent "autocratic peace."

## CONCLUSION

According to most traditional and predominant approaches to the study of foreign policies and international politics, state leaders' primary motive for selecting among policy options has to do with the national interest, the power, or the security of the states in question. We assume instead that policymakers of states, when making foreign policy choices and in their interactions with each other, are motivated primarily by their desire to remain in power. As we noted earlier, J. David Singer long ago took note of the priority national elites give to maintaining themselves in power. Furthermore, he and a coauthor were among the earliest quantitatively oriented analysts of international politics to evaluate the proposition that democratic states have not fought interstate wars against each other (Small and Singer 1976). Singer personally has never chosen to follow up on the implications of the assumption about the priority that state leaders give to remaining in power, or to take very seriously the democratic peace proposition. However, the Correlates of War Project has made a major contribution, in terms of data generation and training a significant number of researchers in systematic empirical methods of analysis, to the development of the stream of research that has focused on the democratic peace proposition and a theoretical framework emphasizing the political ambitions of state leaders.

The focus on the political ambitions of national political elites highlights the impact of domestic political considerations on foreign policy choices and interstate interactions. It also leads us to an increased appreciation of the impact of domestic political structures on international politics. We argue here that there are two aspects of domestic political structures that are of special importance. They are the size of the selectorate, or that portion of the population in a state that participates in the selection of political leaders, and the size of the winning coalition that controls the minimum amount of resources necessary to maintain the incumbent leadership in power. The ratio of the winning coalition's size to the size of the selectorate has particularly important and predictable impacts on policy choices and interactions among states.

In this essay, the impacts of greatest interest are a function of the differences between those states in which both the winning coalition and the selectorate are large (states typically referred to as "democratic"), and states in which the winning coalition is absolutely small, and also quite small relative to the large selectorate ("autocratic states"). These domestic structural attributes, as discussed here in some detail, lead democratic states to focus on the provision of public goods in their efforts to remain in power, while autocratic leaders, in pursuit of the same goal, concentrate on the provision of private goods to the relatively small number of supporters whose loyalty they need in order to stay in power.

These differences between "democratic" and "autocratic" states have important implications for the attitudes of leaders in these different kinds of states toward interstate conflicts. Public policy failures (such as lost wars) are particularly important to the fate of democratic regimes. This means that leaders in such regimes tend to be relatively conservative or cautious in their policies regarding conflicts. They choose targets for disputes carefully, and they exert high levels of effort in order to avoid losing the conflicts in which they become involved. Autocratic leaders, in contrast, are less likely to suffer disastrous consequences from such public policy failures. They tend to be less judicious in their selection of targets in disputes and more willing to engage in risky disputes, even if they are likely to lose in some of those disputes.

This implies, contrary to some recent theorizing in the field that emphasizes the pacifying impact of political similarity (for both "democratic" and "autocratic" regimes), that democratic states are significantly less likely to get involved in risky or violent disputes with each other than are autocratic states. We evaluate this implication of our theoretical approach to the analyses of foreign policies and international politics by analyzing data on over 2,000 militarized disputes that occurred in the years from 1816 to 1992. We find that, if we simply focus on whether or not the "use of force" occurred in these disputes, in a standard dyadic level analysis, the presence of democracies in disputes had no apparent pacifying effect. However, when we focus instead on whether the use of force by one state in these disputes is reciprocated by the target, the results of this directed dyadic level analysis are distinctly different. In short, the reciprocated use of force by both the initiators and the targets in these disputes is significantly *less* likely if both the initiators and the targets in question are "democratic." These results are even clearer if we focus on a set of policy choices more clearly involving high risks of public policy failure, that is, those disputes in which both the initiator and the target suffered at least 100 battle deaths. We find such a dispute occurred not even once in the whole time period from 1816 to 1992, *if* both of the original belligerents in these disputes were "democratic." When combined with the related evidence that democratic states, in that same time period, never fought an interstate war with each other, while autocratic states confronted each other in interstate war some 70 times, we feel that the evidence in favor of a "democratic peace" discussed here is rather compelling. In contrast, the idea that relationships among autocratic states are equally peaceful, in a manner suggesting that it is political similarity rather than particular domestic political structures involving large winning coalitions and large selectorates that has the more important and fundamental pacifying impact, is not supported by the empirical evidence based on data regarding militarized interstate disputes in the nineteenth and twentieth centuries.

## NOTES

1. "Would it not be more . . . consistent with the fundamental notion that political actors will behave in self-interested ways to assume that political elites wish to attain and stay in office'" (Ray 1995, 39).

2. Detailed definitions of these concepts can be found in Bueno de Mesquita, Smith, Siverson, and Morrow's *The Logic of Political Survival* (2003).

3. "A dyadic characterization of regime type . . . must reflect two things simultaneously, namely, How democratic or undemocratic are the members of the dyad? and How different or similar in their regime types are the two states?" (Maoz and Russett 1993, 268).

4. The following is a discursive summary with illustrative examples of an argument presented in a more formal, detailed fashion in Bueno de Mesquita et al. (1999).

5. "Traditional" autocracies, such as monarchies, and also military juntas have small selectorates and small winning coalitions.

6. The software can be downloaded from http://www.eugenesoftware.org

7. We did make one change in these data generated by Maoz, as provided by EUGene. In that data set, "democratic" Turkey and "democratic" Cyprus are reported to have fought an interstate war with each other in 1974. This report results from the fact that because of the structure of our computerized procedure for merging the data on regime type with MID data, even in the more time-specific Polity IIID data, Cyprus is categorized as a democracy when the war begins on the basis of its Polity III score as of July 15, 1974. However, before the war began on July 20, there was a definitely antidemocratic coup in Cyprus (see Ray 1995, 120–21). We changed the democracy score for Cyprus to a 0 to reflect the impact of this coup on its regime type.

8. The qualifying phrase "Once in a dispute with each other" is important. We understand that our hypotheses, analyses, and results here are not applicable to democracies, or autocracies, or states *in general*. Since we focus on states in disputes only, as is appropriate given the theoretical argument we set out, selection effects prevent us from drawing conclusions about states in general. See Reed (2000).

9. Paul Senese has confirmed in electronic correspondence on August 2, 2001, that this reasonable inference is also accurate. That is, the disputes he analyzed were categorized as having escalated to the "use of force" so long as one *or* the other, or both of the disputants used force.

10. These analyses "established definitively that the speculation by Small and Singer (1976) regarding the impact of contiguity on the relationship between regime type and conflict proneness was erroneous" (Ray 1998a, 36).

11. We might acknowledge here that Achen (2002, 446) also stipulates that his rule is applicable when "no formal theory structures the investigation." A formal theory does structure this investigation, but that theory does not suggest that additional control variables are in this case necessary or desirable.

12. The threshold utilized for categorizing states as "democratic" in these analyses is the same as that used here, i.e., states with a score of 6 on the Polity IIID Democracy—Autocracy scale are considered to be "democratic."

# ARMS, ALLIANCES, AND SUCCESS
# IN MILITARIZED DISPUTES
# AND WARS, 1816–1992

*Volker Krause*

From antiquity to modernity, military capabilities have been deemed a vital asset to ensure success in armed conflict. Furthermore, it has been argued that success in armed conflict may not only enhance a state's international security, reputation, and bargaining leverage but also increase its leaders' chances of retaining domestic political control (Bueno de Mesquita and Siverson 1995). Reflecting this line of reasoning, states have devoted substantial human and material resources to the buildup and maintenance of national military capabilities. Given the costs of providing for military preparedness, to what extent do national military capabilities benefit states in terms of increased success in armed conflict? As recently as 1989, the withdrawal of the last Soviet troops from Afghan territory reminded us that not even the vast military capabilities of a superpower like the Soviet Union guarantee success in war against a small state like Afghanistan.

One of the best early quantitative empirical investigations of the extent to which capabilities and military allocations affect outcomes of interstate armed conflict is a 1983 article by Frank W. Wayman, J. David Singer, and Gary Goertz. Considering original parties and entire coalitions on the initiating and target sides in almost 70 wars and about 100 militarized disputes between major powers from 1816 to 1976, the study correlates armed conflict success with a variety of capability and military allocation indicators. As the three investigators find, success in wars and militarized disputes is (1) mostly a function of an advantage in industrial rather than in military or demographic capabilities and (2) predominantly more likely with military underallocations than overallocations. Out of eighteen relations between success in wars and militarized disputes on the one hand and measures of military capabilities and military allocations on the other, eight are statistically insignificant. In brief, contrary to what one might expect, military capabilities are far from a robust guarantee of success in armed conflict.

A critical shortcoming of the study by Wayman, Singer, and Goertz is that it does not take into account that states may rely on some mix of both national and allied[1] military capabilities to ensure success in militarized disputes and wars. It is quite possible that national military capabilities by themselves have a different impact on armed conflict success than national military capabilities considered either in combination with or relative to allied military capabilities.

According to the realist approach to international relations, both armaments and alliances are the most crucial means by which states create, preserve, or reconstruct a balance of power to protect their vital security interests (Morgenthau 1967). A clear example of this point is given by the United States in its Cold War standoff against the Soviet Union. From 1946 through 1990, the United States relied on average not only on 22.5 percent of the global system's national military capabilities but also on 18.4 percent of the global system's military capabilities held by an average of about thirty-eight U.S. allies.[2] It is also important to note that one decade after the end of the Cold War, Condoleezza Rice (2000, 46–47), before becoming National Security Advisor, mentions two key priorities of U.S. foreign policy that focus on the U.S. military and relationships with allies. One priority is "to ensure that America's military can deter war, project power, and fight in defense of its interests if deterrence fails." Another priority is "to renew strong and intimate relationships with allies who share American values and can thus share the burden of promoting peace, prosperity, and freedom."

Assuming that armed conflict involvement and success depend on some combination of national and allied military capabilities, this study extends the work of Wayman, Singer, and Goertz by addressing two fundamental questions. First, to what extent are states with a greater reliance on their own armaments rather than on allies more or less likely to be involved in militarized disputes and wars than states relying on allies rather than on their own armaments? Second, to what extent are states with a greater reliance on their own armaments rather than on allies more or less likely to succeed in militarized disputes and wars than states relying on allies rather than on their own armaments?

In order to generate empirical answers to these questions, I first review some of the prior research on the substitutability of arms and alliances. After this review, I present some theoretical arguments and formulate the hypotheses to be tested. Subsequently, I develop my inquiry's research design. Next, I report and discuss the results from Heckman probit analysis. Finally, I conclude this investigation with a brief summary and evaluation of its findings.

## SUBSTITUTABILITY OF ARMS AND ALLIANCES

Introducing the concept of substitutability in foreign policy, Most and Starr (1989) argue that foreign policy leaders or decision makers have different means of responding to some particular international concern. Hence, "confronted with some problem or subjected to some stimulus," decision makers "could, *under at least certain conditions, substitute one such means for another,*" which suggests that "*similar* factors could lead to *distinct* concrete or empirical foreign policy responses" (102).

So far, the concept of substitutability in foreign policy has been most notably referred to in studies dealing with trade-offs between arms and alliances. According to several scholars (e.g., Altfeld 1984; Morrow 1993; Sorokin 1994b), states choose a combination of arms and alliances that is most efficient in terms of the costs and benefits associated with each of the two foreign policy alternatives. While the costs of arms and alliances are usually internal, arms and alliance benefits tend to be external. The internal costs of arms are that they necessitate dealing with domestic political opposition to increases in taxation and conscription required by arms buildups. The internal costs of alliances are that they necessitate dealing with domestic political opposition to certain policy concessions required to placate alliance partners. The external benefits of arms are that they are more reliable than alliances in improving a state's international security environment, although arms buildups generate security more slowly than alliance ties. The external benefits of alliances are that they improve a state's international security environment more quickly than arms buildups, although alliances are less reliable than arms in generating security.

As states seek the most efficient mix of arms and alliances, they are influenced by their utility for security, wealth, and autonomy or freedom of action. An increased utility for security is likely to generate an increased demand for both arms and alliances. It is when states have a greater utility for autonomy than for wealth that they are more likely to rest their security on their own armaments than on promises of allied support. Also, the more resources states can mobilize easily, the faster their progress in military technology, the more they disagree with potential allies, and the lesser their potential allies' military capabilities, the more likely states are to rely on their own arms than on alliances.

Despite many references to the substitutability of arms and alliances, investigators (e.g., Most and Siverson 1987; Diehl 1994; Morgan and Palmer 2000) do not find any consistent empirical evidence permitting us to generalize that states substitute arms for alliances or alliances for arms. To the contrary, it seems that arms and alliances are often complements rather than substitutes for one another, which has several possible explanations. First, a state may not want to make up for reductions in arms spending by seeking alliances if it is its leadership's intention to reduce military expenditures. Second, it is possible that a state may look for alliances to compensate for unintentional decreases in arms spending but may not find any alliance partners. The rationale here is that reduced military expenditures may render a state unattractive to potential allies due to perceptions that it has problems providing for its own security, let alone the security of alliance partners. Third, substitution or complementary effects of alliances on arms spending depend on alliance types, prevailing defense burdens, and numbers of allies. While nonaggression treaties have a substitution effect on increases in arms spending with high and increasing burdens of military preparedness, multiparty defense pacts have a complementary effect on arms spending increases, most clearly after 1945. Fourth, increases in a state's relative capabilities allow for increases in both arms and alliances. Fifth, a state may rely on increases in both arms and alliances because they help to obtain the same good.

Extending prior research on the substitutability of arms and alliances, this study investigates the impact of arms-alliance substitutability/complementarity on success in military conflict, while also predicting to armed conflict involvement. Specifically, this inquiry examines the extent to which a state's involvement and success in militarized disputes and wars are affected by combinations or trade-offs of arms and alliances, national and allied military capabilities. The focus here is only on military capabilities because I expect foreign policy leaders to have more direct influence over military than industrial or demographic capabilities. There is no consideration of military allocations since their operationalization involves industrial and demographic capability measures together with military capability indicators.

## THEORETICAL ARGUMENTS AND HYPOTHESES

According to most realist and neorealist reasoning (e.g., Morgenthau 1967; Waltz 1979), international anarchy—the absence of a world government with a monopoly over the use of force—compels states to rely on their own efforts to secure their territories and populations against military assaults. As states seek to provide for their security, they may try to maximize their national capabilities in some combination with capabilities of allies. The aggregation of capabilities is expected to either deter armed aggression or ensure military victory once armed conflict gets under way, while enhancing a state's international reputation (Diehl 1994). Given that increased capabilities—specifically military capabilities—are associated with victory or success in military conflict, they may motivate a state to be involved in armed hostilities. This is so because perceptions of possible success in armed conflict make armed conflict involvement an attractive foreign policy option to improve a state's international reputation and strengthen its leadership's grasp on power against domestic opposition.

In brief, when it comes to national military capabilities by themselves:

HYPOTHESIS 1.1:   The greater a state's national military capabilities, the more likely it is to (1) be involved and (2) succeed in militarized disputes.
HYPOTHESIS 1.2:   The greater a state's national military capabilities, the more likely it is to (1) be involved and (2) succeed in wars.

Furthermore, to the extent that national military capabilities are combined with allied military capabilities so that they complement one another:

HYPOTHESIS 2.1:   The greater a state's combined national and allied military capabilities, the more likely it is to (1) be involved and (2) succeed in militarized disputes.
HYPOTHESIS 2.2:   The greater a state's combined national and allied military capabilities, the more likely it is to (1) be involved and (2) succeed in wars.

While a state may rely exclusively on allied military capabilities, this tends to be quite rare. Most states most of the time have some minimum of national military capabilities. Hence, I do not formulate any separate theoretical argument and hypothesis about the impact of allied military capabilities on involvement and success in militarized disputes and wars.

According to Bennett (1997), Morrow's (1991) "security-autonomy trade-off" model challenges the "capability aggregation" approach to alliances. As Morrow argues, states may use alliances less to aggregate capabilities but to exchange security, or the ability to preserve the status quo, for autonomy, or the opportunity to bring about status quo change. Assuming that autonomy is associated with influence or control over alliance partners, even a security-autonomy trade-off may make a state confident of victory or success in armed hostilities, motivating involvement in military conflict. This is so because influence or control over allies may help a state to ensure that allies do not defect and support an adversary in armed confrontations.

Given that many alliances exist for defensive purposes, their encouragement of states to be involved in armed conflict may not be direct but indirect. The point here is that states in defensive alliances, while counting on allied support against aggressors, may see an opportunity to devote their own resources to military action.

There is some prior evidence that the greater a state's national capabilities, the greater its likelihood of militarized dispute involvement as an original initiator or target (Krause and Singer 1997). Also, the greater a state's national capabilities, the greater the likelihood of its war involvement (Bremer 1980). While a state's national capabilities have no statistically significant impact on its success in militarized disputes (Maoz 1983), their increase raises a state's war success (Reiter and Stam 1998).

It is important to consider arms-alliance trade-offs because national military capabilities differ from allied military capabilities in their restraint of armed conflict involvement as well as of the vigorous and uncompromising pursuit of military success. While initial attempts at increasing national military capabilities may be restrained by domestic political opposition, once a state has raised those capabilities, they are likely to generate domestic political support for their use (Diehl 1994). Hence, once national military capabilities have been raised, their availability and reliability for use in armed conflict can be expected to be 100 percent. Increases in a state's national military capabilities may enhance the clout of its military sector, making it more reliant on coercive diplomacy and military force. This means that a state with increased national military capabilities may have an increased willingness to be involved in military hostilities as well as an increased unwillingness to accept anything short of unconditional military success.

Allied military capabilities differ from national military capabilities in that a state has no direct control over their use. It depends on its allies' national interests and on its ability to shape those interests whether a state will encounter allied support or opposition in the event of armed conflict. As Sabrosky (1980) reports, allies honor their agreements reliably in less than 30 percent of war opportunities. By contrast, when considering the specific obligations mentioned in alliance treaties, Leeds, Long, and Mitchell (2000) find that alliance reliability amounts to 74.5

percent. Still, even this increased reliability figure is clearly below the aforementioned 100 percent reliability of national military capabilities. Given that national military capabilities are more reliable than military capabilities of allies, the greater a state's national versus allied military capabilities, the more likely it is to achieve military success and, hence, the greater its motivation to be involved in armed hostilities.

In sum, to the extent that national military capabilities are traded off against allied military capabilities so that they substitute for one another:

HYPOTHESIS 3.1: The greater a state's national military capabilities relative to its allied military capabilities, the more likely it is to (1) be involved and (2) succeed in militarized disputes.
HYPOTHESIS 3.2: The greater a state's national military capabilities relative to its allied military capabilities, the more likely it is to (1) be involved and (2) succeed in wars.

Rousseau et al. (1996) provide evidence that, when controlling for the selection of democracies into international crises, the greater a state's level of democracy, the less likely it is to initiate the use of force and employ more than 1,000 troops against states no matter what their political regimes. Additionally, Reiter and Stam (1998) report that democracies are more likely than states with either autocratic or mixed regimes to win wars, a result that is substantively stronger and statistically more significant for war initiators than for war targets. All these findings suggest that the more democratic a state, the less likely it is to be involved in armed conflict but the more likely it is to achieve military success. Given the line of reasoning here, I control for a state's level of democracy when predicting to its involvement and success in militarized disputes and wars.

In light of the studies by Bueno de Mesquita and Siverson (1995), as well as Reiter and Stam (1998) on democracy, war initiation, and war victory, some states, most notably democracies, may succeed in armed conflict they initiate because they initiate only success-promising armed conflict.[3] Hence, when predicting to a state's militarized dispute and war success, I control for a state's identity as a militarized dispute and war initiator, as opposed to any other participant in militarized disputes and wars.

### RESEARCH DESIGN

In this investigation, I consider all sovereign states, as identified on the basis of the Correlates of War Project's updated list of interstate system members (Small and Singer 1982), between 1816 and 1992.[4] A state-year is the unit of analysis.

For the empirical analysis in this study, I focus on four outcome variables, three predictor variables, and two control variables.[5] The outcome variables are a state's militarized dispute involvement and militarized dispute success as well as its war involvement and war success. The predictor variables are a state's national military capabilities, combined national and allied military capabilities,[6] as well as its trade-off of national versus allied military capabilities. One of the control variables is a state's level of democracy. When predicting to militarized dispute success, an additional control variable is a state's identity as a militarized dispute initiator. A state's identity as a war initiator is an additional control variable when predicting to war success.

Militarized dispute involvement is the probability that a state is involved in militarized interstate disputes. The measure here is a dichotomy, where 1 indicates that a state is involved in at least one militarized interstate dispute, and 0 means that a state refrains from any militarized interstate dispute involvement.

Militarized dispute success is the probability that a state succeeds in militarized interstate disputes. The measure here is a dichotomy, where 1 indicates that a state achieves victory in at least one militarized interstate dispute, and 0 means that a state does not experience any militarized interstate dispute victory.

War involvement is the probability that a state is involved in interstate wars. The measure here is a dichotomy, where 1 indicates that a state is involved in at least one interstate war, and 0 means that a state refrains from any interstate war involvement.

War success is the probability that a state succeeds in interstate wars. The measure here is a dichotomy, where 1 indicates that a state achieves victory in at least one interstate war, and 0 means that a state does not experience any interstate war victory.

The measurement of a state's militarized dispute involvement and militarized dispute success rests on the Correlates of War Project's militarized interstate dispute data (Jones, Bremer, and Singer 1996). The measurement of a state's war involvement and war success rests on the Correlates of War Project's interstate war data (Small and Singer 1982).

The measure for national military capabilities is a scale that captures a state's percentage share of the global system's military capabilities. Specifically, it captures the average of a state's percentage share of the global system's military personnel and a state's percentage share of the global system's military expenditures.

The measure for combined national and allied military capabilities is a scale that adds to a state's national military capabilities the sum of percentage shares of the global system's military capabilities held by all of a state's allies. The latter captures the average of the sum of a state's allies' percentage shares of the global system's military personnel and the sum of a state's allies' percentage shares of the global system's military expenditures. Expressing this indicator more formally, $AAC = NMC + AMC$, where $AAC$, $NMC$, and $AMC$ stand respectively for arms-alliance complementarity, national military capabilities, and allied military capabilities.

A trade-off of national versus allied military capabilities is measured by the ratio of the difference between a state's national and allied military capabilities over the sum of a state's national and allied military capabilities. Expressing this indicator more formally, $AAS = (NMC - AMC) / (NMC + AMC)$, where $AAS$, $NMC$, and $AMC$ stand respectively for arms-alliance substitutability, national military capabilities, and allied military capabilities. The measure of arms-alliance substitutability is a scale that ranges from a minimum of $-1$ to a maximum of 1. A score of $-1$ denotes that a state has only allied military capabilities but no national military capabilities, meaning that allied military capabilities perfectly substitute for national military capabilities. A score of 1 denotes that a state has only national military capabilities but no allied military capabilities, meaning that national military capabilities perfectly substitute for allied military capabilities. A score of 0 denotes that a state has a perfectly balanced mix of both national and allied military capabilities, meaning that national and allied military capabilities do not at all substitute for one another.[7]

For the measurements of a state's national military capabilities, combined national and allied military capabilities, as well as its trade-off of national versus allied military capabilities, I use the Correlates of War Project's data on material capabilities (Singer 1990c). For the measurements of a state's combined national and allied military capabilities as well as its trade-off of national versus allied military capabilities, I also employ the Correlates of War Project's formal alliance data (Small and Singer 1990).[8]

A state's level of democracy is measured by an index of net democracy based on the Polity98 data set's indicators of democracy and autocracy. Here a score of 0 shows respectively minimum democracy and minimum autocracy while a score of 10 reveals respectively maximum democracy and maximum autocracy (Jaggers and Gurr 1995; Gurr and Jaggers 2000). By subtracting autocracy scores from democracy scores and adding the difference to 10, I generate a net-democracy scale ranging from a minimum of 0 to a maximum of 20. A score of 0 denotes maximum autocracy or minimum democracy while a score of 20 denotes maximum democracy or minimum autocracy.

Identity as a militarized dispute initiator distinguishes a militarized dispute initiator from any other militarized dispute participant. It is measured by a dichotomy, where 1 indicates that a state initiated a militarized dispute, and 0 means that a state was either a militarized dispute target or joined a militarized dispute on the side of either another initiator or another target.

Identity as a war initiator distinguishes a war initiator from any other war participant. It is measured by a dichotomy, where 1 indicates that a state initiated a war, and 0 means that a state was either a war target or joined a war on the side of either another initiator or another target.

The measurement of a state's identity as a militarized dispute initiator, like the measurements of the outcome variables concerning militarized disputes, rests on the Correlates of War Project's militarized interstate dispute data (Jones, Bremer, and Singer 1996). The measurement of a state's identity as a war initiator, like the measurements of the outcome variables concerning wars, rests on the Correlates of War Project's interstate war data (Small and Singer 1982).

Since the measures for all outcome variables are dichotomous, probit regression analysis is an appropriate statistical estimation technique (Hanushek and Jackson 1977; Aldrich and Nelson 1984; Greene 2003). A critical issue in this investigation is that a state can only experience armed conflict success if it is involved in armed conflict to begin with. Put differently, armed conflict involvement is a necessary condition for armed conflict success. Furthermore, since some states may succeed in armed conflict because they select involvement in only success-promising armed conflict, attempts at predicting to success in militarized disputes and wars may run into selection bias (Achen 1986; Reed 2000). Selection bias can occur if unobserved variables that affect armed conflict involvement also affect armed conflict success, which means that there is a relationship between the unobserved covariates of involvement and success. Since such related variables are not observed, they are consigned to the error terms of the models predicting respectively to involvement and success in armed conflict. As a consequence, we need to account for the correlation between the error terms pertaining to the outcome variables in a two-stage armed conflict involvement-success selection process.

In order to control for selection bias due to any selection effect of militarized dispute/war involvement on militarized dispute/war success, I test hypotheses 1.1(1) through 3.2(2) with censored probit by relying on Heckman probit analysis (Heckman 1979).[9] Censored probit estimates jointly the probabilities of (1) militarized dispute/war involvement and (2) militarized dispute/war success, with militarized dispute/war involvement coded 1 if a state is involved in a militarized interstate dispute/interstate war and 0 if it is not. Militarized dispute/war success, however, is coded only if militarized dispute/war involvement is coded 1, which indicates that militarized dispute/war involvement is a necessary condition for success in militarized disputes/wars. As Lemke and Regan (this vol.) would put it in their discussion of censored probit, involvement in militarized disputes/wars provides an opportunity for militarized dispute/war success. Overall, there are three possible outcomes: First, a state is not involved in a militarized dispute/war. Second, a state is involved in a militarized dispute/war but does not experience militarized dispute/war success. Third, a state is involved and succeeds in a militarized dispute/war.

By using censored probit, I estimate jointly two types of effects of national military capabilities, combined national and allied military capabilities, and a trade-off of national versus allied military capabilities. First are the predictors' effects on militarized dispute/war involvement as a condition for militarized dispute/war success. Second are the predictors' effects on militarized dispute/war success itself. Furthermore, by employing censored probit, I estimate a statistical link, rho, to control for selection bias due to any selection effect based on inferences about the correlation between the error terms of (1) militarized dispute/war involvement and (2) militarized dispute/war success.

When looking at militarized disputes, I present a combined model including a selection model predicting to militarized dispute involvement *as well as* an outcome model predicting to success in militarized disputes. When looking at wars, I present a combined model including a selection model predicting to war involvement *as well as* an outcome model predicting to success in wars.

In order to control for time dependence, I apply the Beck, Katz, and Tucker (1998) method to all the models in this inquiry. Specifically, the selection models predicting to militarized dispute and war involvement include respectively (1) a time variable for prior state-years with no militarized dispute involvement and (2) a time variable for prior state-years with no war involvement, as well as three splines based on each time variable. The outcome models predicting to militarized dispute and war success include respectively (1) a time variable for prior state-years with no militarized dispute success and (2) a time variable for prior state-years with no war success, as well as three splines based on each time variable.[10]

## RESULTS

Table 1 presents the results of a multivariate Heckman probit analysis of militarized dispute success, with sample selection by militarized dispute involvement. This censored probit estimates jointly a militarized dispute involvement (selection) model and a militarized dispute success (outcome) model.

As for the militarized dispute involvement model, we find that a state's national military capabilities by themselves have a statistically significant and substantively by far the strongest impact on its militarized dispute involvement. A change in a state's national military capabilities from a minimum of 0 to a maximum of 0.43 increases its probability of militarized dispute involvement by 38.0 percent, which supports hypothesis 1.1(1). Neither a state's combined national and allied military capabilities nor its national military capabilities relative to its allied military capabilities have any statistically significant effect on its militarized dispute involvement. This fails to support hypotheses 2.1(1) and 3.1(1). Similarly, a state's level of democracy has no statistically significant impact on its involvement in militarized disputes.

In absolute substantive terms, the impact of a state's national military capabilities on its militarized dispute involvement is over nine times greater than the impact of any other variable considered in the militarized dispute involvement model. This suggests that a state's involvement in militarized disputes is influenced predominantly—almost exclusively—by its own armaments rather than by its allies or its level of democratic governance. One may speculate that an increase in a state's national military capabilities increases its willingness to be involved in militarized disputes by enhancing the clout of its military sector and, hence, making it more reliant on coercive diplomacy and military force.

As for the militarized dispute success model, we find that a state's national military capabilities by themselves have no statistically significant impact on its militarized dispute success, which fails to support hypothesis 1.1(2). Although this finding seems quite counterintuitive, it is important to note at this point that every year from the beginning to the end of a state's militarized dispute involvement is considered a state-year with no experience of any militarized dispute success. To the extent that an increase in national military capabilities may get a state to prolong its militarized dispute involvement, we would observe additional state-years that are not considered successful. Such observations may cancel out any positive effects of a state's national military capabilities on its success in militarized disputes. Hence, it would not be all

**TABLE 1.** Heckman Probit Analysis of Militarized Dispute Success, with Sample Selection by Militarized Dispute Involvement

| Predictors of Militarized Dispute Involvement | Coefficient (Standard Error) | Range of Variable | % Change in Probability of Militarized Dispute Involvement (Baseline: 63.7) |
|---|---|---|---|
| National military capabilities | +4.6743 (1.0937)*** | 0.00–0.43 | +38.0 |
| Combined national and allied military capabilities | +0.1147 (0.1923) | 0.00–0.92 | +3.9 |
| National versus allied military capabilities | −0.0425 (0.0316) | −1–1 | −3.2 |
| Level of democracy | +0.0031 (0.0039) | 0–20 | +2.4 |

| Predictors of Militarized Dispute Success | Coefficient (Standard Error) | Range of Variable | % Change in Probability of Militarized Dispute Success (Baseline: 12.8) |
|---|---|---|---|
| National military capabilities | +0.5300 (0.9472) | 0.00–0.43 | +5.3 |
| Combined national and allied military capabilities | +1.1321 (0.3043)*** | 0.00–0.92 | +30.0 |
| National versus allied military capabilities | +0.2053 (0.0702)** | −1–1 | +8.7 |
| Level of democracy | +0.0134 (0.0046)** | 0–20 | +5.7 |
| Militarized dispute initiator | +0.2032 (0.0865)** | 0–1 | +3.8 |

| | |
|---|---|
| Constant, militarized dispute involvement model | +0.2354 (0.0543)*** |
| Constant, militarized dispute success model | −1.3907 (0.1731)*** |
| Rho (selection effect) | −0.2488 (0.0857)** |
| LL, militarized dispute involvement model | −4948.5388 (−6420.7884) |
| LL, militarized dispute success model | −766.8314 (−829.5980) |
| Number of observations (censored/uncensored) | 10,123 (6,781/3,342) |
| $\chi^2$ | 89.52*** |

*Note:* Models include a variable for prior state-years with no militarized dispute involvement and a variable for prior state-years with no militarized dispute success, as well as three splines based on each time variable, to control for time dependence, using the Beck et al. (1998) method (estimates omitted). Standard errors (in parentheses) are heteroskedastic-robust and account for clustering of observations by state. All significance levels ($p$-values) are based on two-tailed tests, with exceptions of one-tailed tests for predictors that rest on specific directional hypotheses and have coefficients in expected directions. LL is converged log likelihood. Initial log likelihood (in parentheses) is shown for null model. Marginal impacts are computed with predicted values (coefficients). The values of selected predictors are changed while holding all others constant at their means or modes. Each change in position on the cumulative normal distribution underlying a probit model is then translated into a percentage change in the probability of a particular outcome.
*$p \leq 0.05$; **$p \leq 0.01$; ***$p \leq 0.001$

that surprising to find that a state's national military capabilities have no statistically significant impact on its militarized dispute success.

Interestingly, the situation is different when allied military capabilities complement national military capabilities. Unlike a state's national military capabilities by themselves, its combined national and allied military capabilities have a statistically significant and substantively by far the strongest impact on its militarized dispute success. A change in a state's combined national and allied military capabilities from a minimum of 0 to a maximum of 0.92 increases its probability of militarized dispute success by 30.0 percent, which supports hypothesis 2.1(2). This suggests that, once a state is involved in a militarized dispute, its likelihood of militarized dispute success is enhanced by an increase in its allied military capabilities complementing its national military capabilities. Here one may speculate that, as a state increasingly complements its own armaments with militarily strong allies, it increases its chance of militarized dispute success by raising the international legitimacy of its position while reducing potential international support for its adversaries.

The impact of a state's trade-off of national versus allied military capabilities on its militarized dispute success is statistically significant but substantively weaker than the impact of its combined national and allied military capabilities. A change in a state's national military capabilities relative to its allied military capabilities from perfect substitution of allied for national military capabilities $(-1)$ to perfect substitution of national for allied military capabilities $(1)$ increases its probability of militarized dispute success by 8.7 percent, which supports hypothesis 3.1(2). This may be so because the greater a state's national versus allied military capabilities, the greater its influence or control over its allies and the lesser the likelihood that a state's allies will defect and support its adversaries.

Taking into account both combined national and allied military capabilities and a trade-off of national versus allied military capabilities, it seems that a state's chance of militarized dispute success is enhanced most significantly under two conditions. First, there is an increase in a state's allied military capabilities complementing its national military capabilities, raising the amount of allied military resources that may eventually be mobilized against adversaries. Second, there is an increase in a state's national military capabilities relative to its allied military capabilities, raising the likelihood that allied military resources will indeed be mobilized against adversaries, not in their support. Although increases in both combined national and allied military capabilities and in a trade-off of national versus allied military capabilities enhance a state's likelihood of militarized dispute success, the complementary effect is substantively over three times greater than the substitution effect.

The impact of a state's level of democracy on its militarized dispute success is statistically significant but substantively weaker than the impact of a state's trade-off of national versus allied military capabilities. A change in a state's level of democracy from a minimum of 0 to a maximum of 20 increases its probability of militarized dispute success by 5.7 percent. Apparently, once a state is involved in a militarized dispute, the more democratic its political regime, the greater its domestic legitimacy and support, ensuring an increased chance of militarized dispute success.

The impact of a state's identity as a militarized dispute initiator on its militarized dispute success is statistically significant but substantively weaker than the impact of its level of democracy. A state that initiated a militarized dispute tends to be 3.8 percent more successful than a state that was either a militarized dispute target or joined a militarized dispute on the side of either another initiator or another target. Following Bueno de Mesquita and Siverson (1995) as well as Reiter and Stam (1998), one may argue that militarized dispute initiators are successful because they initiate only militarized disputes in which they are likely to succeed.

According to the estimate of the statistical link, rho, there is statistically significant selection bias due to some selection effect of militarized dispute involvement on success in militarized disputes. Specifically, there is a statistically significant negative correlation between the error terms of the two outcome variables, meaning that the effects of unobserved variables on involvement in militarized disputes are in the opposite direction compared with their effects on militarized dispute success.

Table 2 presents the results of a multivariate Heckman probit analysis of war success, with sample selection by war involvement. This censored probit estimates jointly a war involvement (selection) model and a war success (outcome) model.

As for the war involvement model, we find that a state's national military capabilities by themselves have no statistically significant impact on its war involvement, which fails to support hypothesis 1.2(1). While a state with relatively larger national military capabilities may have an increased motivation to be involved in wars, a state with relatively lesser national military capabilities may have an increased likelihood of being involved in wars not of its choice. To the extent that both a militarily stronger state and a militarily weaker state may have, for different reasons, an increased chance of involvement in wars, it would not be all that surprising to find that a state's national military capabilities have no statistically significant impact on its war involvement.

Interestingly, the situation is different when allied military capabilities complement national military capabilities. Unlike a state's national military capabilities by themselves, its combined national and allied military capabilities have a statistically significant and substantively by far the strongest impact on its war involvement. A change in a state's combined

TABLE 2. Heckman Probit Analysis of War Success, with Sample Selection by War Involvement

| Predictors of War Involvement | Coefficient (Standard Error) | Range of Variable | % Change in Probability of War Involvement (Baseline: 69.4) |
|---|---|---|---|
| National military capabilities | −0.7977 (0.6845) | 0.00–0.43 | −12.8 |
| Combined national and allied military capabilities | +1.4696 (0.2745)*** | 0.00–0.92 | +33.7 |
| National versus allied military capabilities | +0.2146 (0.0504)*** | −1–1 | +14.9 |
| Level of democracy | −0.0072 (0.0051) | 0–20 | −5.1 |

| Predictors of War Success | Coefficient (Standard Error) | Range of Variable | % Change in Probability of War Success (Baseline: 21.8) |
|---|---|---|---|
| National military capabilities | −0.9648 (0.9859) | 0.00–0.43 | −10.6 |
| Combined national and allied military capabilities | +1.4150 (0.5794)** | 0.00–0.92 | +44.8 |
| National versus allied military capabilities | +0.1677 (0.1375) | −1–1 | +9.8 |
| Level of democracy | +0.0048 (0.0081) | 0–20 | +2.8 |
| War initiator | +0.6652 (0.1663)*** | 0–1 | +23.7 |

| | |
|---|---|
| Constant, war involvement model | +0.3820 (0.0892)*** |
| Constant, war success model | −1.3934 (0.3950)*** |
| Rho (selection effect) | +0.3102 (0.1104)** |
| LL, war involvement model | −1010.1826 (−1496.0800) |
| LL, war success model | −262.2539 (−278.1988) |
| Number of observations (censored/uncensored) | 3,342 (2,791/551) |
| $\chi^2$ | 28.20*** |

Note: Models include a variable for prior state-years with no war involvement and a variable for prior state-years with no war success, as well as three splines based on each time variable, to control for time dependence, using the Beck et al. (1998) method (estimates omitted). Standard errors (in parentheses) are heteroskedastic-robust and account for clustering of observations by state. All significance levels (p-values) are based on two-tailed tests, with exceptions of one-tailed tests for predictors that rest on specific directional hypotheses and have coefficients in expected directions. LL is converged log likelihood. Initial log likelihood (in parentheses) is shown for null model. Marginal impacts are computed with predicted values (coefficients). The values of selected predictors are changed while holding all others constant at their means or modes. Each change in position on the cumulative normal distribution underlying a probit model is then translated into a percentage change in the probability of a particular outcome.
*$p \le 0.05$; **$p \le 0.01$; ***$p \le 0.001$

national and allied military capabilities from a minimum of 0 to a maximum of 0.92 increases its probability of war involvement by 33.7 percent, which supports hypothesis 2.2(1). This suggests that a state's likelihood of war involvement is enhanced by an increase in its allied military capabilities complementing its national military capabilities. As a state increasingly complements its own arms with militarily strong allies, it may become more motivated to be involved in wars due to expectations of increased allied military assistance in confrontations with adversaries.

The impact of a state's trade-off of national versus allied military capabilities on its war involvement is statistically significant but substantively weaker than the impact of its combined national and allied military capabilities. A change in a state's national military capabilities relative to its allied military capabilities from perfect substitution of allied for national military capabilities (−1) to perfect substitution of national for allied military capabilities (1) increases its probability of war involvement by 14.9 percent, which supports hypothesis 3.2(1). This may be so because the greater a state's national versus allied military capabilities, the greater its influence or control over its allies and the lesser the likelihood that a state's allies will defect and support its adversaries. Taking this argument a step further, the lesser the likelihood that a state's allies will defect and support its adversaries, the greater a state's expectations of its allies' loyalty and, hence, the greater a state's motivation to be involved in wars.

Taking into account both combined national and allied military capabilities and a trade-off of national versus allied military capabilities, it seems that a state's chance of war involvement is enhanced most significantly under two conditions. First, there is an increase in a state's allied military capabilities complementing its national military capabilities, raising the amount of allied military resources that may eventually be mobilized against adversaries. Second, there is an increase in a state's national military capabilities relative to its allied military capabilities, raising the likelihood that allied military resources will indeed be mobilized against adversaries, not in their support. Although increases in both combined national and allied military capabilities and in a trade-off of national versus allied military capabilities enhance a state's likelihood of war involvement, the complementary effect is substantively over two times greater than the substitution effect.

A state's level of democracy has no statistically significant impact on its war involvement. This suggests that a state's war involvement is influenced more critically by its international relationships with allies than by its level of domestic democratic governance.

As for the war success model, we find that a state's national military capabilities by themselves have no statistically significant impact on its war success, which fails to support hypothesis 1.2(2). Although this finding, like the one concerning militarized dispute success, seems quite counterintuitive, it is important to note at this point that every year from the beginning to the end of a state's war involvement is considered a state-year with no experience of any war success. If there were situations in which an increase in national military capabilities might get a state to prolong its war involvement, we would observe additional state-years that are not considered successful. Such observations may cancel out any positive effects of a state's national military capabilities on its success in wars. Hence, it would not be all that surprising to find that a state's national military capabilities have no statistically significant impact on its war success.

Interestingly, the situation is different when allied military capabilities complement national military capabilities. Unlike a state's national military capabilities by themselves, its combined national and allied military capabilities have a statistically significant and substantively by far the strongest impact on its war success. A change in a state's combined national and allied military capabilities from a minimum of 0 to a maximum of 0.92 increases its probability of war success by 44.8 percent, which supports hypothesis 2.2(2). This suggests that, once a state is involved in a war, its likelihood of war success is enhanced by an increase in its allied military capabilities complementing its national military capabilities. Here one may speculate that, as a state increasingly complements its own armaments with militarily strong allies, it increases its chance of war success by raising its amount of potential allied military assistance while reducing potential armed support from allies for its adversaries.

A state's trade-off of national versus allied military capabilities has no statistically significant impact on its war success, which fails to support hypothesis 3.2(2). Once a war is under way, the stakes may be so high that a state's allies may provide military assistance, or at least refrain from defection and support for its adversaries, no matter what the extent of military capability superiority, influence, or control that a state has over its allies. Hence, it may not be all that surprising to find that a state's war success is statistically not significantly affected by its trade-off of national versus allied military capabilities.

A state's level of democracy has no statistically significant impact on its war success. This suggests that a state's war success is influenced more critically by its international allied military capabilities complementing its national military capabilities than by its level of domestic democratic governance.

The impact of a state's identity as a war initiator on its war success is statistically significant but substantively weaker than the impact of its combined national and allied military capabilities. A state that initiated a war tends to be 23.7 percent more successful than a state that was either a war target or joined a war on the side of either another initiator or another target.[11] Following again Bueno de Mesquita and Siverson (1995) as well as Reiter and Stam (1998), one may argue that war initiators are successful because they initiate only wars in which they are likely to succeed.

According to the estimate of the statistical link, rho, there is statistically significant selection bias due to some selection effect of war involvement on success in wars. Specifically, there is a statistically significant positive correlation between the error terms of the two outcome variables, meaning that the effects of unobserved variables on involvement in wars are in the same direction compared with their effects on war success.

## CONCLUSIONS

Contrary to what one might expect, military capabilities are far from a robust guarantee of success in armed conflict. Success in wars and militarized disputes is not only mostly a function of an advantage in industrial rather than in military or demographic capabilities but also predominantly more likely with military underallocations than overallocations. Close to half of all relations between militarized dispute and war success on the one hand and measures of military capabilities and military allocations on the other are statistically insignificant.

This chapter extended the work of Wayman, Singer, and Goertz (1983) by taking into account that states may rely on some mix of both national and allied military capabilities to ensure success in militarized disputes and wars. Given the concept of substitutability in foreign policy (Most and Starr 1989), this study examined the extent to which a state's armed conflict involvement and success are affected by the complementarity or substitutability of its national and allied military capabilities. Put differently, this study examined the extent to which a state's combinations or trade-offs of national and allied military capabilities affect its involvement and success in militarized disputes and wars.

Focusing on all state-years between 1816 and 1992, this inquiry found that an increase in a state's national military capabilities significantly raises its likelihood of involvement in militarized disputes. By contrast, a state's war involvement is statistically not significantly affected by its national military capabilities. Tentative explanations for these findings were provided in the previous section on results.

Increases in a state's combined national and allied military capabilities and in a state's trade-off of national versus allied military capabilities significantly raise its likelihood of war involvement but have no statistically significant effect on its involvement in militarized disputes. This suggests that expectations of allied military support are far more critical in influencing war than militarized dispute involvement.

A state's national military capabilities by themselves have no statistically significant effect on either its militarized dispute or war success. This reinforces the doubt raised by Wayman, Singer, and Goertz about any notion that national military capabilities by themselves are the key to success in armed conflict.

An increase in a state's combined national and allied military capabilities significantly raises both its militarized dispute and war success. In addition to our earlier discussion of results, we may argue that the greater the military capabilities of allies that a state can add to or combine with its national military capabilities, the fewer national military capabilities a state has to invest in the pursuit of success in militarized disputes and wars. This allows a state to keep some national military capabilities in reserve, to be used when a state's allied military capabilities no longer guarantee militarized dispute and war success or when a state's allies become adversaries. At the same time, the greater a state's allied military capabilities, the more likely a state will be abandoned or even opposed by its allies, and the greater a state's need to demonstrate resolve to its alliance partners. By extension, the greater its need to demonstrate resolve to its allies, the greater a state's likelihood of taking a hard line with respect to adversaries and rejecting anything short of unconditional militarized dispute and war success.[12]

The greater a state's national military capabilities relative to its allied military capabilities, the significantly greater its likelihood of success in militarized disputes. This may be largely due to the impact of national and allied military capabilities on alliance politics. As Snyder (1984, 1997) points out, alliance politics involves the fear of either "abandonment" or "entrapment" in military interactions. Additionally, if its alliance partners do not support a state, it may punish those allies by subjecting them to some combination of diplomatic, economic, and military coercion. A state's ability to shape its allies' national interests with threats of abandonment or punishment and its chance of reducing allied resistance to entrapment in unwanted armed conflict depend on its mix of national and allied military capabilities. The greater a state's national versus allied military capabilities, the greater a state's ability to influence its allies' national interests. The greater a state's national versus allied military capabilities, the more credible a state's threats of abandoning or punishing disloyal allies, and the less likely a state is to encounter allied resistance to entrapment in unwanted armed conflict. By implication, the lesser its allies' resistance, the more likely a state is to succeed in armed conflict, that is, at least in militarized disputes.

When it comes to war, a state's national military capabilities relative to its allied military capabilities have no statistically significant impact on its war success, possibly for reasons that I offered in the previous discussion of results.

It should be noted that the analysis of war involvement and success is based on only those cases where states were involved in militarized disputes. This is admittedly a very crude way of considering the selection of cases examined for war involvement and success from a pool of cases of militarized dispute involvement. Further research still needs to develop integrated selection models to take into account more or less simultaneously selection effects both of militarized dispute involvement on war involvement and of war involvement on war success. In further research, I will also seek to explore the optimal mix of allied military capabilities relative to national military capabilities required for a maximum likelihood of success in armed conflict.

## NOTES

*Author's Note:* I gratefully acknowledge Paul Diehl, Douglas Lemke, J. David Singer, Susumu Suzuki, and two anonymous reviewers for constructive comments and helpful suggestions. I also thank Brian Lai and Dan Reiter for sharing their information on alliances beyond 1984.

1. Although Wayman, Goertz, and Singer deal with coalitions in militarized disputes and wars, coalitions are not necessarily alliances. Unlike coalitions, alliances are based on written, mostly voluntary, formal agreements, treaties, or conventions among states pledging to coordinate their behavior and policies in the contingency of military conflict (Bueno de Mesquita and Singer 1973; Ward 1982).

2. The averages reported here in regard to military capabilities and allies are based on the Correlates of War Project's material capabilities and formal alliance data (Singer 1990c; Small and Singer 1990).

3. Gelpi and Griesdorf (2001) make a similar point with respect to democracy, challengers, and success in international crises.

4. The examination begins in 1816 and ends in 1992 because data on *all* variables in this inquiry are available only for the period between 1816 and 1992. As of this writing, the Correlates of War Project is in the process of gen-

erating data beyond 1992 not only on formal alliances, but also on material capabilities and militarized interstate disputes.

5. In order to test for multicollinearity, I look at the tolerance levels among all the predictor and control variables that are supposed to account for a particular outcome variable. The lower the tolerance level of any predictor or control variable, the more likely that variable can be explained by a linear combination of all other predictor and control variables. A common tolerance threshold is 0.30 (Hanushek and Jackson 1977; Menard 1995). There is no serious multicollinearity problem in any of the following analyses because the tolerance levels of all predictor and control variables are consistently above the 0.30 threshold.

6. Including allied military capabilities as a separate predictor variable, in addition to national military capabilities and combined national and allied military capabilities, results in serious multicollinearity. Hence, I omit allied military capabilities from all empirical analyses.

7. It is important to note that a state may also receive a score of 0 for a perfectly balanced mix of both national and allied military capabilities if it has no national and allied military capabilities at all. Despite this caveat, the bottom line is still that a score of 0 denotes that a state's mix of national and allied military capabilities is perfectly balanced.

8. The Correlates of War Project's formal alliance data officially includes alliances between 1816 and 1984. I extended the alliance data for the years between 1985 and 1992 with the help of Lai and Reiter (2000). The Correlates of War 2 Project is currently updating its formal alliance data. Awaiting the completion of this update, the extended alliance data used in this study are not meant to compete with the new official version of the formal alliance data soon to be released by the Correlates of War 2 Project.

9. Reed (2000) cautions that a two-stage probit analysis according to Heckman, although it yields substantive and statistical results that are similar to the ones generated by a full information maximum likelihood (FIML) censored probit analysis, is inefficient due to heteroskedasticity. Heeding Reed's caution, I report standard errors that are heteroskedastic-robust for each analysis in this investigation.

10. In order to focus on the major predictor and outcome variables in this investigation, I omit from the presentation of results all estimates for the time variables and splines created with the Beck, Katz, and Tucker (1998) method. Despite these omissions, it is important to remember that the time variables for prior state-years with no militarized dispute and war involvement, as well as the corresponding splines, are included in the selection models but not in the outcome models. Hence, the variables affecting militarized dispute and war involvement in the selection models are not identical to the variables affecting militarized dispute and war success in the outcome models. This means, according to Sartori (2002), that the Heckman estimators used in this study are appropriate compared with the new estimator introduced by Sartori (2003).

11. Given the evidence by Reiter and Stam (1998) that democratic war ini-

tiators are more likely than any other states to achieve war victory, I replaced a state's identity as a war initiator with an interaction term combining a state's identity as a war initiator with its level of democracy. The results corroborate the Reiter-Stam evidence. As for a war initiator, the higher its level of democracy, the significantly more likely it is to experience war success. A change in a war initiator's level of democracy from a minimum of 0 to a maximum of 20 increases its probability of war success by 30.7 percent. As far as any other war participant is concerned, its level of democracy has no statistically significant impact on its likelihood of war success. Substantively, a change in its level of democracy from a minimum of 0 to a maximum of 20 decreases its probability of war success by 9.9 percent. The additional analysis is available from the author upon request.

12. For an excellent study of alliance and adversary games, see Snyder (1997).

# PART III   DYADIC FACTORS AND INTERACTIVE EFFECTS

# INTERVENTIONS AS INFLUENCE

Douglas Lemke and Patrick M. Regan

J. David Singer (1963) developed a conceptual framework for thinking about when and how states will attempt to manipulate the behavior of other states. His logic develops from the notion of thinking clearly about what the influencer is trying to maximize and the potential strategies best able to achieve this goal. The idea of states as influencers of world events has numerous contemporary and historical applications. The civil unrest in Israel and the occupied territories, for example, is rife with attempts by the United States to modify or reinforce behavior. In Russia, the United States regularly attempts to influence behaviors with regard to political processes and nuclear controls. We suspect any policy initiative could be fruitfully thought through in terms of Singer's conceptual framework. Oddly, though, Singer offered no empirical evaluation of this model. We add to his work by testing implications about civil war interventions based on applying the internation influence model to that activity.

In this chapter we first provide a brief description of the "internation influence" model. After reviewing past research on interventions, we discuss the model in the context of intervention into ongoing civil conflict. In so doing we develop testable hypotheses about interventions based on the internation influence model. We then describe the data set and testing procedures used in evaluating those hypotheses. Along the way we replicate past research on interventions into civil wars, supporting some and recasting other previous findings. Evaluation of one of the hypotheses based on Singer's model generates a wholly new empirical finding, specifically that interventions in support of rebels are bloodier than are interventions in support of governments. Finally, we discuss possible extensions that future intervention researchers might make, and we also speculate about broader applications of the model and the data requirements needed to test the internation influence model more directly.

## SINGER'S "INTERNATION INFLUENCE" MODEL

Although subtitled a formal model, it is best to think of the internation influence model as a conceptual scheme linking the likelihood of influence attempts with their form—or strategy. Central to the internation influence model are the perceptions, predictions, and preferences of the would-be influencer. More specifically, the model centers around the influencer's perception of the target's current behavior, its predictions about the target's future behavior, and its preferences about what that future behavior should be. If the target (referred to by Singer as B) is predicted to behave in ways desired by the potential influencer (designated by Singer as A), then A is very unlikely to take violent steps to influence B. A's interest in such a situation would be to reinforce what B already is expected to do, and this is likely to involve rewards or promises thereof rather than threats and punishments. Were B predicted to behave in ways A disapproves of, then threats and punishments would be more likely. For example, a state contemplating intervening in a civil conflict must consider the current and anticipated behavior of its target. Does it agree with the target's current policy and want to reinforce it, and does it perceive that in the absence of an outside intervention the current policy will change toward a less preferred outcome? Depending on the preferences for the current and anticipated policy of the target, effective options include threats and punishment or reinforcement and rewards. We can observe this interplay of current and anticipated preferences and behavior throughout any number of civil conflicts. Are the Israelis expanding settlements? What is most preferred by the United States? Does the United States anticipate that Israeli policy will move into line with U.S. preferences, and if not, what actions are available to move Israeli policy?

We are especially attracted to Singer's conceptual model because its generality incorporates both conflict and cooperation. When perceptions of B's current behavior and predictions about its future behavior are consistent with A's preferences, we expect A and B to get along well and interactions between the two to be cooperative. When B's behavior is perceived now or predicted later to diverge from A's preferences, coercive efforts to influence B to modify its behavior are increasingly likely. By considering possibilities of modification and reinforcement within a framework running the gamut from threats and punishment to promises and rewards, Singer systematically relates situations and incentives for

| | Persuasion Situations: A Prefers X | | | | Dissuasion Situations: A Prefers O | | | |
|---|---|---|---|---|---|---|---|---|
| | 1 | 2 | 3 | 4 | 5 | 6 | 7 | 8 |
| Preferred Future Behavior | X | X | X | X | O | O | O | O |
| Predicted Future Behavior | X | X | O | O | O | O | X | X |
| Perceived Present Behavior | X | O | X | O | O | X | O | X |
| Reinforce or Modify | R | M | R | M | R | M | R | M |
| Punish? | No | P | No | Yes | No | P | No | Yes |
| Reward? | Yes | No | Yes | No | Yes | No | Yes | No |
| Threaten? | P | Yes | Yes | Yes | P | Yes | Yes | Yes |
| Promise? | Yes | Yes | Yes | Yes | Yes | Yes | Yes | Yes |

KEY: R = REINFORCE, M = MODIFY, P = PERHAPS

Fig. 1.  Hypothesized relevance of influence techniques

states to use carrots or sticks to influence the target nation. The internation influence model is thus a tremendously general and flexible scheme with which to make sense of interactions between states.

It is perhaps easiest to understand the internation influence model by consulting figure 1 (a reproduction of fig. 3 from Singer's original article). It begins with all of the possible combinations of preferences, predictions, and perceptions about B's behavior. For simplification, Singer dichotomizes the target's behavior into X and O, where O simply represents "not X," although clearly actual behaviors could run along a continuum.

Consider column 1. In this scenario A prefers B do X, predicts B's likely future behavior is X, and perceives its current behavior also is X. In this situation A is likely to get a satisfactory outcome in terms of B's behavior and thus need not take steps to influence B to modify its behavior. Consequently Singer hypothesizes any actions taken by A to influence B would be to reinforce current behavior. More specifically, Singer hypothesizes influence strategies involving punishment will not be undertaken, but rather rewards and promises are most likely to be used. In contrast, column 4 offers a scenario in which A prefers B do X, but it perceives B as currently doing O and predicts that it will likely continue to do O in the future. As a result, A is not likely to observe its preferred outcome unless something is done to modify B's behavior. In this scenario Singer predicts threats, promises, and punishment are likely influence strategies, and it is unlikely we would observe A using a reward strategy to influence B.

By presenting each possible combination of preferences, predictions and perceptions, figure 1 lays out hypothesized relationships between influence situations and the expected types of influence attempts. The internation influence model summarized in this figure offers a logical and persuasive scheme about when and how states will take steps to influence each other's behavior.

As logical and persuasive as the scheme is, however, it lacks the specificity needed to articulate precise hypotheses. That absence of specificity makes empirical testing problematic, even though the conceptual framework retains redeeming value. What is required to make it useful is the inclusion of a context within which states might find themselves presented with specific preferences, predictions, and perceptions.

## CIVIL WARS AS INFLUENCE ENVIRONMENTS

Civil wars are usually extremely violent events disrupting not only the states suffering through them but also those interacting with the beleaguered victims. Frequently, civil wars represent cultural or ideological conflicts in which the characteristic of the post–civil war society will be heavily influenced by which side wins the contest. For this reason, not only those involved but also those concerned about the ethnic or ideological stakes have an interest in the course and outcome of the civil war. For instance, a civil conflict in a bordering country may lead to instability among its neighbors. And if the "causes" of the conflict are rooted in manipulable behavior by the state, a neighboring state may try to influence that behavior (see Gurr 1970; Collier, Hoeffler, and Soderbom 2001; Sambanis 2001). Civil conflicts thus are situations in which many states may have powerful incentives to try to influence the outcome. Civil conflicts, viewed as intervention opportunities for other states, are an important category of potential influence situations, and thus a context within which Singer's internation influence model can be tested.

For example, the policy community frequently struggles over questions of whether and how to intervene in civil conflicts. The most glaring instance might be Rwanda in 1994. There have been many public expressions of regret since then. As the atrocities began to unfold, members of the world community contemplated taking action, but ultimately they could not satisfy the condition that an intervention would have a reasonable chance of success. On a less dramatic scale this type of decision calculus has played out in the Congo, East Timor, Liberia, Israel, and a host of other countries over the past decade. Policymakers are riveted to these problems but lack a coherent plan of action. Such might begin to be provided by Singer's internation influence model. We believe it adds considerably to thinking about when and how interventions into civil conflicts might take place.

In order to move Singer's framework from the abstract to the specific we use as our point of reference recent scholarship on interventions in civil conflicts. While there are numerous policy treatments focusing on a limited number of historical cases, much of this genre of work is geared toward prescriptive advice without the support of broad-based evidence or a logical theoretic framework. We believe Singer's model can contribute by showing how to organize evidence within such a framework. The internation influence model can aid our understanding of interventions in civil conflicts and provide a framework for evaluating evidence about the relative success of outside efforts. At the core of Singer's model is a rationally calculating decision maker who attempts to maximize utility given expectations, preferences, and current information. Regan (2000) applies this type of argument to civil conflicts by adopting a decision-theoretic model largely consistent with Singer's work. Building on Regan's research on interventions into civil conflicts, we add to its theoretical and empirical rigor by explicitly adopting Singer's framework and then testing hypotheses against the data developed by Regan.

Like Singer's, Regan's (1996, 1998, 2000) studies treat potential intervenors as rational actors who evaluate the likely costs and benefits of intervening, heavily influenced by whether they expect their interventions to succeed in stopping the fighting. Stopping the fighting is treated as the goal of all potential intervenors because a cease-fire is the proximate goal without which no other goal can be achieved. In a framework informed by Singer's model an intervention is an attempt to influence the actors in a civil war to terminate their fighting, in effect to alter their current and/or anticipated future behavior.

In his work, Regan articulates a decision-theoretic model of the cost-benefit calculations that potential intervenors face when deciding whether to intervene. By careful consideration of variables plausibly anticipated to affect the costs and benefits of fighting or laying down arms, Regan is able to develop hypotheses about five conditions for intervention success. He analyzes these five hypotheses against the record of 189 foreign interventions into civil wars, finding reasonably strong support for three of them and moderate support for the other two (1996, 2000, chap. 4).

In our investigation of Singer's internation influence model, Regan's work on interventions into civil wars is an obvious referent because he consciously structures his analyses consistent with Singer's model. He not only repeatedly makes reference to it but actively constructs his argument along the lines of Singer's discussion of the model. For example, when describing how would-be influencers/intervenors consider the consequences of not attempting to influence/intervene, Singer writes, "If A's decision makers are *reasonably confident* that nation B either *will* behave in a fashion *desirable* to A or *not* behave in an *un*desirable fashion, the incentive to attempt to influence B will diminish" (1963, 421, emphasis in original). In describing the potential intervenor's considerations, Regan writes, "The question is posed as to the likely outcome of the conflict without an outside intervention. If the subjective estimate of the probability of a successful settlement is high without an intervention, then the expected utility for not intervening is high and the decision process stops there" (2000, 44). In either case, if the influencer/intervenor expects the target to behave as desired without interference, no interference is expected. Such similarities make connections between Singer's and Regan's work easy to draw, and thus make Regan's interventions into civil conflicts an attractive empirical beginning into evaluation of Singer's model.

Replication and extension of Regan's (and others') past work on interventions is an important justification for our study. However, we wish to reiterate that our main goal is to use the analysis of interventions into civil wars as an empirical place to start evaluating Singer's model. We believe interventions are an important topic for study. However, we use them here not out of intrinsic interest, but rather because we claim they represent efforts by states to influence the future behaviors of other states. If this reasonable claim is true, then Singer's model should offer important insights into interventionary behavior. Those insights are developed in the next section, then evaluated empirically in the rest of the chapter.

### HYPOTHESES ABOUT INTERVENTIONS AS INFLUENCE

Singer's model can offer many hypotheses about foreign intervention into ongoing civil wars. For example, as presented in figure 1, the model suggests promises are always an appropriate reaction in any influence attempt. Threats are also common, albeit not as common as promises. As a result, we might hypothesize would-be intervenors are very likely to threaten to intervene militarily or promise to intervene economically as first steps at encouraging civil war participants to stop the fighting on their own. Additionally, Singer's model can generate a hypothesis that interventions on the government side will be rare when the government is preponderant over the opposition. Therefore there is little if any incentive for a foreign state favoring the government to come to its assistance. Singer writes, "No nation has the resources to engage in serious efforts to influence a great many of the others at any given time" (1963, 423). Consequently, states favoring the government, if able to predict with high probability that the government will win the civil war, can preserve their resources for other influence/intervention cases yet still enjoy satisfactory outcomes. Many similar hypotheses can be drawn from Singer's model about likely interventions; we leave them for future research. Instead, we turn to hypotheses about the violence of civil wars with interventions and about the identity of foreign intervenors.[1]

Figure 1 indicates that the goal of reinforcing never coincides with a strategy of punishment but instead always coincides with a reward strategy. This means the internation influence model only anticipates punishment when the influencer's goal is to modify the target's behavior. If an intervention opposes the government, then it is effectively trying to alter the pre-conflict status quo, in effect attempting to modify the state's behavior. This suggests a hypothesis that civil wars in which the opposition is aided by a foreign intervention are bloodier than civil wars in which foreign intervention aids the government. The logic is as follows. When foreign intervention aids the government it is plausible to assume the intervening state prefers the government's policies and way of ruling to what it predicts the opposition would institute if it were to win. By intervening on behalf of the government the intervenor seeks to reinforce the government already in power and by connection to reinforce its existing policies. Intervention on behalf of the opposition is consistent with assuming the foreign intervenor prefers the opposition's alternate policies and/or mode of governing. Such intervention is thus geared toward modifying the policies and/or mode of governance existing in the civil war state. Conceptually altering or restoring the pre-conflict status quo reflects modifying or reinforcing state behavior, and these preferences always involve rewarding or punishing strategies (fig. 1). Since punishment is an influence strategy appropriate to situations in which the influencer wants to modify rather than reinforce, we expect to see punishment in interventions on behalf of the opposition. Putting some real-world context on the abstract category of "punishment" gives us our first hypothesis.

*The Scourge of* **WAR**

HYPOTHESIS 1: Interventions on behalf of the opposition will co-incide with more violent civil wars than will be the case when interventions occur on behalf of the government.[2]

There is a second way to justify this hypothesis. In general the government is likely to be stronger—at least initially—than the opposition. Consequently, if the foreign state intervenes on behalf of the government it is reinforcing the behavior of the state by reinforcing the likely outcome of a governmental victory in the civil war. If, in contrast, it intervenes in favor of the opposition, it is attempting to modify the likely outcome so an opposition victory will occur. Thus, if the opposition is the underdog, interventions on its behalf are influence attempts to modify the likely outcome of the civil war, and punishment is thus an appropriate strategy according to the internation influence model.[3] More important, an intervention on behalf of the opposition might not have as the objective an opposition victory, but rather a goal of making the opposition strong vis-à-vis the government, though not necessarily strong enough to prevail on the battlefield. Estimates of victory by either side will contribute to concessions at the negotiating table. When the opposition is strong it can extract compromises consistent with the intervenor's preferred future behavior.

Perhaps the most fruitful area within which the internation influence model offers hypotheses concerns the identity of intervening states. In his analyses of what makes intervention more likely, Regan (1996; 2000, chap. 3) analyzes what makes at least one intervention into an ongoing civil war more likely, ignoring which states specifically might intervene. Regan's argument about cost-benefit calculations of potential intervenors does not give any indication of which states are likely to bother to undertake the cost-benefit calculations in the first place. There are two types of states that do not intervene. First, there are those who undertake the cost-benefit calculation and decide intervention is not a rational response because the costs are too high or the probability of success too low. But there is also a second group of non-intervenors: those who don't even bother to undertake the cost-benefit calculation because they do not care about the civil war state. Unable to distinguish between these two types of non-intervenors, Regan's empirical emphasis is on the civil war as the unit of analysis, using as the dependent variable the presence or absence of *any* outside intervention.

Singer's internation influence model offers more robust expectations about which states are likely to undertake the cost-benefit calculations about whether to intervene. Specifically, Singer writes: "The first prerequisite for an influence attempt is the perception on the part of A's decision-makers that A and B are, or will be, in a relationship of significant interdependence, and that B's future behavior consequently could well be such as to exercise either a harmful or beneficial impact on A" (1963, 423). States interacting regularly and significantly with the civil war state are likely to care more about the civil war's outcome, are thus more likely to undertake the cost-benefit calculation, and ultimately are more likely to intervene. That is, the pool of potential intervenors can be thought of in terms of their geographic relationship and/or their previous political and economic interactions. Thus we hypothesize states that have significant interaction with the civil war state are more likely to intervene in its civil war, which gives us our next hypotheses.

HYPOTHESIS 2: States bordering the civil war state are more likely to intervene.
HYPOTHESIS 3: States allied with the civil war state are more likely to intervene.
HYPOTHESIS 4: If a state is the former colonial metropole of the civil war state, it is more likely to intervene.

Neighbors, allies, and former colonial powers of the civil war state are likely to interact frequently with the civil war state, anticipate they will continue to do so in the future, and thus be more likely to think about and actually intervene. Including such variables in our analysis, based on the internation influence model, allows us to address the question of who are the *potential* intervenors.

In sum, we motivate two categories of hypotheses about interventions from Singer's internation influence model. The first anticipates that interventions on behalf of the opposition or insurgent forces will be bloodier or at least more aggressive than interventions on behalf of the government. This hypothesis is suggested by the fact that Singer's model identifies punishment as the appropriate strategy in situations where the influence effort seeks to modify a target's predicted future behavior. We envision interventions on behalf of the opposition as efforts to modify a state's future policies and anticipate bloodier and more aggressive activity to represent a strategy of punishment. The second category of hypothesis is represented by three specific hypotheses about characteristics of states associated with a greater likelihood they will intervene into an ongoing civil war. Singer very clearly anticipates that, due to limited resources, actors will be picky about when and where they will attempt to exert influence. Since influence attempts are costly, states are more likely to bother to try to influence others when they anticipate a high likelihood of future interactions with those others. Our specific hypotheses anticipate that neighbors, allies, and former colonial powers of civil war states are more likely to expect to interact with civil war states in the future, thus care more about what civil war states will do in the future, and consequently are more likely to intervene to influence the outcome of the civil war. These hypotheses are so far untested in the larger literature on civil war interventions and thus are unique and original contributions of our application of Singer's internation influence model to the topic of interventions.

## RESEARCH DESIGN

The analyses to follow rely on extensions to the data set generated by Regan to study interventions in civil conflicts (Regan 2000, chap. 2). The data set includes all civil conflicts between 1944 and 1994, defined as "armed combat between groups within state boundaries in which there are at least 200 fatalities" (21). Regan identifies 138 civil conflicts meeting these criteria. He also provides information about whether the civil war triggered a humanitarian crisis, indicated by the flow of at least 50,000 refugees (23). The basis of the conflict is also of interest, and consequently the data set indicates whether the primary disagreement between the belligerents was rooted in identity issues, recorded in terms of the ethnic, religious, or ideological orientation of the opposition group. In addition, the level of violence of the conflict is also of interest, and thus the data set indicates the number of fatalities as well as the intensity of the conflict (fatalities/year). The final characteristic of the conflicts is whether they occurred during the Cold War, defined as ending on January 1, 1989. Thus, in the analyses to follow we include a number of variables about the characteristics of civil wars (Ethnic Conflict, Ideological Conflict, Refugees, Casualties, Intensity, and Cold War) drawn directly from Regan's previous work.

Regan's data set also includes information on the intervenors and the characteristics of their interventions. He defines "third-party intervention in intrastate conflicts as convention-breaking military and/or economic activities in the internal affairs of a foreign country targeted at the authority structures of the government with the aim of affecting the balance of power between the government and opposition forces" (2000, 10). The data set lists 197 interventions into the 138 civil wars. Of critical importance is the outcome of the intervention. In the data set "success" is operationalized as the cessation of fighting for at least six months. In addition to this outcome variable, Regan's data set also includes information on other aspects of the interventions that occurred, such as whether the intervention was of a military, economic, or mixed nature, whether the intervenor was a major power, and whether the intervention was in aid of the government or the opposition. Thus, in the analyses to follow we include a number of variables about actual interventions (Success, Mixed Intervention, Supporting Government, Major Power Intervenor, Mixed Support for Opposition, Mixed Support for Government, and Economic Support for Opposition) drawn directly from Regan's previous work. All of this allows us to replicate his past studies, but importantly we do so within the framework of the internation influence model.

To this existing data we add cases of potential intervention by foreign states and variables representing what we think, based on the internation influence model, makes such interventions more likely. For the additional cases, we treat each civil war as an intervention opportunity for every member of the international system (as defined by COW) in existence while the civil war occurred. Thus, instead of the Greek civil war of 1944–49 having only five cases of actual interventions (by the United States, United Kingdom, Albania, Yugoslavia, and Bulgaria), our data reflect seventy-five cases of possible interventions, with five actually occurring. The Correlates of War Project lists seventy-six members of the international system between 1944 and 1949, and since Greece cannot launch a foreign intervention into its own civil war, we have seventy-five "intervention opportunities." That is, we treat each civil war as an intervention opportunity for every other system member. As a result the 138 civil wars expand to 19,533 cases of intervention opportunity, in which only 197 actual interventions occurred.

Not all system members are equally likely to intervene, of course. Consequently, based on the internation influence model, we include a number of new variables designed to help us weed through the potential intervenors and highlight a subset of likely intervenors. The first new variable "Neighbor" is a dichotomous indicator of whether the potential intervenor is directly contiguous to the civil war state at any point during the civil war. By excluding contiguity by sea we do not mean to suggest India, for instance, would not be interested in Sri Lanka's civil wars. Rather, we are trying to keep our analysis simple. Some states might be quite close, separated by only a small amount of water, but without a substantial flotilla be nevertheless unable to intervene (at least militarily). We suspect different specifications of neighbors, including sea contiguity or perhaps simple intercapital distances, would produce results very similar to the ones we found.

The second new variable, "Allied," simply indicates whether the potential intervenor and the civil war state shared a defense pact, neutrality pact, or entente at any time during the civil war. We rely on

Correlates of War alliance data in coding this variable, specifically the compilation included in EUGene (Bennett and Stam 2000a). As with Neighbor, Allied is purposefully kept simple. We can envision justifications for including variables indicating the type of alliances potential intervenors may have had with the civil war state. For instance, potential intervenors with defense pacts may be interested in the civil war state and interact with it regularly but also happen to hold preferences consistent with the current behavior of the government. It would seem reasonable that if a potential intervenor promised to defend the civil war state's government in the past, it would come to its defense when the enemy is domestic. In contrast, neutrality pacts historically have coincided with a certain enmity between governments, and thus when they exist we might expect any interventions by neutrality-pact allies to favor the opposition. It might prove interesting in subsequent studies to investigate such relationships, but our goal here is more preliminary.

Finally, we also include a variable, "Colonial History," indicating whether the potential intervenor was previously the colonizer of the civil war state. If the civil war state was never a colony, this variable equals 0 for all potential intervenors. Occasionally a civil war state had a history of being colonized sequentially by various imperial powers, and in such cases all former colonizers are coded the same. Data for coding this variable are drawn from the Issue Correlates of War Project (Hensel 2001b).

The new expanded version of Regan's data set thus has over 19,000 cases, each of which is an intervention opportunity for a specific potential intervenor into an ongoing civil war. For each case we have data representing the characteristics of the civil war, data about whether an intervention occurred, if so its form, and whether or not it succeeded. Based on our interpretation of the internation influence model, we have added data providing information about the relationship between the potential intervenor and the civil war state. We use these data to evaluate our four hypotheses about foreign intervention based on the internation influence model, and in the process we replicate and extend the second author's past research on this topic.

In addition, we also include information in the data set about the regime types of the civil war state and potential intervenor, and also indicate whether the potential intervenor is African. We do this to evaluate other hypotheses in broader literatures that are of interest to us. The regime type variables are suggested by a pair of articles published by Margaret Hermann and Charles Kegley (Hermann and Kegley 1996; Kegley and Hermann 1995). They find democracies are no less likely to intervene militarily than are nondemocracies and also that democracies are disproportionately unlikely to be the targets of interventions, regardless of the regime type of the intervenor. The general body of democratic peace research suggests democracies should be unlikely to intervene against each other. Thus we indicate whether the civil war state is a democracy (at the time the civil war starts) and whether the potential intervenor is a democracy (at the time of its initial opportunity to intervene in the civil war). We use Polity III data, supplemented by Freedom House's reports for those states not included in the Polity data sets. "Democratic Intervenor" equals 1 if the potential intervenor scores 6 or greater on the Polity III index of institutionalized democracy (or if it is listed as "Free" by Freedom House), "Democratic Government" equals 1 if the government of the civil war state is a democracy according to these criteria, and "Joint Democracy" equals 1 if both potential intervenor and civil war state are democracies.

The final variable added to the data set, "African Intervenor," is recorded dichotomously, equal to 1 if the potential intervenor state is located on the African continent (or is an immediately adjacent island). Lemke finds that even controlling for an array of known and suspected correlates of interstate conflict, African states are disproportionately peaceful in their interstate relations (2002, chap. 7). But Africa is also rife with civil wars, and thus we wonder if Africans are also disproportionately peaceful with regard to interventions into ongoing civil wars. A negative coefficient on this variable in the following analyses indicates they are.[4]

These then are the cases and variables comprising our data set. We now describe the specific form of the estimations and address a few issues raised by our choice of estimator. In analysis of hypothesis 1 we offer only descriptive statistics, and little or no explanation is likely required. In order to analyze hypotheses 2, 3, and 4, we employ censored probit. Censored probit simultaneously estimates the impact of covariates on two binary dependent variables. Our first dependent variable, "Intervention," indicates whether the potential intervenor intervened. Our second dependent variable, "Success," is coded only if the first dependent variable equals 1. Success indicates whether an intervention that occurred was successful.

The simultaneous estimation of censored probit allows us to determine the direct effects of the independent variables on the dependent variables while controlling for prior indirect effects. We often think about this as "selecting into an opportunity," though many quite often fail to take into account the conditions leading states to this choice. We model this first set of conditions as indirect effects. The indirect effects are the influence of the independent variables on the probability of Intervention equaling 1 and thus creating the *opportunity* for Success to equal 1. In addition to these direct and indirect effects, there can be other linkages between the two dependent variables. Censored probit allows for these other linkages by estimating a parameter, rho, which is the correlation between the disturbance terms of the two dependent variables. The rho parameter is sometimes referred to as a "selection effects" parameter, and the censored probit is often seen as a diagnostic tool allowing correction of selection bias possibly existing if the impact of the independent variables on one dependent variable is estimated independently of the other dependent variable. For these diagnostic and/or corrective purposes we estimate the impact of the covariates on the two dependent variables simultaneously within a censored probit. The censored probit is increasingly commonly used in world politics research for similar reasons (e.g., Reed 2000; Lemke and Reed 2001a, 2001b; Nooruddin 2002).

Concerns about selection bias affecting past research on foreign intervention into civil wars are important. For instance, if we were to find major powers are more likely to be successful at interventions than are minor powers, but we do so only considering the populations of civil war interventions that actually occurred, we might simply be observing the results of a process whereby states choose to intervene based on expectations of success. If major powers know they are likely to be successful and are thus more likely to intervene at all, then there are direct and indirect effects of major power status on the probability an intervention succeeds. Without explicitly controlling for this self-selection process—with an estimator like censored probit that can account for direct and indirect effects—we might reach erroneous conclusions.[5]

Regan's work is informed by such concerns. At the beginning of his book he writes, "Rarely would one expect political leaders to choose to intervene under circumstances where they expected the intervention to fail," and then, "It is clear . . . states self-select themselves into or out of interventions for a variety of identifiable reasons" (2000, 4–5, 16). However, since his framework did not address the question of "who are the potential intervenors," he was unable to estimate a selection model. Thus a great benefit to us of combining Regan's work with Singer's internation influence model is that Singer's framework allows us to address the question of identifying potential intervenors that arises out of other research designs. We are thus able to employ a statistical technique appropriate to the selection bias problem identified by Regan.

EMPIRICAL ANALYSES

We begin with evaluation of hypothesis 1, that interventions on behalf of the opposition will correspond with bloodier civil wars than will interventions on behalf of the government. We address this hypothesis through descriptive statistics.

Table 1 offers first a difference-of-means test comparing the casualty levels of instances in which interventions favored the government and those in which they favored the opposition.[6] If "punishment" corresponds with bloodiness, then we would expect the mean casualty level to be higher in opposition-support situations than in government-support ones. As seen in table 1, the average casualty level is more than a third higher in interventions in support of the opposition, and this difference is statistically significant (albeit only at the $p < 0.1$ threshold).[7] We know that civil wars without interventions are dramatically less violent than those with interventions (Regan 2000, 3). Yet even within this more deadly category of civil conflict (those with interventions) support for opposition forces results in an average of 27,000 more fatalities per conflict. This is also largely consistent with evidence of interventions supporting the opposition leading to conflicts of longer duration (Balch-Lindsay and Enterline 2000; Regan 2002). We interpret this as support for hypothesis 1. Presumably this finding would be of interest to policymakers. Supporting the rebels in order to punish a government appears to come at higher human cost than does intervention to reinforce governments.

Punishment need not correspond with blood, of course. Recognizing this, we also present in table 1 a pair of cross-tabulations comparing whether the intervenor assisted the government or opposition with whether the intervention was militarized.[8] Here we find 70 of 88 interventions in support of the opposition were militarized while only 61 of

TABLE 1. Support for Opposition as a Punishing Strategy

| Intervention Supporting Government | | | Intervention Supporting Opposition | | |
|---|---|---|---|---|---|
| Militarized Intervention | No | Yes | | No | Yes |
| No | 20 | 31 | No | 33 | 18 |
| Yes | 75 | 61 | Yes | 66 | 70 |
| $N = 92$ | | | $N = 88$ | | |
| Average Casualty = 61,385 | | | Average Casualty = 88,845 | | |

Note: Odds Ratio: 1.2.
$F = 2.853, p = 0.093$

92 interventions in support of the government were militarized. This generates an odds ratio of 1.2, meaning interventions in support of the opposition are 20 percent more likely to be militarized than are interventions in support of the government. This result might be a more appropriate evaluation of hypothesis 1 than the difference-of-means test. As mentioned in note 2, we do not know if the casualty figures represent bloody conflicts into which bloodless interventions occur or relatively bloodless civil wars made gory by the intervention. With the categorical analysis, however, we offer information about the intervention separate from the civil war itself. If military action is a prerequisite for "punishment," then this too supports hypothesis 1.

We turn now to our evaluation of hypotheses 2 through 4. Table 2 presents two censored probit models indicating the influence of 21 variables on whether interventions into civil wars occur and if so whether the interventions are successful at stopping the fighting for at least six months. In column 1 the correlates of successful intervention include general categories of intervention (Mixed Intervention, Supporting Government). In column 2 the correlates of successful intervention include more specific target-and-type categories (Mixed Support for Opposition, Military Support for Government, Economic Support for Opposition). Collinearity between the general and specific variables is high, and it seems prudent to follow Regan's earlier example and estimate separate models (hence columns 1 and 2). Attentive readers may note the sample size in our censored probits drops from the original 19,533 to just below 16,000. Almost all of the dropped cases are lost due to missing data on the "Refugees" variable. We lack comprehensive data on Refugees, and thus including it causes almost 20 percent of the cases to be deleted. We think Refugees is an important variable and thus include it even though we lose many cases by doing so. We have replicated table 2 omitting Refugees, and there are only minor changes.[9]

We begin evaluation of table 2 by discussing what these results say about each of the three hypotheses pertinent to it, then make some general comments about its meaning for empirical patterns in civil war intervention occurrence and about whether such interventions succeed. We also consider what its results say relevant to past studies of interventions and close with specific comments about table 2's results and Singer's internation influence model.

The results of our multivariate analyses strongly support hypotheses 2 through 4. Recall those hypotheses all concern the likely identity of civil war intervenors, and based on the internation influence model we anticipate states likely to interact frequently with the civil war state in the future are most likely to intervene. Consistent with these expectations we find the coefficients for Neighbor, Allied, and Colonial History are all large, positive, and statistically significant. Each of these conditions substantially increases the probability of intervention. States with repeated interaction with the civil war state are more likely to intervene, precisely as anticipated by our interpretation of the internation influence model.

Turning to more general questions of when intervention opportunities are more likely to actually have interventions, we find results consistent with past research. Major powers are more likely to intervene in

TABLE 2. Censored Probits of Intervention and Success

|  | Column 1 | Column 2 |
|---|---|---|
| **Intervention** | | |
| Constant | −3.73*** | −3.72*** |
| Intensity | −0.13 | −0.12 |
| Refugees | 0.32*** | 0.32*** |
| Cold War | 0.53*** | 0.52*** |
| Casualties | 6.17e-07** | 5.95e-07** |
| Neighbor | 1.36*** | 1.37*** |
| Allied | 0.47*** | 0.47*** |
| Colonial history | 0.81*** | 0.81*** |
| Major power intervenor | 1.37*** | 1.37*** |
| African intervenor | −0.14* | −0.13* |
| Democratic intervenor | 0.06 | 0.07 |
| Democratic government | 0.27** | 0.26** |
| Joint democracy | −0.14 | −0.14 |
| Ethnic conflict | 0.25** | 0.25* |
| Ideological conflict | 0.28** | 0.28** |
| **Success** | | |
| Constant | −2.22*** | −2.32*** |
| Ethnic conflict | −0.08 | −0.01 |
| Ideological conflict | −0.18 | −0.11 |
| Mixed intervention | −0.38* | — |
| Supporting government | 0.42** | — |
| Casualties | −6.28e-07 | −9.96e-07 |
| Major power intervenor | 0.97*** | 0.94*** |
| Mixed support for opposition | — | 0.58 |
| Military support for government | — | 0.75*** |
| Economic support for opposition | — | 0.20 |
| Number of cases | Y1:15931, Y2:156 | Y1:15931, Y2:156 |
| Model $\chi^2$ | 19.63*** | 22.61** |
| Rho | 0.71** | 0.61** |

*$p < 0.10$, **$p < 0.05$, ***$p < 0.01$, one-tailed significance tests with robust standard errors.

civil wars than are minor powers. Civil wars with many refugees, with high numbers of casualties, and with ethnic or ideological motivations behind the fighting are also more likely to draw interventions. We find Intensity negatively related to the probability of an intervention (although it is not statistically significant). Finally, civil wars during the Cold War were more likely to experience interventions than were civil wars after that period. All of these general results are consistent with Regan's past findings even though our unit of analysis (the intervention opportunity) differs from his (the civil war).

When we turn our attention to what increases the probability intervenors will enjoy success, far fewer variables seem to matter. Major power intervenors enjoy a greater probability of success than do minor power intervenors. Supporting the government, either generally or specifically with military assistance, is associated with a greater probability of success. Finally, the general category of Mixed Intervention decreases the odds of success.

In our analysis of the correlates of intervention success, our unit of analysis is the same as Regan's, but the big difference now is that our censored probit allows us to determine if the selection bias concerns he talked about affect the results. We find that even controlling for the indirect effects of many of our variables on the prior stage of whether an intervention occurs in the first place, interventions by major powers and those favoring the government generally, as well as those specifically with military assistance, are more likely to be successful than are those by minor powers or those not bringing aid to the government's cause. There are no major differences between Regan's past studies and this one, only marginal variation in coefficient size likely attributable to the more appropriate estimator used here. For example, we suspect that being allied, having a history of prior colonial interaction, or being a neighboring country probably predispose intervenors to come to the government's aid. If true, then most of the statistical oomph of the Supporting Government variable will be felt at the prior stage of whether an intervention occurs at all. It is possible this explains why our Supporting Government coefficient is only one-third the size of Regan's earlier estimate. The statistically significant rho parameter suggests there are other linkages across the two dependent variables, bolstering suspicions of selection bias causing the minor differences between the earlier work and that reported here.

We included a series of variables representing the regime types of the civil war state and the potential intervenor. We find democracies involved in civil conflicts are more likely to experience foreign intervention. We also demonstrate democratic potential intervenors are no more likely to intervene than are nondemocratic potential intervenors, and jointly democratic potential intervenor-civil war state dyads are no more or less likely to involve interventions than are other types of dyads. That is, democratic linkages do not determine the outcome of internation influence opportunities. These results run counter to Hermann and Kegley's previous findings. In contrast to our estimates, they report democracies are more likely to intervene than are nondemocracies, and democracies are less likely to experience interventions than are nondemocracies. A number of possible explanations may be offered for the disparity between our and their findings. First, Hermann and Kegley study a shorter time span than we do. Second, Hermann and Kegley restrict themselves to military interventions, while we include economic and mixed interventions along with the military category. Finally, we consider only interventions into ongoing civil wars, whereas Hermann and Kegley employ data sets about interventions across a larger range of intervention opportunities. With so many differences it is not surprising we produce different results. What is of interest, however, is the clues our research and theirs might jointly offer about the democratic peace and internation influence strategies. If our democratic civil war states with interventions are disproportionately drawing economic interventions, then our results do not contradict Hermann and Kegley's. What's more, it might be that civil war democracies disproportionately experience economic interventions because military interventions are believed unlikely to succeed since democracies are hard to defeat (as argued by, among others, Bueno de Mesquita et al. 1999). Closer analysis of such issues might be an interesting avenue for future research.

Finally, what of international pacificity among African states (Lemke 2002)? Our results include a negative and statistically significant coefficient for African Intervenor. Given the rather small coefficient size and modest statistical significance, support for our expectation is present, but tentative. This result is perhaps consistent with one of Regan's more puzzling findings. He reports that as the number of bordering states increases, the probability of an intervention declines. African states have more common borders than countries on other continents with significant amounts of armed civil violence, and if African states are more pacific internationally, the higher number of common borders in Africa could account for Regan's result. Even though the substantive and statistical significance of our result is marginal, this may suggest an explanation for a puzzling finding in Regan's earlier work regarding the number of borders and an unanticipated lower probability of intervention.

Moreover, this uncommon continental control variable also might suggest Singer's internation influence model has a narrower range of applicability than we initially thought. Lemke's work focuses on Africa because he investigates whether underdeveloped states are able to respond to international stimuli as developed states do. After all, if the treasury is empty or there is no road by which soldiers can be transported to the border, *can* a state decide to go to war with another? If underdevelopment reduces the range of options that third world leaders face internationally, we might be better off *not* expecting them to behave like leaders of developed states. Singer's internation influence model suggests states attempt to influence each other given the resources to do so and an anticipation of interaction in the future. If underdevelopment coincides with reduced resources and shorter time horizons, perhaps some level of development must be achieved before states worry about influencing each other. In that case, perhaps Singer's model will apply to developed states well, but underdeveloped states poorly. This interpretation is consistent with the negative African Intervenor estimate, as well as with Lemke's (2002) investigation.[10]

In this section we offered a variety of analyses running from simple difference-of-means tests through somewhat more complicated censored probit analyses. We find support for all four hypotheses about foreign intervention into ongoing civil wars based on the internation influence model. Our results successfully replicate Regan's earlier findings but may contradict Hermann and Kegley's studies. Finally, there is some evidence of African aversion to intervening in civil wars. Again, all four hypotheses are supported by our analyses here.

### DISCUSSION AND CONCLUSIONS

In this chapter we tested two implications of J. David Singer's internation influence model, one being the role of interest in the likelihood of interventions into civil conflicts and the other questioning the destructiveness of punishment as an influence strategy. Our empirical analyses support our expectations. States with continuing interests in civil war states are more likely to intervene in those civil wars. Situations that the internation influence model leads us to expect to be ones in which punishment is the appropriate influence strategy are demonstrably bloodier than instances in which less aggressive influence strategies are expected. But Singer's model has a considerably broader range of applications that we do not address. We return later to Singer's model to discuss other applications and explore some requirements for future empirical verification.

By focusing on the decision to intervene in civil conflicts we neglect a host of other potential influence environments. For example, our focus on civil conflicts narrows the scope to conflictual behavior. However, it is clear from Singer's model that states also attempt to influence cooperative policies and interactions. In fact, the distribution of conflictual behaviors may constitute but a small fraction of the total range of behaviors that states attempt to manipulate. We miss all forms of cooperative trade, immigration policies, triangular interactions among states A and C of interest to state B, as well as other diplomatic activities potentially useful to the influencer. Furthermore, by narrowing our analysis we fail to capture influence attempts involving interstate conflict, possibly the main interest behind Singer's initial inquiry.

Empirical verification of the broad range of applicability, however, must confront some rather knotty issues. Two key components of Singer's model—and we concur with their conceptual necessity—are the preference and prediction parts of the decision calculus. Both preferences and predictions, especially ex ante, are difficult to observe. We can readily observe current behaviors but have a much harder time knowing what the potential influencer's prediction of future behavior is, let alone its preferences about current and anticipated behavior. What we have done in our analysis is to make an indirect inference from an aspect of structural conditions (proximity, alliance, etc.) to preferred behavior. This may obscure much of what Singer was trying to illuminate. The difficulty lies in identifying systematically empirical traces to form the backbone of reliable and valid indicators. Presumably the strength of any influence attempt would be directly related to the magnitude of the difference between predicted and preferred behavior. If we think about these two conditions in spatial terms, then the distance between them would help predict the type of influence attempt and the amount of resources a state invests.

We do not offer an empirical solution to this vexing problem but rather point it out as a challenge for future scholarship. This challenge, moreover, has a more modern-day corollary. Regardless of whether we employ a 1960s version of a formal model or one articulated in the twenty-first century, we need to come to grips with the empirical centrality of preferences and predictions.

Finally we end with a word about the generalizability of Singer's model. That is, we speculate as to whether the model is too general and instead requires contextual—or contingent—modifications in order to be widely applicable. For instance, information is critical to the model, and the information required may transcend the capabilities of all but the most technologically sophisticated states. This might be changing with time and modern communication technology, but the demands of preferences and predicted future behavior mean the confidence intervals around predictions from the model may vary systematically with a number of conditions found in both the potential intervenor and the target. It also may be that as the behavior of interest moves from "normal" diplomatic relations to trade to security issues the demands of information required by the model decrease its reliability. This might suggest Singer's model—or an empirical extension—may be more directly applicable to major power interactions and trade issues than to those of minor powers and conflictual behavior. The negative African Intervenor coefficient is consistent with this possibility.

In the final analysis Singer's influence model provides a conceptual framework within which to think about when and why states attempt to manipulate the behavior of others. Moreover, his work also extends conceptually the categories of actions available to the influencer. By making, for instance, the distinction between promise and reward, threat and punishment he allows for the subtleties of internation influence to be at the forefront of the policy agenda. A promise can be less easily observed than a reward, though under a certain set of conditions a promise may be sufficient to achieve the desired outcome. Much of the emphasis in international politics has been on the more directly observable, and consequently we might be simply failing to observe many or most efforts by states to influence each other. Our analyses shed light on the empirical validity of Singer's model, but they remain far from definitive tests of this rich theoretical framework.

### NOTES

1. We apologize for discussing untested hypotheses. Tests would require data collection neither of us has undertaken, and thus they are left to future research. However, we nevertheless discuss such hypotheses here in order to demonstrate that Singer's model has utility beyond the few hypotheses we actually do test. We regard fertility as a desirable characteristic of models, and much of our enthusiasm for Singer's model is related to its fertility.

2. Our analysis of this hypothesis is far from perfect. Ideally we would like to observe the violence associated with the intervention alone rather than the total violence (as indicated by the number of casualties) in the entire civil war. Unfortunately, our data are not amenable to such detailed evaluation, and thus the support we uncover for hypothesis 1 is tentative pending the eventual collection of more appropriate data.

3. We recognize that both of these justifications for this hypothesis potentially contradict the second author's previous assumption of stopping the fighting as the goal of interventions. It is possible intervenors would like the oppo-

sition to win but calculate that helping the government is most conducive to speedy institution of a cease-fire. In such a situation the proximate goal and long-term preference may be at odds.

4. We recognize our efforts to replicate various past studies might distract readers from our primary goal of using civil war intervention behavior to test Singer's internation influence model. However, we believe this risk worth taking because, in a volume honoring his contributions to the scientific study of world politics, replications demonstrating where his work fits within cumulative research traditions is important.

5. Of course, if the causes of civil wars themselves are also causes of interventions and of interventionary success, then our omission of the logically prior stage of civil war onset could introduce selection bias even though we are so careful to avoid it subsequently. Three points are relevant. First, there is an infinite regress of possible linked causation because we have no ultimate starting point for international or domestic politics. That there always could have been something previous does not mean that correcting for subsequent selection bias is undesirable. Second, our uninformed sense is that the "decision" to start a civil war is not one made with much consideration given to the likely course of subsequent foreign intervention. We have trouble envisioning the prospects of foreign intervention playing a large role in the decision calculus of opposition parties as they launch civil wars. Surely there may be cases in which potential external support (or opposition) weighs large, but generally so? Third, studies of civil war onset (Collier and Hoeffler 1998; Hegre et al. 2001) suggest civil wars are not "caused" by variables important to our analysis. Collier and Hoeffler's "ethno-linguistic fractionalization" variable may be related to our "Ethnic Conflict" variable, but if so it is the only connection across our analyses. Like us, Hegre et al. use an indicator of how democratic the civil war state is, but otherwise our analyses do not overlap. Readers may want to be suspicious of our Ethnic Conflict and Democratic Government variables if they believe potential interventions are an important part of the opposition's calculus (or the government's) in starting civil wars.

6. Attentive readers will note that 92 interventions in support of the government plus 88 in support of the opposition equals 180, not 197, interventions. The omitted interventions were neutral ones favoring neither the government nor opposition. As such they do not provide any information relevant to this first test.

7. An OLS regression with casualties as the dependent variable and "support opposition" as the independent variable generates a positive and statistically significant coefficient. The overall regression is also significant, but the $r^2$ is tiny.

8. This comparison requires two cross-tabulations because there are some interventions that support neither the government nor the opposition.

9. Clearly, 75 cases of intervention opportunity within just the Greek civil war (for example) are not independent of each other. Recognizing this, the results in table 2 are calculated with robust standard errors. Being able to guess

something about the likely non-independence of cases, we also reran both analyses with robust standard errors clustered on each civil war and on each potential intervenor. Nearly identical results obtain across the three different standard error calculations.

10. Alternatively, one might argue the African pacifism is explained by other forms of underdevelopment, lack of power projection capabilities, difficult terrain, etc. Lemke (2002, chap. 7) considers all of these factors and concludes none adequately accounts for Africa's disproportionate pacificity.

# THE SLOW ROASTING OF SACRED COWS
## J. David Singer and the Democratic Peace

*Errol A. Henderson*

As one of the architects of the behavioral revolution, J. David Singer argued forcefully yet skillfully for a more positivistic orientation in world politics. Dismayed by the poor record of scientific advancement in the field, he proffered not only a spirited defense of the use of scientific method in world politics (1969b) but also provided the strategy and framework for the type of experimentation that should be undertaken (1977). Singer not only sought to provide the basis for scientific cumulation in world politics, but he was (and is) convinced that findings derived from scientific analyses should occupy pride of place in the field, and conclusions drawn from them should be relied upon to inform foreign policy. Probably the most robust nontrivial, nontautological finding in world politics to emerge from the research of behavioralists is that democracies rarely if ever fight each other. Moreover, in a manner consistent with Singer's effort to have findings garnered from rigorous systematic analyses of world politics guide foreign policy, the democratic peace thesis has become the centerpiece of the U.S. post–Cold War strategy of "democratic enlargement," which is aimed at expanding the community of democratic states. President Clinton (1996, 9) made it clear that such a strategy would help engender peace because democracies are "far less likely to wage war on one another." President George Bush, while giving less credence to the Wilsonian idealism that undergirds Clinton's assessment, nonetheless has colored his self-styled "war on terrorism" as an attempt, in part, to assist more democratic elements to assume control of states such as Afghanistan and Iraq, with the explicit assumption that once transformed these states will be more peaceful and less likely to support forces aligned against Western states.[1] Nevertheless, Singer remains one of the most consistent critics of the democratic peace thesis, even as the research in support of it—a fair share of it conducted by his former colleagues and students (e.g., Russett 1993 and several of his coauthored works; Bueno de Mesquita in several coauthored works; Ray 1995; Maoz 1997a; Henderson 1998)—continues to pile up.[2]

More than any other author, Singer, along with Melvin Small, provided both the major empirical and theoretical justifications for the democratic peace thesis in world politics. To be sure, scholars have long been concerned about the relationship between a state's regime type and its probability of war involvement, with systematic analyses of the relationship between democracy and war evident in Quincy Wright's research published during World War II and Dean Babst's empirical analysis of the absence of war between democracies first published in two rather obscure journals in 1964 and 1972 (*The Wisconsin Sociologist* and *Industrial Research*, respectively). The 1976 Small and Singer study, which sought to refute key aspects of Babst's (1972) findings, introduced his research to mainstream political scientists. In their study, Small and Singer found—as Wright's (1942, 841) research had shown—that democracies were no more peaceful than nondemocracies, and they noted almost in passing that democracies rarely fight each other, thereby substantiating Babst's (1972) findings. Nevertheless, they did not seem too impressed by the latter finding, reasoning that the relative absence of such wars in the 1816–1965 period was probably due to the rarity of democratic government and the lack of contiguity among democratic states. Since states that are not contiguous are, in general, less likely to fight each other, and democracies were rarely contiguous, they conjectured that infrequent contiguity more than regime type accounted for the relative absence of war between democracies.

Subsequent studies using multivariate analyses, and thus providing controls for a host of factors including contiguity, have refuted Small and Singer's argument that contiguity vitiates the democratic peace. In fact, scholars have built a veritable research program around what Small and Singer regarded as a largely spurious inference drawn from the correlation between joint democracy and peace. Democratic peace advocates have proffered two major theoretical arguments to account for the democratic peace, which, in turn, emphasize the conflict-dampening role of structural/institutional or cultural/normative factors in preventing war between democracies (see discussion in Russett 1993; Ray 1995; Russett and Oneal 2001).[3] Even more interesting—and rarely noted—is the fact that Small and Singer anticipated these theoretical arguments in the first paragraph of their study, where they ponder "whether the allegedly pacific nature of [democracies] is a result of bureaucratic slug-gishness or of a more fundamental humaneness on the part of the masses (as opposed to the moral insensitivity of dictatorial leaders)" (1976, 50). Similarly, the structural/institutional approach posits that institutional constraints (evocative of their reference to "bureaucratic sluggishness") on the decision-making choices of democratic leaders make it difficult for them to opt for the use of force in their foreign policies, which acts as a brake on conflict with other democracies; while the cultural/nor-mative perspective assumes that democracies are less disposed to fight each other due to the impact of their shared norms that proscribe the use of violence between them (evocative of their reference to "fundamental humaneness").

How, then, does one reconcile Singer's skepticism regarding the em-pirical and theoretical arguments in support of the democratic peace, which he himself has largely supplied? Well, Singer's skepticism is rooted in several factors. First, in what his students recognize as Singer's First Law, he is hesitant about monocausal "theories" of war and peace that assign to a single variable, such as democracy, a chief explanatory role in what are often complex relationships such as the processes leading to international war. Second, Singer has not been very keen on the ex-planatory ability of variables that focus on state-level attributes, such as democracy, in accounting for international war, sensing, as he does, that arguments with respect to these types of variables will be weighed less by evidence and more by the propaganda of elites who reside in—or are otherwise positively disposed to—a particular political, social, or cul-tural arrangement. Therefore, he has been more inclined to examine the relationships and interactions between and among entities across vari-ous levels of aggregation. For example, in 1971, prior to the burgeoning democratic peace literature, Singer took a sanguine view of research ori-entations that focused on the "similarities and differences between and among entities in order to see whether they help account for the war-proneness of particular pairs" (63). He also stated that "we may profit-ably ask to what extent we can predict to the frequency and magnitude of war for a given nation if we know something about its links and bonds to other nations, or to the war-proneness of a pair of nations on the basis of the interdependence and connections between them" (64). In these statements Singer was pressing for, among other things, analy-ses of dyadic relationships such as those that dominate democratic peace research. Further, they are consistent with a focus on both the conflict-dampening impact of regime similarity and trade interdependence, which would come to dominate analyses of the democratic peace (dis-cussed later). But Singer was not as positively disposed to studies that sought to account for war by analyzing the "structural" attributes of the state—"the institutions and configurations normally associated with the labels 'political, economic, and sociological'" (62)—a category in which regime type falls. He assumed that studies of this type could serve more as brush-clearing exercises: "helping to clear away the debris of political folklore, they will eventually fit into analyses which look at other classes of independent and intervening variables at the same time" (63).

Nearly thirty years later, and now focusing specifically on the role of democracy in the war-proneness of individual states, he does not equivocate: "Regime type turns out to be unimportant [as a correlate of war], with autocratic and democratic regimes showing an equal propensity to enter into or to initiate war over the past century and three-quarters" (1999, 467). As for the role of democracy in the war-proneness of pairs of states, Singer acknowledges that regime type "turns out to be a fairly powerful factor at the dyadic level, and the data-based literature is massive and growing" (467). But, at this point, he stubbornly returns to the rationale he offered in 1976: "There are quite a few plausible explanations for this dramatic correlation, but it may simply be a spatial-temporal artifact in the sense that up to 1945 there were very few democratic regimes in the interstate system, and few of them were geographically contiguous. And since World War II, most of the world's democracies were bound together in a U.S.-dominated collective defense and collective security coalition" (467).

In a larger sense, Singer's skepticism provides a deeper insight into his philosophy of science. It clearly belies the notion that behavioralists are barefooted empiricists exalting only what they can quantify. Those types of charges were never applicable to his research in the first place (see Singer 1969b), and his skepticism further reminds us that our research should not be guided by a simple search for correlations but by a search for explanations. In *The Scientific Study of Politics: An Approach to Foreign Policy Analysis,* Singer (1972b) clearly lays out what he views as the primary path for the development of a scientific study of world politics that could provide cumulation in the field and also serve as a basis for a more informed foreign policy. For him, these objectives require the accumulation of several types of knowledge: existential, correlational, and explanatory. *Existential* knowledge refers not only to facts and data, but to "empirical regularities or patterns," which, for Singer, "constitute the bedrock of knowledge" without which "we cannot make predictions or explanations with any degree of confidence (5). *Correlational* knowledge provides information on the degree of association between two or more factors—such as two or more observations drawn from our existential knowledge—and "to the extent that we can predict to the future by observation and analysis of the past . . . correlations provide the basis for successful prediction" (6). Finally, *explanatory* knowledge is causal knowledge, which addresses "the extent to which a given class of outcomes or events was 'caused' by a given sequence of prior conditions and events" (1).

He argues that all three types of knowledge are important in predicting foreign policy behavior; however, he maintains that while existential and correlational knowledge are important, they can "carry the decision makers only so far." He makes it clear that "the more explanatory knowledge that is available—especially in the form of well-tested models and theories—the better one can predict in complex or unfamiliar situations. That is, in the absence of good correlational knowledge, one many nevertheless deduce such principles from a good theory, and use them as the basis for prediction" (2). He continues: "Without denying, then, the tremendous value of correlational and predictive knowledge in the conduct of foreign affairs, we must nevertheless recognize that causal and explanatory knowledge is ultimately essential" (6). He reemphasizes these assertions in his later work in which he states that "despite the folklore to the contrary, *prediction* is neither the major purpose nor acid test of a theory; the goal of all basic scientific research is *explanation*" (1979d, 52). He remains convinced that "a strong explanatory theory will—because it is better able to account for and explain the effects of changing conditions—provide a more solid base for predicting than one that rests on observed covariations and postdictions alone" (52).

For him, a theory consists of "a body of propositions that: offer a credible explanation of the outcome phenomena, are logically compatible with one another, are essentially consistent with other relevant knowledge, are stated in testable language, and—most of which have been successfully tested" (71). He insists that "using these criteria, it is clear that social scientists have produced, so far, precious few theories, despite audacious or careless claims to the contrary" (71). While Singer is doubtful that theories worthy of the name exist in social science, he is even less sanguine about theories in world politics: there aren't any. For Singer, while existential knowledge was expanding in world politics, the breadth of correlational knowledge was very poor, offering little empirical bedrock upon which to rest explanatory models that could, in turn, provide the building blocks of scientific theory. In the absence of explanatory knowledge, what often passed as theories were often little more than informed guesses, speculations, hunches, or, at best, hypotheses, waiting to have their main premises substantiated by rigorous systematic analysis. But even with support provided by correlational evidence, the explanation of the relationships invoked by the theories in world politics such as "balance of power" or "power transition" left Singer unconvinced. For him, correlational knowledge could provide the basis for our explanation of allegedly causal processes, but it could not substitute for explanatory knowledge: what was needed was sound theory. Finding the theoretical arguments of democratic peace advocates as unconvincing today as he did when he first suggested them in 1976, he is skeptical of the correlational evidence used to support democratic peace claims. Basically, Singer is compelled by the absence of what he perceives as sound theoretical support for the democratic peace thesis to reject the explanatory claims that rely mainly on the statistical evidence. Therefore his skepticism with regard to the democratic peace findings is consistent with his larger epistemological orientation.

To be sure, Singer is not alone in his skepticism regarding the democratic peace; however, although skeptics continue to challenge the theoretical basis of the democratic peace (e.g., Layne 1994; Oren 1995; Gowa 1999), neither they nor Singer have been able to refute the statistical evidence that democracies rarely if ever fight each other (e.g., Maoz and Abdolali 1989; Ray 1995; Maoz 1997a; Oneal and Ray 1997; Russett and Oneal 2001)—remember that even Singer's own research supports it. It is the meticulous statistical evidence in support of the democratic peace that has been most persuasive. Nevertheless, Singer appears convinced that other factors will vitiate the democratic peace relationship if and when more fully specified models are introduced into research designs that test for the phenomenon. In this chapter, I show how Singer's skepticism is borne out: by slightly modifying the prominent research design among democratic peace advocates and paying particular attention to Singer's concern with similarity and interdependence as factors contributing to our understanding of international conflict, even utilizing a widely used data set among democratic peace advocates, one can demonstrate that joint democracy is not significantly associated with the probability of international conflict. In this way, I provide the empirical substantiation for Singer's theoretical agnosticism.

The chapter proceeds in several sections. First, I discuss the basic research design used in important studies of the democratic peace. Second, using this research design, I replicate one of the most important studies of the democratic peace. Third, using the data from that study, I slightly modify the research design by introducing an additional control variable—one of the relational variables to which Singer alluded in his earlier research—into the model and, in so doing, show that joint democracy is not significantly associated with the absence of international disputes for pairs of states. Fourth, I briefly discuss the implications of the findings for future research aimed at explaining war along the lines suggested by Singer and his colleagues.

## THE EVOLVING DEMOCRATIC PEACE RESEARCH DESIGN

The empirical support for the democratic peace thesis is voluminous; however, Oneal and Russett's (1997) "The Classical Liberals Were Right: Democracy, Interdependence, and Conflict, 1950–1985" has been rightly viewed as a definitive empirical substantiation of the democratic peace thesis using multivariate analyses controlling for alliance membership, geographic contiguity, economic development, and trade interdependence. Focusing on the post–World War II era, which is more amenable to statistical analyses of the democratic peace given the greater number of democratic states as compared to the pre–World War II period, they established the significance of the conflict-dampening impact of joint democracy (coded as a continuous variable) when controlling for trade interdependence. No other study up to that time had been successful in accomplishing this. Further, their research design has become one of the most widely utilized, cited, and respected approaches in the analysis of the democratic peace thesis. The significance of this study was recognized immediately after its publication, and several authors replicated its findings.

The research design utilized in studies of the democratic peace such as Oneal and Russett's draws on a "weak link" assumption, which presumably allows one to draw inferences about the relative war-proneness of dyads by focusing on the regime score of the least democratic state in the dyad. This approach derives from Dixon's (1993) assertion that by focusing on the weakest link in the dyad one can better grasp the motive forces compelling the states to conflict (also see Bueno de Mesquita and Lalman 1992). These theorists tend to agree that "the likelihood of conflict [is] primarily a function of the degree of political constraint experienced by the less constrained state in each dyad" (Oneal and Russett 1997, 274). To better appreciate the importance of the weak-link specification and its centrality to democratic peace research, a discussion of the evolution of scholarly reliance on this approach is warranted.

## THE WEAK-LINK THESIS AND THE SEARCH FOR A
## CONTINUOUS MEASURE OF JOINT DEMOCRACY

The main theoretical arguments on the democratic peace suggest that the greater the extent of shared democracy between two states,[4] the greater the ability of shared democratic norms and/or institutions to prevent conflict (see Rummel 1983; Russett 1993).[5] This is an argument with respect to the magnitude of democracy and not simply its presence or absence; therefore, an appropriate operational measure of joint democracy should be scaled as a continuous rather than a discrete (i.e., dichotomous or trichotomous) variable (Henderson 1999). But many early studies of the democratic peace utilized noncontinuous—mainly dichotomous—measures of democracy (even my own, Henderson 1998). A dichotomous or discrete measure of joint democracy implies that the conflict-dampening impact of joint democracy is only evident above some threshold value. But such thresholds have been largely atheoretical and arbitrary, leading Oneal et al. (1996, 24) to remark that "our confidence in a democratic peace would have to be tempered . . . if the pacific influence of democracy were strong only above a high threshold." Even with more widely accepted measures of regime type garnered from the Polity datasets, analysts continued to caution against the use of dichotomous measures in evaluating the democratic peace because "any threshold used to distinguish democratic from non-democratic states in the Polity data is bound to be largely atheoretical," since "all but the highest and lowest values on the Polity democracy-autocracy scale can be achieved by different combinations on the constituent dimensions making the resulting sums of uncertain meaning" (Oneal and Ray 1997, 771). Nevertheless, it soon became apparent that variables derived from the Polity measures that had been used in important studies of the democratic peace had some unattractive characteristics.

For example, one of the most widely utilized continuous measures of joint democracy was Maoz and Russett's (1993) *JOINREG*, which they used in their influential *American Political Science Review* article, which presumably demonstrated the greater salience of normative than institutional factors in accounting for the democratic peace. According to Russett (1993, 76–77), this indicator was constructed to "reflect two things simultaneously: How democratic or undemocratic are the members of the dyad, and how different or similar in their regime types are the two states?" Accordingly, *JOINREG* is a ratio with a numerator that measures the degree of joint democracy between the states and a denominator that gauges the difference between the regime scores. However, it is unreliable as a measure of joint democracy for the very reasons that it was found useful to Russett. That is, since *JOINREG* measures both the average level of democracy and the similarity of the regimes, interpreting the results from analyses that utilized it were very difficult because, as Ray (1995, 26) noted, "a pair of states will attain a high score on [*JOINREG*] *either* because they are relatively democratic *or* because they are relatively similar in regime type." An even more troubling feature of *JOINREG* is that it does not increase monotonically with increases in the constituent states' democracy scores. That is, in certain cases where a dyad becomes more democratic, its *JOINREG* score decreases.

Rummel initially pointed out this inconsistency in the *JOINREG* measure. *JOINREG* is measured as the ratio between the sum of the two states' regime scores (taking the highest score first) and the difference of the two states' regime scores plus 1: $(\text{Democracy}_{HI} + \text{Democracy}_{LO})$ / $(\text{Democracy}_{HI} - \text{Democracy}_{LO} + 1)$. As Oneal and Russett (1997, 274) point out, if one takes a pair of states whose regime scores are both 50 (well above the democracy threshold of Maoz and Russett 1993, which is +30), then *JOINREG* is $(50 + 50)$ / $(50 - 50 + 1)$, or 100. If one state becomes more democratic and now scores 70, while the other state remains at 50, *JOINREG* for this more democratic dyad now equals $(70 + 50)$ / $(70 - 50 + 1)$, or 5.7. The continuous measure of joint democracy *decreases* substantially as one of the two states— and, therefore, the dyad—becomes *more democratic*. Once this shortcoming was recognized, scholars sought more reliable measures of joint democracy, such as the sum or product of the individual state's regime scores as recorded in the Polity data sets.

At the same time, they also began to examine the impact of trade on the democratic peace. In another groundbreaking study, Oneal et al. (1996), still relying on *JOINREG*, found that trade interdependence had a more robust conflict-dampening impact than joint democracy. Their findings presented a quandary for democratic peace advocates since they also revealed that only a dichotomous democracy variable was significant when controlling for trade interdependence, while continuous democracy variables were not significant in such models. In attempting to address the failure of continuous democracy variables to remain significant in models that controlled for trade, democratic peace scholars redoubled their efforts to devise a measure that captured both the degree to which two states were democratic and the degree to which they were politically dissimilar (they called the latter attribute "political distance"), while avoiding the problems associated with *JOINREG*. One potential source of problems was that which Ray (1995) observed earlier: they were attempting to fuse two attributes, each of which, they believed, had an independent impact on international conflict. Of these two attributes, joint democracy was viewed as reducing the probability of conflict, and political distance was seen as increasing the probability of conflict. Put another way, theorists were fusing what Singer (1971, 62–64) called a "structural" variable, regime type, with a "relational" variable, political distance, hoping that their impact would not be vitiated by another "relational" variable, trade interdependence.

Appreciating the contrasting effects of joint democracy and political distance and seeking to resolve the quandary of Oneal et al.'s findings, Oneal and Ray (1997) evaluated several indicators of joint democracy to test their robustness in models that included a measure of trade interdependence. When different results were garnered from estimations using a joint democracy variable measured as the sum of the states' regime scores and one measured as the geometric mean of the states' regime scores, they thought they could explain why Oneal et al.'s dichotomous measure of joint democracy had been robust while their continuous measure had not.[6] Oneal and Ray (1997) noted that the geometric mean measure—which was the most robust of the continuous measures they used initially—was more sensitive to changes in the differences of the two regime scores and increased more with an increase in the less democratic state's regime score than with a similar increase in the more democratic state's regime score. For Oneal and Ray (764), "this suggests that the prospects for peace improve more when the less democratic nation in a dyad becomes more democratic, which reduces the political distance along the democratic-autocratic continuum separating the two states." On the other hand, their joint democracy variable measured as the sum of the two states' regime scores "is affected equally by an increase in either regime score," therefore, "its poor performance suggests that a high level of democracy in one state does not compensate for a low level in a strategic partner." They reasoned that "the absolute difference in regime scores—the political distance separating the members of a dyad along the autocracy-democracy continuum—is important for understanding the influence of political regimes on the likelihood of conflict" (764). They concluded that "a discrete measure of joint democracy lends more support for the democratic peace because it identifies those dyads for which political distance is a minimum and the sum of the states' democracy scores is a maximum." They expected pairs of states with these characteristics to be the most peaceful because "the probability of a dispute is not only a function of the average level of democracy in a dyad, but also the political distance separating the states" (768).

Since Oneal and Ray (1997, 771) were clear that scholars should "not rely on a dichotomous measure of regimes because it masks the separate effect of democracy and political distance," they opted for a "weak-link" specification of joint democracy because with such a specification there was "no need . . . to postulate that the effect of democracy on conflict is discontinuous—involving a threshold—or that a club good is involved." In addition, they thought that it captured both the level of democracy of the two states as well as the "political distance" between them. When they included their weak-link joint democracy variable(s) in models that also included a trade interdependence variable, the coefficient of the joint democracy variable(s) was statistically significant. These findings replicated those of Oneal and Russett (1997), which were published just months prior to Oneal and Ray (1997). Both sets of findings overcame the statistical quandary of Oneal et al.'s results. Oneal and Ray (1997) explained that the problem with previous continuous joint democracy measures was that analysts did not fully appreciate that "combining states' regime scores into a single dyadic measure entails a loss of information, however it is done," therefore, "it is preferable simply to identify the higher and lower democracy scores and to use these" (770). They noted that "Maoz and Russett's (1993) instincts were correct; they erred only in combining these two factors into a single variable (*JOINREG*)" (768).

As noted previously, Oneal and Russett (1997, 274) adopted the weak-link approach for much the same reasons as Oneal and Ray, although they were even more emphatic that the likelihood of a dispute is "a function of the lower democracy score in the dyad" (274) and that "the probability of a dispute is strongly associated with the continuous measure of the political character of the less-democratic state" (288). Therefore, in their basic equation, Oneal and Russett include only the regime score for the less democratic state, while introducing the regime score for the more democratic state when their interest turns to the specific impact of political distance on conflict involvement. In fact, in their subsequent study (Russett and Oneal 2001) all of their estimations of the democratic peace rely on models that include only the democracy score for the less democratic state in the dyad. Clearly, for both sets of authors, the weak-link specification was viewed as a huge improvement over previous continuous measures of joint democracy because it was theoretically derived, reliable, and remained statistically significant in models that controlled for the impact of trade interdependence.

So the adoption of the weak-link specification of joint democracy should be seen as part of a process aimed at generating a more theoretically consistent, reliable, robust, continuous measure of joint democracy that could be utilized to systematically evaluate democratic peace claims. Within this context, Oneal and Russett's (1997) findings served as a reaffirmation and extension of democratic peace research that had faced a serious empirical quandary—the impact of joint democracy was vitiated by trade interdependence. The weak-link specification gained greater acceptance, in large part, because it allowed for the substantiation of democratic peace claims; and it is not surprising that in relatively short order it became a standard operationalization for joint democracy in systematic studies of the link between democracy and international relations.[7]

As is evident from the previous discussion, earlier democratic peace advocates argued in favor of a measure of joint democracy that reflected both the level of democracy of two states as well as the "political distance" between them. However, since both of these factors are assumed to predict to international conflict, it strikes me as a much simpler—and a more methodologically consistent—task to construct one measure of joint democracy and a separate measure of political distance. It is assumed that a weak-link specification enables one to determine the impact of political distance on the likelihood of conflict, which is important because democratic peace advocates assert that the difference in the regime scores of both states also contributes to the conflict-proneness of the dyad. That is, "making a dyad more democratic by increasing the [regime] score of the less democratic state reduces the likelihood of conflict; but raising the level of joint democracy by increasing democracy in the more democratic state, increasing the political distance separating the pair, makes the dyad more prone to conflict" (Oneal and Russett 1997, 281–82). Such a research design seems to conflate both the allegedly conflict-dampening impact of joint democracy and the presumably conflict-exacerbating impact of political distance in the regime variables (or as is often the case, in the single regime variable for the less democratic state). Fusing these two contrasting attributes in a single variable makes it difficult to distinguish between the competing processes. To be sure, if political distance—or "political dissimilarity"—is an important factor in international conflict, one should simply include it as a separate variable in the analysis. Such a specification would allow us to better determine the independent impact of political distance on conflict and to determine whether the effect of joint democracy is robust once one controls for this variable. Therefore, I also include a political distance variable, *Political Distance,* which is measured as the absolute value of the difference between the two states' regime scores. In addition, by including a political distance variable we will also be able to examine the extent to which "structural" variables such as regime type are less important than "relational" variables such as trade interdependence, as Singer (1971) surmised. If Singer is correct, then the impact of the "relational" variable, trade interdependence, should supersede that of the "structural" variable, joint democracy. More important, if Singer is correct, in the more fully specified model, the coefficient for the joint democracy variable should not be significant.

The only other modification of Oneal and Russett's research design is that whereas they code ongoing years of militarized disputes as additional cases of conflict, I do not. Not including subsequent years of multiple-year disputes as additional cases of conflict is consistent with the coding used in previous studies of the democratic peace, and it simply reflects the view that the factors that contribute to the onset of a dispute are often distinct from those factors that affect its continuation. Most of the research on international conflict from the Correlates of War Project substantiates this view (see Vasquez 1993). Moreover, Oneal and Russett (1999) maintain that their findings are consistent even when subsequent dispute years are excluded; therefore, in the final model, I do not include ongoing dispute years as additional cases of conflict. With these modest changes in mind, we now turn to the data analyses.

### Data Analysis

A multivariate logistic regression model is estimated to replicate Oneal and Russett's (1997) findings. This is the identical statistical method that they used. The basic model takes the following form:

$$\Pr(MID_{ij,\,t}) = 1\,/(1 + e^{-Z_i}).$$

$\Pr(MID_{ij,\,t})$, is the probability that the outcome variable (the onset of a militarized interstate dispute) equals 1; and $Z_i$ is the sum of the product of the coefficient values $(b_j)$ across all observations of the predictor variables $(X_{ij,\,t})$, that is:

$$\beta_0 + \beta_1 Democracy_{LO} + \beta_2 Economic\ Growth_{LO} + \beta_3 Allies$$

$$+ \beta_4 Contiguity + \beta_5 Capability\ Ratio + \beta_6 Trade\ Ratio_{LO}.$$

### Findings

Equation (1) in table 1 replicates Oneal and Russett's (1997) results found in equation (1) of their table 2 (278), which regresses MID involvement (including ongoing years) on the less democratic state's regime score ($Democracy_{LO}$), the lower economic growth rate of the two states ($Economic\ Growth_{LO}$), whether or not the states are allies ($Allies$), whether or not the states are contiguous ($Contiguity$), the ratio

TABLE 1. Logistic Regression of the Relationshp between Democracy and MIDs, 1950–85

| | (1)<br>(Replication) | (2)<br>(Drop Ongoing MIDs) | (3)<br>(Add Political Distance) | (4)<br>(Drop Ongoing MIDs,<br>Add Political Distance) |
|---|---|---|---|---|
| Democracy$_{LO}$ | −.05*** (.001) | −.03*** (.008) | −.035*** (.008) | −.011 (.009) |
| Economic Growth$_{LO}$ | −.02*** (.01) | −.03*** (.01) | −.03*** (.01) | −.04*** (.01) |
| Allies | −.82*** (.08) | −.64*** (.09) | −.64*** (.09) | −.51*** (.10) |
| Contiguity | 1.31*** (.08) | 1.67*** (.10) | 1.42*** (.08) | 1.80*** (.10) |
| Capability ratio | −.003*** (.000) | −.002*** (.001) | −.003*** (.000) | −.002*** (.000) |
| Trade ratio$_{LO}$ | −66.13*** (13.44) | −43.82*** (12.08) | −68.82*** (13.74) | −45.13*** (12.28) |
| Political distance | — | — | .02*** (.005) | .04*** (.007) |
| Constant | −3.29*** (.08) | −3.99*** (.10) | −3.57*** (.10) | −4.36*** (.12) |
| −2 Log Likelihood | 6,955.14 | 4,979.55 | 6,925.64 | 4,945.77 |
| N | 20,990 | 20,990 | 20,990 | 20,990 |
| χ² | 764.043*** | 560.36*** | 793.54*** | 594.14*** |

Standard errors are in parentheses; all p-values are estimated using two-tailed tests.

*p ≤ .10, **p ≤ .05 level, ***p ≤ .01 level

of the two states' relative capability scores (*Capability Ratio*), and trade interdependence measured as the lower of the two states' ratio of dyadic trade to GDP (*Trade ratio*$_{LO}$).[8] The results of equation (1) are identical to those in equation (1) of Oneal and Russett (1997), and they show that their democratic peace findings are robust. The results are also consistent when one modifies the analysis and focuses on the onset of disputes, excluding ongoing dispute years, as in equation (2), which substantiates the authors' claims that their findings were robust even in light of the dropping of these cases. Extending the analysis further, the findings reported in equation (3) allow us to isolate the impact of political distance on dispute involvement, and as expected, political distance has a significant conflict-exacerbating impact, even as the impact of joint democracy remains significant.

But the findings reported in equation (4), which control for political distance but exclude ongoing years of disputes in the outcome variable, tell a much different story. They reveal that the impact of *Democracy*$_{LO}$ is not significantly associated with the probability of dispute onset. This lack of consistency with respect to the democracy variable across the models is even more surprising since the other predictor variables (i.e., *Economic Growth*$_{LO}$, *Allies*, *Contiguity*, *Capability Ratio*, and *Trade ratio*$_{LO}$) are quite robust across the various equations. The results indicate that when controlling for political distance and dropping ongoing years of disputes—two straightforward modifications that are widely accepted in the democratic peace literature—the heretofore-significant

TABLE 2. Logistic Regression of the Relationship between Democracy and MIDs, 1950–85, Excluding Continuous MIDs

|  | (2a)<br>(Drop Ongoing MIDs) | (4a)<br>(Drop Ongoing MIDs,<br>Add Political Distance) |
|---|---|---|
| Democracy$_{LO}$ | −.03*** (.008) | −.012 (.009) |
| Economic Growth$_{LO}$ | −.03*** (.01) | −.04*** (.01) |
| Allies | −.68*** (.09) | −.54*** (.10) |
| Contiguity | 1.70*** (.10) | 1.83*** (.10) |
| Capability ratio | −.002*** (.001) | −.002*** (.001) |
| Trade ratio$_{LO}$ | −46.22*** (12.31) | −47.60*** (12.52) |
| Political distance | — | .04*** (.007) |
| Constant | −3.96*** (.10) | −4.33*** (.12) |
| −2 Log Likelihood | 4,932.34 | 4,908.55 |
| N | 20.656 | 20,656 |
| $\chi^2$ | 577.61*** | 611.41*** |

Standard errors are in parentheses; all *p*-values are estimated using two-tailed tests.
*$p \leq$ .10, **$p \leq$ .05 level, ***$p \leq$ .01 level

TABLE 3.  General Estimating Equation (GEE) of the Relationship between Democracy and MIDs, 1950–85

| | (1) (Replication) | (2) (Drop Ongoing MIDs) | (3) (Add Political Distance) | (4) (Drop Ongoing MIDs, Add Political Distance) |
|---|---|---|---|---|
| Democracy$_{LO}$ | -.05*** (.01) | -.03* (.016) | -.003*** (.001) | -.01 (.02) |
| Economic Growth$_{LO}$ | -.02** (.01) | -.03** (.013) | -.02** (.01) | -.04*** (.01) |
| Allies | -.82*** (.22) | -.65*** (.21) | -.77*** (.21) | -.52*** (.20) |
| Contiguity | 1.24*** (.23) | 1.66*** (.21) | 1.31*** (.23) | 1.78*** (.22) |
| Capability ratio | -.003*** (.001) | -.002*** (.001) | -.003*** (.001) | -.002*** (.001) |
| Trade ratio$_{LO}$ | -40.64** (20.52) | -41.23*** (23.02) | -43.26** (21.17) | -42.36** (23.55) |
| Political Distance | — | — | .02 (.01) | .04*** (.01) |
| Constant | -3.26*** (.18) | -3.97*** (.17) | -3.44*** (.22) | -4.33*** (.22) |
| Deviance | 6,957.57 | 4,974.48 | 6,931.83 | 4,940.70 |
| N | 20,985 | 20,985 | 20,985 | 20,985 |
| $\chi^2$ | 78.20*** | 110.77*** | 81.21*** | 112.00*** |

Standard errors are in parentheses; all $p$-values are estimated using two-tailed tests.

*$p \leq .10$, **$p \leq .05$ level, ***$p \leq .01$ level

impact of joint democracy washes out. Moreover, the findings in equation (2) and equation (4) of table 1 are not affected by completely excluding the ongoing years of MIDs entirely from the analyses or by simply making the observation 0 as is done in table 1. The values for equation (2) and equation (4) when dropping the values entirely are shown in table 2 as equation (2a) and equation (4a), respectively. Again, the results indicate that joint democracy is not a significant factor in international conflict.

Table 3 includes additional tests using the general estimating equation (GEE) to control for both serial and spatial autocorrelation, and the results reveal that the main findings are confirmed.[9] In light of these findings, it appears that Singer's skepticism is borne out; but why should we be able to observe this rare finding in the democratic peace literature when so many other studies find just the opposite? To my mind, the key lies in two factors. First is the obvious tenuous relationship between joint democracy and peace, which is well documented. For example, Ray (1997, 14) reminds us that the relationship between joint democracy and war "is in fact so modest in strength . . . that it is something of a minor miracle that it has yet to be eliminated by most of the controls' to which it has been introduced."

Second, the slightly modified research design utilized in this study serves to separate the two tendencies captured in the variable commonly used to measure joint democracy. In so doing, it excises the conflict-dampening impact of low political distance from that of joint democracy, such that only the impact of joint democracy remains; and in light of trade interdependence, this impact washes out just as it did in the earlier models of Oneal et al. (1996). One is left to question whether the extent to which continuous joint democracy variables such as the weak-link variable(s) have been significant may be largely due to the fact that they capture aspects of regime similarity, especially at the two extremes of their ranges (i.e., at total democracy or total autocracy where $Dem_{HI}$ and $Dem_{LO}$ are at their respective maximum and minimum values of democracy/autocracy. That is, where $Dem_{HI}$ and $Dem_{LO}$ both have values of +10, or where $Dem_{HI}$ and $Dem_{LO}$ both have values of $-10$, they are not simply measuring the regime score of the two states but they are also capturing the absence of political distance between the two states (i.e., either full democracies or full autocracies).[10] Once one includes a political distance variable in the same model with the weak-link variable, the greater conflict-dampening impact of low political distance is excised from the weak-link democracy measure, and what is left is the nonsignificant relationship between joint democracy and the probability of conflict that Singer assumed. One might conjecture that common regime type is largely significant to the extent that it also takes into account political similarity, but when one evaluates the effect of regime type qua regime type—in this case, joint democracy—one finds that it is not significant. In sum, earlier tests of the democratic peace thesis that utilized continuous measures of joint democracy in the presence of trade interdependence failed because the democratic peace thesis failed: joint democracy does not appear to be a significant factor in reducing the likelihood of international conflict once one controls for political distance and trade interdependence, and excludes subsequent years of ongoing disputes.

## CONCLUSION

In this chapter, I've discussed Singer's agnosticism toward the democratic peace thesis in light of the overwhelming statistical evidence in support of it. I noted that Singer's skepticism is ironic since he has been key in establishing both the empirical and theoretical framework for studying the democratic peace. I situated Singer's skepticism in his philosophy of science and argued that it was consistent with his approach to theory building in world politics. Drawing on his discussions of the significance of "structural" and "relational" variables in analyses of the correlates of war, I replicated the findings of one of the most important studies on the democratic peace thesis and then reexamined them in light of several straightforward modifications of the basic research design, which were consistent with Singer's basic logic. Importantly, the modifications that I presented here have each been utilized in previous studies of the democratic peace; however, those studies have not examined these modifications in combination. Further, the modifications are not arrived at arbitrarily to stack the deck against the democratic peace; on the contrary, they derive consistently from the theoretical arguments on the democratic peace voiced by liberal advocates themselves and capture the relationships assumed by democratic peace supporters in a much more straightforward fashion than the "weak-link" specifications currently in vogue. Utilizing this more straightforward specification, I find that the results contradict the democratic peace finding and provide statistical support for Singer's skepticism.

In addition, the results from this chapter also suggest that the arguments of those who've maintained that the democratic peace is epiphenomenal of factors related to any of the control variables that are consistent throughout the models presented here (alliance membership, trade, relative capability, growth, etc.) should be reconsidered. Importantly, one of these variables is contiguity—which Singer thought was the key to the apparent relationship between joint democracy and peace. Its impact remains significant even as that of joint democracy fades—an important vindication of Singer's skepticism. The results also call into question the accuracy of deductive models that derive the democratic peace relationship from their rational choice assumptions (e.g., Bueno de Mesquita and Lalman 1992; Bueno de Mesquita et al. 1999). Most significant, the findings seem to suggest that Singer was right insofar as democracy does not appear to be significantly associated with international conflict.

What is probably needed to push our understanding of the causes of international conflict forward is the complex, process-oriented analysis of foreign policy decision making that Singer (1958, 1963, 1985) has supported for decades. Such rich analyses may provide the bedrock for the type of explanatory knowledge that is necessary for theory building in world politics. The accumulation of more and more correlational studies of basically monocausal models is not an auspicious path toward a more scientific and policy-relevant world politics. Even less auspicious are recent and recurrent assertions that war has changed so fundamentally that large-*n* studies of wars across long time periods are inherently flawed if not fruitless (see Henderson and Singer 2002 for a response). Beyond research, the most important policy implication of the findings in this chapter is that the post–Cold War strategy of "democratic enlargement," which is grounded in the Wilsonian idealist aim of ensuring peace by enlarging the community of democratic states, is quite a thin reed upon which to rest a state's foreign policy—much less, the hope for international peace.

## NOTES

1. Several authors observe presidential support for spreading democracy as a means of encouraging peace back to the nineteenth century. Such assessments, however, are difficult to reconcile with U.S. imperialism and antidemocratic interventions epitomized in its rapacious policies against American Indians and Filipinos during the Second Philippines War of the nineteenth century; and a plethora of interventions to overturn incipient democracies in Iran, Guatemala, and Chile, among the most notable during the twentieth century (Henderson 2002).

2. Russett was an early postdoctoral student on the COW Project while at Yale, while the others were Singer's students at the University of Michigan.

3. For a fuller discussion of the divergent strands of theorizing on the democratic peace, see chapter 1 of Henderson (2002).

4. The following argument draws on Henderson (2002, 26–30).

5. Russett (1993, 77) states that "our hypothesis . . . says that the more

democratic both members of the pair are they [*sic*] less likely they are to become embroiled in a militarized dispute." Rummel (1983) makes a similar point.

6. The geometric mean is measured as the $n$th root of the product of $n$ values. Unlike a simple arithmetic mean (i.e., an average), it takes into consideration the difference in the values.

7. An often overlooked finding of both these studies is that *individual* democracies are more peaceful than other types of states. Both Oneal and Ray (1997, 770) and Oneal and Russett (1997, 288) explicitly state that there is a *monadic* as well as a dyadic democratic peace.

8. See Oneal and Russett (1997, 277) for the coding rules for the variables in the original model.

9. Also see Henderson (2002, appendix).

10. Although one can make this case for any point along the democracy-autocracy continuum where the regime scores for the two states are identical, the points of full democracy and full autocracy are important because it is by focusing on their relative conflict-proneness that scholars have argued most profusely in support of the democratic peace thesis.

# ALLIANCES, TERRITORIAL DISPUTES, AND THE PROBABILITY OF WAR
## Testing for Interactions

*Paul D. Senese and John A. Vasquez*

## SINGER AND THE STUDY OF ALLIANCES AND WAR

For centuries international relations thinkers have mused on the role of alliance in peace and war. Thucydides, in the Melian dialogue, relates how the Athenians counsel the Melians not to rely on the Spartans to save them. Similarly, ancient China saw alliances play an important role (Chi 1968; Cioffi-Revilla and Lai 1995). This is not surprising since coalition building has deep, if not primordial, roots within humans going back at least to our primate cousins (see de Waal 1989). Despite this history, it was not until the work of J. David Singer and Melvin Small that systematic scientifically replicable data on interstate alliances were collected (Singer and Small 1966a; Small and Singer 1969). Those data and their initial statistical analysis of them remains the single most important watershed in our collective attempt to understand the role of alliances in international politics.

Prior to their work there was much theorizing and speculation on alliances, but little evidence. Some of this work, particularly in diplomatic history, was very important (see Langer 1935, 1950), but much of it that tried to generalize about patterns relied on anecdotal evidence and followed a method David Singer characterized as an attempt to "ransack history for those cases that seem to support our hypotheses" (2000, 4; see also 1969b, 79) without regard, and sometimes with disregard, for those examples that did not.

Singer and Small (1966b) provided the first systematic evidence on the relationship between alliance making and war involvement. They found, for the 1816–1945 period, that states that had many alliances also had many war involvements (both in terms of the number of wars and the number of years at war). They also found that a high rank in alliances was associated with a high rank in battle deaths. At the system level, they found that states in the central system had more alliances than those in the total system, and that war was more prevalent in the central system. They also found that the longer a state was a member of the system the more apt it was to have had an alliance, and that some of the relationship between alliance and war was a function of length of system membership, but that not all of it was.

These findings were important at the time because they were among the first the field had that moved us "beyond conjecture" (Singer and Jones 1972) to identifying and documenting patterns of behavior. Some saw this movement as too inductive, and Waltz (1979, 12) was to later disparage it as "correlational labors." These criticisms miss the point, as well as mischaracterizing induction and its importance. Induction is rarely theory-free, and Singer had plenty of theory from which to choose in his attempt to find the correlates of war. Often this theory had realist components to it, and the attempt to see if alliances were associated with war was the subject of a long philosophical and political debate between realism and idealism (see Walker 2000). Before, during, and after Singer collected data, he always addressed questions of theory. Frequently, this involved examining and/or testing contradictory hypotheses within the literature, as in Singer, Bremer, and Stuckey (1972). More important, it involved Singer using some of the insights of social psychology to undermine traditional realist analyses based on power and to come up with alternate explanations of war (e.g., Singer 1958, 1970a, 1982). Many of these early theoretical pieces are collected in Singer (1979a), and an examination of them will show that not only was Singer guided by theory in his collection of data and his testing, but that he frequently compared various and often contradictory realist hypotheses with those that could be derived from a different perspective—that provided by social psychology and the emerging field of peace research.

Even though Singer's work was far from theory-free, his main defense of induction was that first one had to delineate patterns before they could be adequately explained (1979b, xviii–xix). There were just too many contradictory claims being made by scholars with no real way of empirically assessing which were historically accurate. One must remember that in international relations, most work at the time was conducted in what was a "data-free" environment. Much of the discourse of the 1950s and early 1960s assessed hypotheses by evaluating their logic in terms of how well a hypothesis did in comparison to the dominant realist assumptions of the time—namely, that power is the key to all politics. For example, Claude (1962) and Organski (1958) looked at balance-of-power explanations and criticized them for being inconsistent with what one would expect about the effects of power on behavior. Similarly, Morgenthau (1960) criticized various peace proposals (like world government or the balance of power) because they were inconsistent with his realist assumptions about states acting in terms of the national interest defined in terms of power. He also saw these peace proposals as being contradicted by empirical examples drawn (not very systematically) from the historical record. What was missing, however, was the systematic examination of the historical record. For Singer, this could be best done by applying the most appropriate avenue of inquiry available, the scientific method (see Singer 1969b). He was concerned with how the mass of the historical record could be converted to replicable evidence that could then be made into *data* (see Singer 1965). Once the data were collected, then the path to truth lay with establishing the correlates of war; in other words, which factors are associated with war and which factors thought to be associated with it are actually statistically insignificant. Once these were known, then explanation would be easier.

This strategy of inquiry is a sound one. It uses existing theory to collect data and empirically probe hypotheses, then it reformulates the explanation in light of tests. It then retests and collects new data, reformulates or develops new theory in light of new patterns, and so forth. True induction always goes hand in hand with theorizing. In many ways, it is a strategy for building theory and plays an important part in the logic of discovery. A potential problem with deduction is that the familiarity of certain theoretical assumptions can lead it to become a doctrine, where claims are rejected by comparing them to the theory's assumptions or its logic rather than some body of empirical evidence, a danger exhibited in the 1950s and 1960s first with classical realism and then with nuclear deterrence. This danger is especially the case when some of the assumptions embody empirical patterns that have never been established. Then theorists can end up explaining a "law" that never existed, something Kenneth Waltz probably ended up doing in *Theory of International Politics* (1979) (see Vasquez 1997; Vasquez and Elman 2003, esp. chaps. 8, 9, 11, 12, 17 ).

It is essential that part of the field always be devoted to establishing empirical patterns, even if the theory used to get at these may not be as explicit or as formal as some would like. Empiricism, "with and without shoes," is important for understanding and for constructing better theory. Without it we are awash in a sea of speculation without any anchor (Wallace 1985, 109). One of Singer's most important legacies is understanding this lesson. He created data in international relations when little existed and had a strategy of inquiry that made sense then and does now. The alternative is armchair philosophizing, or worse—sophistry that assumes empirical patterns to make political points. A reasonable blend of inductive and deductive theory building, always guided by the scientific method, is certainly a road map worth utilizing.

The other contribution to theory that Singer and his early associates made that is often neglected by criticizing induction is that in trying to follow the scientific method, Singer, as well as other early behavioralists, had to reformulate and systematize existing hypotheses. Thus, in the study of alliances and war, one of the first things done was to review the literature for propositions as a prelude to testing them (Bueno de Mesquita and Singer 1973; see also Ward 1982). The attempt to operationalize concepts and derive testable hypotheses led scholars to often find several hypotheses where traditional scholars only saw one (see Siverson and Sullivan 1983). Nowhere was this more evident than in Singer's attempt to test the various claims associated with power, polarization, and war (cf. Singer and Small 1968a; Singer, Bremer, and Stuckey 1972).

This brief overview should make it clear that the Correlates of War Project was a highly ambitious one that attempted to bring the scientific method to bear upon the most central questions in international relations—why war occurs and how peace can be built. The secrecy that shrouded foreign policy decision making naturally made Singer turn toward the historical record as a source of evidence. His collaboration with Melvin Small, a diplomatic historian, was no accident. Together they assembled data on the main dependent variable (war) (Singer and Small 1972) and independent variable (alliances) in the field. The selection of the latter along with capability as the two main independent variables is quite consistent with what one would expect of a field being guided by the realist paradigm, as international relations was at the time (see Vasquez 1998b, chap. 5).

Data were never an end in themselves for Singer or the project. As soon as data were collected they began to be analyzed, and the reason this was possible was that the data were collected with certain analyses in mind. Thus, as soon as Singer and Small (1966a) had collected alliance data for a reasonable time period (1816–1945), they tested hypotheses. They did not wait for more data. As they completed their data collection to 1965 (Small and Singer 1969), they shifted to studying how alliances affect polarization and polarity and how that in turn affects war (Singer and Small 1968a). This study focused on the polarity debate, examining key differences between Deutsch and Singer (1964) on the one hand and Waltz (1964) on the other. A more explicit incorporation of capability was the focus of Singer, Bremer, and Stuckey (1972), another classic study in the field. In this study they uncovered their famous intercentury difference, which finds that the concentration of power (in the system) has one effect in the post-1815 nineteenth century and another in the twentieth century.

## RECENT LITERATURE ON ALLIANCES AND WAR

What is important about Singer's work, generally and not only with regard to the study of alliances, is that it was a research program that brought in a number of people, especially graduate students, who then went on to do their own studies and collect more data. Some of these, like the extensive refining of the alliance data by Sabrosky (1976), were done under Singer's direction. Others, like Levy's (1981, 1983) extension of the alliance data back to 1495, were done separately and without his knowledge. Data collection on alliances in recent years has seen another spurt. Gibler has collected data on new alliance variables that he has used to create new typologies of alliances (1997b; see also 1996), as well as refining the data by using the new treaty series published by Parry (1978) and extending the data back in time (Gibler 1999). Leeds, Long, and Mitchell (2000) have collected new data on alliances by identifying the precise conditions under which a state is committed to defending its ally. Finally, Gibler and Sarkees (2002) have led the effort to update the official Correlates of War data on alliances to the end of the twentieth century.

The early work of Singer and Small on alliances and war gave rise to a host of interesting studies. Sabrosky (1980) examined the reliability of alliances and found that many alliances are unreliable in that allies do not go to war against those that attack their ally, and in many cases actually go to war against their allies. Smith (1995, 1996) used the idea of alliance reliability to try to explain why some alliances are followed by war and others by peace. The former, he argued, is the result, in part, of potential attackers believing that the ally is unreliable (i.e., it is not credible that the ally will intervene in an ongoing war), whereas the former is a function of the ally being seen as not reliable. Part of the supposition of this explanation is undercut, however, by Leeds, Long, and Mitchell (2000), who found that if the actual *casus belli* of alliance treaties are examined, Sabrosky's (1980) unreliability finding is overturned. They found that approximately 75 percent of alliances from

1816 through 1944 are in fact reliable (Leeds, Long, and Mitchell 2000, table 5).

Levy (1981) provided further evidence on the war proneness of alliances involving major states. He found, with the important exception of the nineteenth century, that most alliances involving major states tend to be followed by at least one war involving a signatory within five years. Vasquez (1993, chap. 5) used Levy's findings and Singer and Small (1966b) to argue that alliances are a form of power politics that increase threat perception and therefore increase the probability of war. He maintained that alliances rarely prevent war the way some balance-of-power explanations expect. Wayman (1990), however, provided findings that cast doubt on the propensity of alliances to be followed by war.

Gibler (1996, 2000) and Maoz (2000b) took a different tack. They tried to explain why some alliances are followed by war and others are not by taking a more empirical approach. Gibler delineated the characteristics that he thinks make certain types of alliances war prone and others associated with peace. He found that a certain class of alliances are not associated with attempts to balance power but rather are the outcome of settling a host of territorial disagreements and then sealing those with an alliance. He argued, on the basis of the territorial explanation of war, that these territorial settlement treaties, since they resolve territorial disputes, will be followed by peaceful relations. Although there are only a few such alliances, he found that they are overwhelmingly followed by peace (Gibler 1996; see also 1997a). Conversely, he found that alliances composed of major states that are dissatisfied with the status quo and have been successful in their last major war have a much higher probability of going to war than those that lack these attributes. Maoz (2000b) also maintained that different types of alliances have different effects. He agreed with Gibler that if major states are in an alliance this has an impact, but for him what made the major difference is whether the alliance is composed of democratic or nondemocratic states. Depending on the politically relevant environment of states, alliances consisting of democratic states have patterns of behavior different from those consisting of nondemocratic states.

A number of empirical and theoretical studies have been conducted that look at how alliances expand war. Siverson and King (1979) documented, early on, the tendency of alliances to expand war, and they have investigated the type of attributes in an alliance associated with expansion (1980). Siverson and Starr (1991) replicated and extended this finding. Bueno de Mesquita (1978) found that when alliances tighten, this is associated with the subsequent expansion of war. Sabrosky (1985) also used the alliance data to do important studies on polarization and the expansion of war. A number of other studies also looked at how polarity affects the expansion of war (e.g., Wayman 1984; Levy 1985).

Several studies have suggested that alliances and military buildups are foreign policy practices that are substitutable for one another. Most and Starr (1984) were among the first to suggest this, although elements can be found in Waltz (1979) who referred to this as external and internal balancing. Most and Siverson (1987) provided an early test of the claim, while Morrow (1993) looked at the dynamic in more detail. Palmer, Wohlander, and Morgan (2002), as well as Morgan and Palmer (n.d.), developed a "two-good" model of foreign policy that assesses the general trade-off between change and maintenance-seeking behavior. One of the specific policies examined through this substitution approach is the decision to enter into alliances, compared to other substitutable policy options, as a means of achieving foreign policy goals (see also Morrow 1991, 2000).

In the remainder of this chapter, we continue to build upon the initial work of Singer and Small (1966b) that has been so influential over the past thirty-eight years. We do this by examining some of the specific conditions under which alliances are associated with the outbreak of war, with our main focus directed at the contingent role of territorial disputes. Very little research has been conducted on how alliances might play a role in the escalation of territorial disputes. We argue on the basis of the steps-to-war explanation (Vasquez 1993; Senese and Vasquez 2003) that alliances are most apt to be associated with war when states that are contending over territorial questions have militarized disputes and have outside allies that presumably can be relied on to support them in these disputes. We specify and test a hypothesis that maintains that outside alliances among states that are disputing territory increase the probability of war. We are particularly interested in determining whether there is a statistical interaction between territorial disputes and the presence of outside allies that produces an increased probability of war.

## THEORETICAL ANALYSIS

The territorial explanation of conflict and war outlined in Vasquez (1993, chap. 4) and Senese and Vasquez (2003) maintains that territorial disputes typically have a higher probability of escalating to war than expected by chance and in comparison to other types of disputes, such as disputes over general foreign policy or regime questions. Several pieces of evidence have been adduced to document this pattern (Hensel 1996, 2000; Huth 1996a, 1996b, 2000; Senese 1996, 2002; Senese and Vasquez 2003; Vasquez 1993; Vasquez and Henehan 2001). The reason territorial disputes are more war prone undoubtedly has something to do with human inheritance of a sense of territoriality, which in vertebrates generally involves the use of aggressive displays to keep and gain territory (see Valzelli 1981). Such biological factors are treated as exogenous by the explanation; rather the emphasis is on the political implications of territoriality (Vasquez 1993, chap. 4). These include a division of the world into territorial units, the tendency of neighbors to fight over borders, and the greater willingness to incur fatalities over territorial disputes than other disputes—which in turn may be related to the creation of hard-line domestic constituencies that keep territorial issues at the forefront of a state's political agenda, especially if these involve territorial ethnic questions (see Huth 1996b; Roy 1997). Since this explanation has been detailed elsewhere (Vasquez 1993, chap. 4), suffice it to say here that territoriality and its political consequences are seen as making territorial issues more prone to war, if they are handled in a certain fashion. The explanation does not maintain as some determinists do (e.g., Ardrey 1966) that territory always gives rise to war. Instead, it maintains that these issues give rise to war only if they are handled in a particular fashion; indeed, many territorial disagreements are resolved without states going to war (Kacowicz 1994; Kocs 1995; Hensel 2001a; Zacher 2001; see also Simmons 1999).

The territorial explanation of war maintains that if territorial disputes are handled in a power politics fashion the probability of escalation to war will increase. Realist diplomatic culture, which has dominated international relations in the West since 1648, provides a variety of foreign policy practices for decision makers. Key within this discourse is the idea that as security issues arise, states should increase their power by making alliances and/or building up their military (Vasquez 1993, chap. 5). The steps-to-war model maintains that such actions often increase the probability of war because they produce a security dilemma that leads each state to feel more threatened and more hostile toward the other side. Adopting one or more of these practices leads to a repetition of disputes and an increased level of escalation across disputes (see Leng 1983; Brecher and Wilkenfeld 1997, 826–28, 837–38, for some evidence on this proposition).

This analysis will examine the impact of alliance formation on the probability of war breaking out among states that have territorial disputes with one another. It is posited that states that dispute territory have a higher probability of going to war with each other than states that have other kinds of disputes. It is further posited that if a state with a territorial dispute makes an alliance with an outside party that can be used to aid it in its territorial dispute, this will increase the probability of war. In this sense, having a territorial dispute can be considered a first step to war, because it increases the probability of war, and making or having an alliance relevant to the dispute can be considered a second step to war, because it further increases the probability of war. This analysis will test the proposition that dyads with territorial disputes where one or both sides have an outside alliance partner will experience an increased probability of going to war compared to (1) dyads that contend over territorial disputes but do not have an outside alliance or (2) dyads that contend over policy or regime disputes and have an outside alliance (or have no alliance). This proposition assumes that certain types of alliances do not have any "deterrent" effect; instead, they increase the probability of war.[1] The alliances that are most dangerous are those that increase threat perception and thereby often provoke a hostile response (Gibler and Vasquez 1998; Gibler 1997b, 2000; Walker 2000).

We approach the testing of our core proposition through the use of both additive and multiplicative modeling techniques. Before specifying how these propositions will be tested, however, it is important to elaborate the various ways in which alliances might affect the probability of war between two states that are contending with each other by resorting to the threat or use of force. Generally, it is believed that states that are allied to each other should have a lower probability of fighting each other, even if they have a dispute, than states that are not allied to each other (see Bremer 1992, 2000). The reasons given for this expectation may vary, but one logic is that states within the same alliance may want to mute their dispute because of a fear of a third party that is seen as more threatening to both parties than they are to each other. If this were not the case, then they might not make the alliance in the first place. Huth (1996b, 119–22) provides some evidence to indicate that the rise of a dispute with a third party can reduce the probability of escalation and war between parties that have an ongoing disagreement over territory. Such a logic, however, assumes that these states are in a bilateral alliance where they have actually chosen to ally with each other even in the presence of a territorial dispute. It might be the case that the dispute arises after the alliance forms or that they are rivals who find themselves in a large multilateral alliance (e.g., Greece and Turkey in NATO). In such a case, a different logic might be operating. Rather than an external threat reducing the probability of war, the multilateral alliance itself may have a muting effect on conflict by providing an incentive to other allies to mediate or otherwise limit the conflict potential of the dispute in order to keep the alliance together. From these two logics, it is plausible to expect that states allied to each other (that also have a dispute with one another) should have a lower probability of war than states that have disputes with one another, but are not allied to each other. This expectation is contrary to the finding that allies often fight each other—the so-called friends-as-foes hypothesis (Bueno de Mesquita 1981, 73–83, 159–64). Bueno de Mesquita, on the basis of an expected utility argument, predicts that states that are allied to each other have a greater probability of fighting one another. Ray (1990) raises questions about these findings, but while his research design reduces the strength of the findings, he too finds a statistically significant relationship. Others, however, have rejected this finding, seeing it as a function of the contiguity of states; namely, that contiguous states have a comparatively greater propensity to both fight and ally with each other (see Ray 2000, 300; see also Maoz and Russett 1992; Bremer 1992).

While contiguity may have an impact on the friends-as-foes hypothesis, to dismiss this finding merely as spurious and therefore theoretically uninteresting may be too quick. Schroeder (1976) points out that states frequently use the practice of alliance making to try to control their rivals (such alliances are called *pacta de contrahendo*). These alliances might very well break down and lead to war, compared to the more straightforward defense pacts that are the exemplar alliance in realist thinking. Similarly, nonaggression pacts deviate from the theoretical expectation that allies will not fight each other. Since these partners are often rivals, if not enemies, they may be engaged in a pact of expediency, which can break down at any moment, as witnessed by the Hitler-Stalin Pact. Of the various alliance types in Correlates of War data, Sabrosky (1980) finds that nonaggression pacts are most apt to have "unreliable" allies, that is, those who end up in war with one another or not aiding their ally if it is attacked.[2]

These two contradictory theoretical streams raise a problem of how alliance pacts should be ranked in terms of their propensity for war, as well as posing an empirical puzzle. The steps-to-war explanation maintains that alliance formation that follows a realist logic of trying to aggregate power (thereby preventing an attack by building peace through strength) will in fact fail, even if it succeeds in "balancing power." Alliances that pose threats are seen as increasing the probability of war by giving rise to a cycle of increasingly hostile interactions. Conversely, alliances that do not pose threats and do not follow a realist logic of trying to balance power may not have such consequences. Alliances that seek to manage relations or create a security regime or system of governance among major states are alliances of a different sort (see Schroeder 1976; Kegley and Raymond 1986; Vasquez 1993, 170–71). The alliance system growing up around the Congress of Vienna is an example of such an alliance. A related example is the territorial settlement treaty, identified by Gibler (1996) as an alliance that does not seek to balance power and counter threat but instead to resolve territorial disagreements among two states. Gibler finds that such alliances are rarely followed by a politically relevant war. In this analysis it will be posited, theoretically, that alliances that do not pose threats will not be prone to war, but those that do pose such threats will be prone to war. Therefore, only certain types of alliances are expected to increase the probability of war, a conclusion that is consistent with what is known about the relationship between alliance formation and the onset of war; namely, that certain types of alliances are followed by war but that others are not (Gibler 1997b, 2000; Maoz 2000b, 2003).

A second conceptual problem with specifying the relationship between alliance formation and the onset of war is that not every alliance is relevant to every dispute or war an ally might be involved in. If a state has an alliance with a state that only commits it to fight in a circumscribed set of conditions these conditions may not be relevant to a situation that arises in another region or issue area. Leeds, Long, and Mitchell (2000) begin to address this problem in their data collection, but the problem may be more severe than they suggest. For example, Britain and Portugal signed an alliance in the nineteenth century dealing with the colonial situation in Africa. Such an alliance is not relevant to British actions outside Africa. It does not help Britain in Asia or in Latin America, nor would any of the principal states at the time expect it to. Yet a typical analysis of dyadic militarized disputes might simply ask if Britain had a formal ally while it was involved in a dispute. Active countries, like Britain and the United States, would be classified as having an ally for many of the years between 1816 and 1992, but many of these alliance commitments would not be relevant to the dispute at hand.

The research design that we propose and carry out here is designed, in part, to separate out the impacts of various types of alliance scenarios by focusing on their relevance to the dispute at hand. The causal logic of realism purports that states make alliances in order to increase their power and help balance the power of opponents, which under some versions of realism should lead to a reduction in the probability of war by increasing the risk that an attacker will lose the war. Such a logic could only be assumed to be at work *if* the alliance was politically relevant to the dispute at hand and seen that way by the participants. To test the relationship between alliance formation and war properly, it is necessary to have some idea of whether the alliances are relevant.

One solution is that provided by Leeds, Long, and Mitchell (2000). They confine relevant alliances to the legal commitments made by states in their formal treaty. Their analysis has been pathbreaking in making data collection more closely attuned to diplomatic documents. Their data collection and analysis are very appropriate (indeed long overdue) for the question they are addressing—the reliability of alliances. For the kind of question we are addressing, however, such an operational rule can be overly legalistic; it ignores the more behavioral expectation that allied states usually have shared diplomatic concerns and a relationship that should not be constrained by a resort to legalistic nitpicking. True allies or friends will not resort to the legal conditions of their alliance when one is in danger but will allow the underlying political relationship to govern their decision. From a realist perspective they will do what is in their interest, which may or may not be what they are legally bound to do. From a nonrealist point of view (e.g., cognitive psychology or constructivism) their "interests" or preference ordering will be determined by a variety of factors and not just the distribution of capability.

This suggests that the underlying political relationship can often outweigh the legal technicalities when it comes to deciding whether to intervene in a war. To confine oneself to those technicalities may be to miss an important part of the historical record. This conclusion points out the need to develop a more behavioral measure of politically relevant alliances that could supplement the treaty-based measure of Leeds, Long, and Mitchell (2000); but that is no mean feat. The analysis herein will attempt to examine whether the presence of a politically relevant alliance increases the probability of war among states that have territorial disputes. More formally, the following hypothesis will be tested.

HYPOTHESIS: Dyadic disputes over territorial questions where one or both sides have outside politically relevant alliances have a greater probability of going to war than dyadic disputes over other questions (ceteris paribus) or territorial disputes in the absence of outside politically relevant alliances.

The research design will outline how each of these concepts is operationalized and present a test design that will permit inferences to be made about the accuracy of the hypothesis.

### Research Design

To test the claim that alliances increase the probability of war among states that are contending over territorial disputes, it is necessary to compare the probability of war for states that are contending over territorial disputes and have alliances with those that do not. Thus, one test is simply to see if states that dispute territory in the presence of outside alliances have a higher probability of going to war than states that do not have an alliance. Such an analysis tests an important aspect of the explanation, but not all of it, since the steps-to-war model also maintains that while territorial disputes are more apt to go to war than other types of disputes when they are handled by the practices of power politics, that power politics itself, regardless of the issue under question, can increase the probability of war. In principle, the steps-to-war model maintains that there are two separate roads to war—one beginning with territory and one beginning with power politics.

This raises the question of which has a greater impact on the probability of war—the presence of territorial disputes or the use of power politics. The theory assumes that once territorial issues are handled by the threat or use of force (i.e., once there is a militarized dispute), they will have a greater probability of going to war than other disputes handled by the threat or use of force. Likewise, additional resorts to the foreign policy practices of power politics will have this differential effect. This means that the increasing use of power politics raises the likelihood of all types of disputes going to war, but it has more of an impact on territorial disputes. It is also assumed that territorial disputes by their very nature will give rise to a greater use of power politics. Put another way, the explanation assumes an interaction effect between territorial disputes and the use of power politics. Not all these intricacies can be tested here, so the focus will be on comparing the relative impact of having an outside alliance on the probability of war in territorial disputes, on the one hand, and policy and regime disputes, on the other.

The clearest way to test this aspect of the explanation is to begin by examining the probability of war for territorial disputes compared to policy and regime disputes. Two recent studies have done this, and both have found, using various controls (Vasquez and Henehan 2001), as well as testing for selection effects (Senese and Vasquez 2003), that, in general, territorial disputes have a higher probability of going to war than policy or regime disputes. The question in this analysis is whether the probability of war for states engaged in territorial disputes will increase with the presence of certain types of politically relevant alliances. Two related questions are whether the same effect will be present for policy and regime disputes and, if so, whether territorial disputes will still have a higher probability of going to war than policy or regime disputes.

The sample for the analysis will be all dyadic militarized interstate disputes (MID 2.1 data) from 1816 through 1992. This sample is derived by taking the 2,034 MIDs in the data and breaking them down into each pair of states in the dispute. This increases the number of cases to 3,045 disputes.[3] The most pronounced effect of this procedure is to place more weight on multiparty disputes, particularly those related to the two world wars. This procedure, however, probably increases the validity of the data because otherwise the onset of each of these wars would have the same weight as a simple tuna boat chase.

## The Dependent and Independent Variables

The dependent variable in the analysis will be whether any given MID involving two or more states escalates to war. This approach presents a rather severe test because it sees the outbreak of war as a process with the probability of war increasing as disputes recur, and the dependent variable we employ looks only at whether the current MID escalates. Specifically from the theory's perspective, it is unlikely that the first dispute over territory will go to war, especially for major states, which tend to have a long fuse. This supposition is consistent with what is known about crisis escalation (see Leng 1983). Because this is often the case, early territorial disputes between the same pairs of states that do not go to war will count as evidence against the hypothesis, even if the two states eventually go to war within a reasonable time frame. The current test, therefore, may very well underestimate the strength of the explanation. In other analyses (Senese and Vasquez 2001), our dependent variable has been whether the current MID *and any within five years* go to war. This dependent variable produces results similar to those here for the entire period, but (as would be expected) with much higher probabilities of war.

The two major independent variables in our tests will be the type of dispute and the type of politically relevant alliance. For the first variable, we will employ the revision type variable in the MID 2.1 data of the Correlates of War Project. This variable classifies actors involved in militarized disputes from 1816 through 1992 in terms of revisionist and nonrevisionist states. The revision the former is trying to bring about by its resort to force is then classified in terms of whether it is over territory, a general foreign policy question, the regime of its opponent, or some "other" miscellaneous question (Jones, Bremer, and Singer 1996, 178). We will report the findings on "other" disputes, but not place great emphasis on them because they tend to mirror territorial disputes. This is not an accident: a previous analysis of these disputes reveals that although they are coded correctly, 3 of the 4 "other" disputes that go to war (out of the 32 disputes for which there are complete data) have an underlying territorial element (for a detailed analysis and discussion of these cases, see Vasquez and Henehan 2001, 127–33, esp. footnotes 9, 15).

For the second variable, we are generating a new measure based on the Correlates of War alliance data that determines for any given case whether the alliance ties of each disputant are politically relevant to any dispute that might occur between them. Simply put, an alliance with a major state is always relevant because it is assumed that a major state is able to project its capability beyond its own region.[4] An alliance with a minor state, however, is only seen as relevant if the alliance partner is in the same region as the target in the dyad, because it is assumed that an ally that is a minor state cannot easily project its capability beyond the region in which it is located and/or that it may not be inclined to do so. A hypothetical example may make this rule clearer: if the United States and Brazil are in a dispute and the United States has an alliance with Argentina then that alliance is relevant, since Brazil (the target in the dyad) is in the same region as the United States' ally. If Brazil has an alliance with Portugal this is not relevant, because Portugal is a minor state and is not in the same region as either Brazil or the United States. However, if Brazil had an alliance with the USSR, the latter would be relevant because the USSR is a major state. In order to make this determination, first side B is treated as the target and the relevant alliances for it are computed, and then side A is treated as the target and its relevant alliances are computed. Regions are determined by the state membership list of the Correlates of War Project with a couple of emendations to include some states in more than one region.[5]

More formally, an alliance is classified as politically relevant to a specific dispute if any of the following conditions are met:

1. If the state in question is a minor state, then any alliance it has with a major state is relevant.
2. If the state in question is a minor state, then any alliance it has with another minor state is relevant, if that minor state is in the same region as the target in the dyad. This has the effect of dropping those minor states as politically relevant allies if they are not in the region of the target of the dyad, which might happen in a large multilateral alliance.
3. If the state in question is a major state, then any alliance it has with a major state is relevant.
4. If the state in question is a major state, then any alliance it has with a minor state is only relevant if that minor state is in the same region as the target in the dyad.

Once the data on the politically relevant alliance measure were collected, then each dyadic MID was coded on the basis of:

0. Both states in the dyad are allied to each other and have no allies outside the alliance of which they are joint members
1. No [politically relevant] alliance in the dyad
2. One side has an outside alliance
3. Both sides have an outside alliance
4. Any combination of 0 and (2 or 3).

Except for category 4, this ranking is also a theoretically informed ranking of the probability of war. Given the theoretical discussion in the previous section, it was predicted that states that are allied to each other, but have no outside alliances, should not pose a threat to each other, all other factors being equal, and therefore should have the lowest probability of war. Conversely, states that are not allied to each other should have a higher probability of war, all other factors being equal. On the basis of this assumption, dyads without a politically relevant alliance would be ranked second. For all the reasons outlined earlier, a considerably higher probability of war is assumed to occur if one side has an outside alliance. Lastly, if both sides have an outside politically relevant alliance, this is assumed to have the highest probability of going to war, because each side is threatened by the other.

Category four was originally included to make the classification mutually exclusive, in a manner that would identify states that were allied with each other and that also had an outside alliance. It was felt that states that fell into this category might be of a different sort than those that were only allied to each other. States that also had an outside alliance might be states that were not really friends but foes that were using the practice of alliance making to control their rival. Having an outside alliance while being allied to a state might be seen as hedging one's bet, and also as a possible indicator of this complex phenomenon without having to make a judgment that the alliance was a *pacta de contrahendo*. Having developed this indicator, however, it was unclear on the basis of the theory where such dyads might rank in their probability of war. Obviously, it would be above 1, but how much above could not be logically derived.

In this analysis we have used the newly released Correlates of War alliance data (version 3) (Gibler and Sarkees 2002) in calculating all our alliance measures. In order to capture the correct theoretical sequence posited by the explanation, a politically relevant alliance must precede the territorial dispute; otherwise it could not be seen as increasing the probability of war. Therefore, any alliances that came into effect after the first day or after a dispute concluded are dropped from the analysis of the given MID.

## Measuring Interaction Effects

Since the analysis is concerned with examining the effects of the specific values on the revision type and politically relevant alliance variables, each category of the two variables was broken down into dummy variables. Table 1 lists the frequencies across the groupings of the two categorical indicators. It can be seen from table 1 that the most frequent MIDs in the 1816–1992 period are policy disputes (1,310), followed by territorial disputes (964), and then after a very sharp drop, regime disputes (253). "Other" disputes, as a miscellaneous category, has just under 50 cases. What is of more theoretical interest is that only 212 of 964 cases that dispute territory do so in the absence of any alliance. Most territorial disputes (410) have one outside relevant alliance partner, and a good number, but fewer (187), face a situation where both sides have an outside relevant ally.

The main thrust of this analysis, however, is to see if there is an interaction effect between the presence of territorial MIDs and politically relevant alliances. The steps-to-war explanation maintains that these are separate steps to war and that taking one in the presence of the other increases significantly the probability of a militarized interstate dispute escalating to war. The combined effect could be of two types—additive or multiplicative. An additive model posits that each independently adds to the probability of a militarized interstate dispute escalating to war. A multiplicative model posits that only when both are present is there a great increase in the probability of war. The latter model sees the increase in the probability of war as contingent on the presence of both

TABLE 1. Frequency Distribution for Revision Type and Politically Relevant Alliance Variables (COW alliance v3 data)

| | Revision Type | | | | |
| Alliance Configuration | Territory | Policy | Regime | Other | Total |
| --- | --- | --- | --- | --- | --- |
| Only allied to each other | 59 | 15 | 9 | 5 | 88 |
| No alliances | 212 | 166 | 51 | 18 | 447 |
| One side has outside alliance | 410 | 605 | 82 | 12 | 1,109 |
| Both sides have outside alliances | 187 | 374 | 73 | 4 | 638 |
| Allied to each and one outside | 96 | 150 | 38 | 10 | 294 |
| Total | 964 | 1,310 | 253 | 49 | 2,576 |

variables. The peculiar combination of territorial disputes and the presence of outside alliances in a multiplicative model is seen as having a much more explosive effect than the independent effects of territorial MIDs and politically relevant alliances, and it therefore predicts that there would be a statistical interaction between the two variables. While the explanation suggests that there is an interaction effect between the two variables, a simpler additive model would still be consistent with the logic of the explanation, although it requires a slight reformulation of the explanation.

We will test for several different types of statistical interaction. The explanation itself posits that when one or both sides have outside allies there will be a greater probability of war, because an outside alliance increases threat perception and hostility between the contending parties. The effect of both sides having an outside alliance is seen as more dangerous because it is assumed that the situation is a result of one side making an alliance and the other responding with a counteralliance. The presence of a counteralliance, rather than reducing the probability of war through balancing, is seen as increasing threat perception, hostility, and insecurity, and thereby being an additional step to war. The explanation then would posit a possible statistical interaction with territorial MIDs and *two* of the dummy alliance variables— "one side having an outside ally" and "both sides having an outside ally" with the latter having a higher probability of escalating to war than the former.[6]

To test for statistical interaction, first a base model without any interaction terms will be examined. Then interactive models will be tested, inclusive of interaction terms between territory and one side or both sides having an outside alliance. Inclusion of these interaction variables allows us to assess the contingent nature of the alliance impact; namely, whether alliance configuration effects are stronger or weaker in the presence of a territorial dispute.

Logistic regression will be used to test the hypothesis, since the dependent variable is binary (no war, war) and the analysis wants to determine the relative effects of territory (etc.) while controlling for type of alliance. To determine the relative probability of war, simulated probabilities are calculated on the basis of the logit analysis. Given the theoretical model, using this maximum likelihood technique is more appropriate than a conventional correlation analysis, especially since the independent variables being examined are posited as only increasing the probability of war and not posing a sufficient condition for war (Vasquez 1993, 9, 155, 195–96; Senese and Vasquez 2003; Vasquez and Henehan 2001).

## Controls

In addition to the two independent variables of primary interest and the interaction terms, a control for historical period will be included in the logistic regression models. To see if the post-1945 (Cold War) era is fundamentally different from others, as several explanations of international politics suggest, we explicitly consider our expectations across the pre-1946 and post-1945 historical eras. Among the most prominent of these suggestions pointing to a need for care in generalizing across eras are those focusing on the role of nuclear weapons, the alliance structure and dynamics of the Cold War struggle, and the impact of the democratic peace. It behooves us, therefore, to examine whether the impact of territorial disputes and various alliance configurations differ for the 1816–1945 and 1946–92 periods. This approach allows us to assess any differences between the two subperiods and to compare them to findings derived from the full time span.

This research design is complicated enough so we have not tested for possible counterhypotheses by introducing further controls. One such counterhypothesis, based on a selection effect argument, maintains that the inference we make from the presence of outside alliances and the increased probability of territorial disputes going to war may be invalid because studying solely MIDs is a potentially biased sample. According to this criticism, the sample is biased because the cases in it are in there for a reason (i.e., they are not randomly selected). It is possible that the factors that make dyads have MIDs in the first place may also be the variables that increase the probability of war, and not those in the model that is being tested.[7] From this perspective some other factor(s) might be seen as producing both alliances and territorial MIDs that escalate to war, and therefore controlling for that factor(s) would wipe out the relationship we test. The most likely factor that might do this is the presence of a territorial claim (or disagreement) that has not yet given rise to a militarized interstate dispute. This explanation, which is embodied in Huth (1996b), would posit that territorial claims would create alliances and MIDs and war.

While such a hypothesis is logically possible, it is not the same as the steps-to-war explanation, which sees the actions that states take *after* they have territorial claims as crucial for their involvement in war. The steps-to-war explanation clearly states that it is not territorial issues that lead to war, but how they are handled (Vasquez 1993, 124). From our theoretical perspective it only makes sense to test for counterhypotheses, such as those based on possible selection effects or spurious inference, once the hypothesized relationship has been established.

This is especially the case if there are data availability problems for testing the counterhypothesis, and earlier empirical tests of parts of the selection effect counterhypothesis have shown that selection effects do not have an impact on the results. In terms of data availability, territorial claims are available only back to 1919 (see Huth and Allee 2002). Elsewhere, we (Senese and Vasquez 2003) have use these data to test whether territorial claims both give rise to MIDs and make territorial MIDs more likely to go to war, or whether (as posited by our theory) it is territorial MIDs (not claims per se) that increase the probability of war. We do this by conducting a Heckman two-stage analysis that controls for the effect of the first stage (the onset of a militarized interstate dispute) on the second stage (the escalation of MIDs to war). We find that the variables at the first stage do not substantively affect the results of the second stage (i.e., the signs and significance remain the same). Generally, the error terms are also not correlated (rho is not significant), and the one instance where it is can be attributed to omitted variables and not to the impact of territorial claims on the escalation of a militarized interstate dispute. These results mean that territorial MIDs have a higher probability of going to war than policy or regime disputes. They imply that the increased probability of going to war is a result of how territorial claims are handled once they become militarized and not a result of their mere presence between states. Further, they suggest that while comparing MIDs that escalate to war with those that do not might logically be prone to selection effects, empirically this is not the case with regard to territory and war. Given these previous results, we confine our tests here to the behavior of states once they have militarized disputes.

### THE FINDINGS

We begin our discussion by considering the additive influences of revision type and alliance relevance over the full time span. Table 2 presents logit analyses of the base model and permits a determination of whether each of the revision type and alliance dummy variables has a statistically significant impact on the probability of a dyadic MID involving a war, without looking at any possible interaction effects. The standard technique for estimating the impact of categorical independent variables is to select one grouping of the variable as a reference (or comparison) category. The other categories of that variable are then represented by dummy indicators. Policy MIDs (the modal category) and "no alliance" have been selected as the reference categories.

As the signs and significance levels of the coefficients show, territorial, regime, and "other" disputes significantly increase the probability of a militarized interstate dispute going to war when compared to policy MIDs for the entire 1816–1992 period. These findings provide support for the steps-to-war model's expectation that territorial revision attempts will be significantly more war prone than revision attempts centered around policy disputes. A separate analysis (not reported in the table) shows that territorial disputes are also more likely to escalate to war than regime disputes.[8]

Table 2, column one, also presents the results for the impact of the various types of politically relevant alliances, compared to dyadic disputes where there are "no politically relevant alliances." We find, for the entire period, that only having "both sides with an outside politically relevant alliance" has a positive significant impact on the probability of the current MID escalating to war. For the other two outside alliance variables, there is no significant difference between the no alliance reference grouping and disputants that have either "one side with an outside alliance" or that are "allied to each other and at least one side has an outside alliance," during the full time period. The only alliance condition showing a clear pacifying effect on disputing states' tendency to wage war is when the two are formally allied to each other (and neither has an outside alliance), which is a perfect predictor of no war.

Taken together, these findings for the 1816–1992 span are partially

TABLE 2. Logistic Regression Results: Territorial Disputes, Politically Relevant Alliances, and Escalation of a Current MID to War (reference category = policy revision, no alliance)

| Base Model | | | |
|---|---|---|---|
| Variable | 1816–1992 | 1816–1945 | 1946–92 |
| Territorial revision | 1.781 (.123)*** | 1.745 (.158)*** | 2.537 (.294)*** |
| Regime/government revision | .471 (.219)** | −.045 (.401) | 1.928 (.358)*** |
| Other revision | 1.411 (.368)*** | 1.242 (.420)** | 1.418 (1.069) |
| Only allied to each other | Perfect predictor[a] | Perfect predictor | Perfect predictor |
| One side has outside alliance | .212 (.156) | .716 (.196)*** | .118 (.301) |
| Both sides have outside alliances | .440 (.173)**+ | 1.336 (.228)*** | −.309 (.345) |
| Allied to each and one outside | .012 (.209) | .555 (.271)** | .035 (.370) |
| Constant | −2.615 (.170)*** | −2.377 (.211)*** | −3.906 (.361)*** |
| Wald $\chi^2$ (df = 6) | 231.43*** | 134.98*** | 82.26*** |
| Pseudo-$R^2$ | .1038 | .1258 | .1439 |
| No. of observations | 2,488 | 1,115 | 1,373 |

*Note:* Entries are unstandardized parameter estimates; robust standard errors are in parentheses. (COW alliance v3 data)
[a]Only allied to each other is a perfect predictor of no war.
*$p \le .10$; **$p \le .05$; **+$p = .011$; ***$p \le .001$

in line with the expectations derived from the steps-to-war explanation. Territorial disputes are significantly related to conflict escalation, compared to policy disputes (the reference category); so too are regime disputes. In terms of the impact of the alliance variables, dyadic disputes where both sides have an outside alliance have a significant impact on the occurrence of war, which is a key prediction in the steps-to-war explanation. However, the other two conditions where outside alliances are present are not significantly related.

Lastly, being allied only to each other reduces the probability of war. This finding is tangential to the main hypothesis being tested in the analysis, but it does show that the friends-as-foes hypothesis does not apply to dyads that are allied only to each other. Hedging one's bet about the loyalty of a state one is allied with by making an alliance with another state can and does result in war in the right circumstances. If there are no hedges, however, then states that are truly allied only to each other can be expected to avoid war. From 1816 to 1992, this variable is a perfect predictor of no war,[9] which supports the more common notion in the literature that being allied to each other helps reduces the likelihood that a militarized interstate dispute between the two states will escalate to war (see Bremer 1992, 2000).

The tests in columns two and three control for historical era to see if there is a difference between the classic international politics 1816–1945 period and the nuclear Cold War post-1945 period. Across the two time periods there are some similarities, as well as some dissimilarities. As expected, territorial disputes are significantly more likely than policy disputes to escalate to war in each of the two historical eras. This is the most consistent finding. The same is true for "other" disputes during the full and pre–Cold War spans, which mirror territorial disputes. Interestingly, regime disputes are more likely to go to war than policy disputes only in the Cold War period. This certainly fits into a portrayal of this later period as one characterized by extreme ideological divides.

The next four rows in table 2, columns two and three, compare the various alliance classes to the reference category of no alliance. Here we see stark differences. In the 1816–1945 period, the alliance variables generally work as anticipated and are fully consistent with our theoretical expectations, unlike the findings for the full period. Having any outside ally has a significant impact on the likelihood that a given dyadic dispute will go to war compared to those dyadic disputes that do not have any politically relevant alliances. For the 1816–1945 span "only allied to each other" again reduces the chance of war. These findings support our hypothesis in that the two main independent variables, "one side having an outside alliance" and "both sides having an outside alliance," are positively and significantly related to a given MID escalating to war.

When we turn to the post-1945 period things are quite different. Here, all the alliance variables except "allied only to each other" (which is a perfect predictor of no war) are statistically insignificant. These results reveal important deviations from our expectations about the role of alliance. They suggest that in terms of alliance behavior the steps-to-war explanation best fits the classic international politics period of 1816–1945, and the nuclear Cold War period is an anomaly. Territorial disputes, however, remain more war prone than policy disputes. As a whole, the results in table 2 support the territorial explanation of war and show that in the earlier period there is at least an additive effect for the combination of territorial disputes and having any outside alliance. Before reaching any final conclusions, however, we turn to an examination of potential statistical interactions between states that have territorial disputes and an outside politically relevant alliance.

Table 3 presents the main results on the tests for statistical interaction for each of the three time periods. We have tested several different

TABLE 3. Logistic Regression Results: Interaction Test for Territorial Disputes, Politically Relevant Alliances and Escalation of a Current MID to War (reference category = policy revision, no alliance)

| Interaction Model | | | |
|---|---|---|---|
| Variable | 1816–1992 | 1816–1945 | 1946–92 |
| Territorial revision | 1.573 (.163)*** | 1.182 (.196)*** | 2.814 (.386)*** |
| Regime/government revision | .437 (.222)** | −.192 (.402) | 1.968 (.362)*** |
| Other revision | 1.356 (.367)*** | 1.098 (.406)** | 1.510 (1.079) |
| Only allied to each other | Perfect predictor[a] | Perfect predictor | Perfect predictor |
| One side has outside alliance | −.093 (.225) | −.073 (.272) | .475 (.411) |
| Both sides have outside alliances | .397 (.171)** | 1.160 (.211)*** | −.289 (.347) |
| Allied to each and one outside | −.015 (.207) | .498 (.260)*+ | .061 (.373) |
| One side has outside alliance × Territorial revision | .457 (.232)** | 1.310 (.306)*** | −.493 (.421) |
| Constant | −2.465 (.184)*** | −1.972 (.212)*** | −4.113 (.404)*** |
| Wald $\chi^2$ (df = 7) | 232.32*** | 155.85*** | 78.89*** |
| Pseudo-$R^2$ | .1055 | .1397 | .1455 |
| No. of observations | 2,488 | 1,115 | 1,373 |

*Note:* Entries are unstandardized parameter estimates; robust standard errors are in parentheses. (COW alliance v3 data)
[a]Only allied to each other is a perfect predictor of no war.
*$p \leq .10$; *+$p = .056$; **$p \leq .05$; ***$p \leq .001$

interaction models and find the most consistent to be that which includes the single interaction term of territorial MID and "one outside alliance," and only this model is reported in table 3. This model shows that there is a statistical interaction between disputing territory and having one side with an outside alliance and the likelihood that the MID will go to war. This holds for the 1816–1992 period as a whole and for 1816–1945, where the findings are particularly robust. They do not hold, however, for the post-1945 Cold War period.

These findings show that when states contend over territory and one side has an outside alliance this increases the probability of the current MID escalating to war. This interaction effect is peculiar to the presence of territorial disputes and having one side with an outside alliance. This can be seen by the interaction term wiping out the significant relationship between one side having an outside alliance and escalation to war (which was significant in table 2 for 1816–1945 at $p < .001$, but is not in table 3).

Table 3 also shows that when both sides have an outside alliance in the presence of any dispute or when they are allied to each other and also have an outside alliance there is a significant likelihood of war for only the 1816–1945 period. As will be seen later, the effect of both sides having an outside alliance when the parties are contending over territory has a probability of going to war as much as when one side has an outside alliance, but the effect for "both sides" is better seen as additive rather than multiplicative.[10]

These findings provide support for the steps-to-war explanation and show that the effects of having outside allies while contending on territorial disputes significantly increase the likelihood of war during the 1816–1945 period. While this relationship is generally additive, there is a multiplicative effect between contending on territory and one side having an outside ally. The latter findings show that it is not just territorial MIDs and "one or both sides having an outside alliance" that independently increase the likelihood of war, but it is also the peculiar combination of territorial MIDs and "one side having an outside alliance." On the basis of the second column in table 3, we can tentatively conclude that there is a statistical interaction between contending on territorial questions and the escalation to war when one side has outside allies during the 1816–1945 period. This means that for the 1816–1945 period dyads that dispute territory while one side has an outside politically relevant alliance can expect to see an explosive (multiplicative) effect on the probability of war. This evidence is consistent with our expectations and the steps-to-war explanation.

Table 3 tells a different story for the post-1945 period. Here, none of the alliance variables, including the interaction term of territorial disputes and "one side having an outside alliance" is statistically significant. In terms of the impact of "outside allies" on escalation to war, the Cold War period deviates from the theoretical expectations of the steps-to-war explanation. Despite these alliance deviations for the Cold War period, it is important to point out that the territorial effect is still quite significant during this span. Compared to policy disputes, territorial disputes (as well as regime and other disputes) are more likely to escalate to war. Likewise, dyads where the states are allied only to each other never have a war in any of the periods under study.

The findings in table 3 for outside alliances are quite clear; they appear to be very meaningful predictors of war for the 1816–1945 period, while imparting no meaningful effect after World War II. In the earlier period, when dyads have an outside alliance this significantly increases the likelihood of war when states are contending over territory. The exact nature of these effects is more appropriately discussed later through presentation of simulated probabilities of war under the varying conditions. It will suffice to say for now, however, that a dyad's alliances while contending on territorial questions do provide purposeful clues to its propensities to engage in more intense conflict from 1816 through 1945. After that they do not.

While these logit analyses reported in tables 2 and 3 reveal the general direction and statistical significance attached to the relationships of interest, they do not provide a measure of the strength of the relationship, nor what is of central interest—a substantive idea of how the probability of war might vary for the 1816–1945 and 1946–92 eras. To address these questions, it is necessary to estimate simulated probabilities for each of the combinations of categories associated with the revision type and alliance indicators across each of the temporal subperiods. This is done in table 4, which lays out the simulated probabilities of MIDs escalating to war depending on whether they are disputing territorial, policy, regime, or "other" questions in either the 1816–1992, 1816–1945, or 1946–1992 periods. The simulated probabilities are derived from the interaction models reported in table 3.[11] Table 4 examines the entire 1816–1992 period, with breakdowns for the 1816–1945 period and the post–1945 era. Column one in tables 4A, 4B, and 4C provides information about how likely war is when states dispute territory under varying conditions of alliance formation. The second row in each table can be used as a benchmark for comparison. It shows the probability for war occurring when there are no politically relevant alliances present in the dyad. The overall base probability of war for each sample is shown at the top of the table.[12] For dyads that are involved

**TABLE 4.** Simulated Probabilities of the Current Dyadic MID Escalating to War with One Interaction Term Included: Territory and One Side with an Outside Ally and All Other Dummy Variables

| Alliance Configuration | Revision Type | | | |
| --- | --- | --- | --- | --- |
| | Territory | Policy | Regime/Government | Other |
| | PERFECT—NO WAR | PERFECT—NO WAR | PERFECT—NO WAR | PERFECT—NO WAR |
| **A.** Interaction Territory—One Side Outside Ally and Dummy Variables, 1816–1992; Base Probability = 464/2,488 = .186 | | | | |
| Only allied to each other | | | | |
| No alliances | .292 | .079 | .119 | .257 |
| One side has outside alliance | .371 | .072 | .109 | .239 |
| Both sides have outside alliances | .379 | .113 | .166 | .337 |
| Allied to each and one outside | .288 | .079 | .117 | .254 |
| **B.** Interaction Territory—One Side Outside Ally and Dummy Variables, 1816–1945; Base Probability = 335/1,115 = .300 | | | | |
| Only allied to each other | | | | |
| No alliances | .312 | .124 | .109 | .299 |
| One side has outside alliance | .609 | .115 | .102 | .284 |
| Both sides have outside alliances | .593 | .311 | .276 | .569 |
| Allied to each and one outside | .427 | .188 | .166 | .409 |
| **C.** Interaction Territory—One Side Outside Ally and Dummy Variables, 1946–92; Base Probability = 129/1,373 = .094 | | | | |
| Only allied to each other | | | | |
| No alliances | .220 | .017 | .109 | .099 |
| One side has outside alliance | .212 | .027 | .162 | .142 |
| Both sides have outside alliances | .170 | .013 | .082 | .077 |
| Allied to each and one outside | .230 | .019 | .115 | .106 |

*Note:* These simulated probabilities are derived from the interaction model estimates provided in table 3; alliances must be in effect on the first day of the dispute to be counted (COW alliance v3 data).

in territorial disputes (from 1816 to 1992) but have no politically relevant alliance, the simulated probability of going to war is .292 (table 4A, column 1, row 2). If they have a politically relevant alliance of any kind, the probability of war breaking out increases substantially—to .371 if one side has an outside alliance and to .379 if both sides have an outside alliance. These are the highest probabilities of war occurring for the entire period, which is consistent with the predictions of the steps-to-war explanation in that having one or both sides with an outside alliance has a significantly higher probability of going to war than disputing territory in the absence of alliances.[13]

Two other findings relevant to the hypothesis being tested can be gleaned from table 4A. First, for policy and regime disputes, the presence of any outside alliance does not significantly increase the probability of war over disputing these issues in the absence of alliances, even though when states have both sides with outside alliances there is, technically, a higher probability of war. This suggests, contrary to our hypothesis, that the use of power politics (at least in terms of having an outside ally that presumably supports or aids a state) has no or little effect on the probability of a nonterritorial dispute escalating to war. This conclusion is not contradicted by the findings on the few "other" MIDs, since these, as noted earlier, have a territorial component.

Second, it is clear from the simulated probabilities that territorial disputes are consistently more likely to escalate to war than nonterritorial disputes. As our hypothesis predicted, territorial disputes always have higher probabilities of going to war than policy or regime disputes. Further evidence that territorial disputes are more war prone can be derived by comparing the probabilities for territorial disputes in column A with the overall base probability of war for the sample—.186—listed at the top of the table. Here, we see that even where two states dispute territory without alliances the probability of escalation to war is .292, which is higher than the base probability. Also noteworthy is that the probability of policy or regime MIDs going to war in the absence of alliances is below the base probability (.079 and .119, respectively).

Table 4B presents the findings for the 1816–1945 period. The breakdown of the sample into two periods results in the simulated probabilities for the first period going way up. This is especially the case for territorial disputes in the presence of outside politically relevant alliances. In table 4A (for the entire period) dyads that dispute territory and have one outside alliance have a probability of going to war of .371, but in the 1816–1945 period this increases to .609. Similarly, dyads that dispute territory when both sides have an outside alliance have a probability of going to war for the entire period of .379, but in the 1816–1945 period this increases to .593. This appears to be a function of the combined effect between territorial disputes and having outside allies. Note that the probability of war without any alliances does not substantially increase between the entire period and the 1816–1945 period, .292 and .312, respectively.

The evidence in columns two and three in table 4B also provides considerable support for the claim that territorial disputes are more war prone than policy or regime disputes. The probabilities in both these columns are much lower than those in the territory column. For instance, dyads contending over policy or regime disputes where both sides possess an outside politically relevant alliance have a simulated probability of escalating to war of .311 and .276, respectively; but dyads that contend over territorial disputes in which both sides have an outside alliance have a probability of .593. A comparison with the overall base probability of war for the 1816–1945 period—.300—shows that territorial MIDs have a significantly higher probability of war when any of the three outside alliance types are present (.609, .593, .427, respectively). In addition, policy and regime disputes generally have a probability of war lower than the overall base probability with the exception of "both sides having an outside alliance" (which is in the same range as the base probability).

The probabilities in table 4B on the use of power politics, in terms of having a politically relevant alliance while contending on policy or regime questions, are more complicated than those in table 4A. When both sides have outside alliances there is an increase in the probability of war compared to when policy or regime questions are disputed in the absence of alliances (.311 vs. .124 for policy disputes and .276 vs. 109 for regime disputes). When only one side has an outside alliance there is no significant effect of having an outside alliance. This pattern is partially consistent with what is predicted by the steps-to-war explanation in that both sides having an outside alliance is more war prone than just having one side with an outside alliance.[14] The findings on policy and regime disputes suggest that the use of certain alliance configurations does increase the probability of war. However, it is clear, given the lower simulated probabilities for policy and regime disputes, that the presence of outside alliances on both sides is not as dangerous as when used with territorial disputes.[15]

The evidence in tables 4A and 4B provides considerable support for both the territorial explanation of war and the steps-to-war model. The evidence is very consistent with the hypothesis that territorial disputes are more war prone than policy or regime disputes and that their probability of going to war will increase if one or both sides have an outside politically relevant alliance. Anywhere from 37 to 61 percent of these cases can be expected to go to war. The evidence also shows that the use of power politics practices, at least in terms of the presence of outside alliances, increases the probability of war when territorial disputes are under contention; when policy or regime disputes are under contention the use of power politics has this effect only when both sides have outside alliances. All of these findings are stronger for the 1816–1945 period than for the entire period, which means that they can be expected to be weaker for the post-1945 period.

Table 4C presents the findings for the post-1945 Cold War period (1946–92). The most obvious difference between this period and the rest of the sample is that the probability of war is much lower. The highest probabilities for this period are .230 (territorial disputes in the presence of being allied to each other and also having an outside alliance) compared to .609 in table 4B.[16] This finding is consistent with the absence of a major world war in the post-1945 span compared to two world wars in the earlier period. Nevertheless, for a period of intense conflict and the Korean and Vietnam Wars, the shift in the probability of war across all types of disputes is stark and underlines the comparative reduction in the amount of war.

The major difference from the 1816–1945 period in terms of our expectations is that in the post-1945 period having one side or both sides with outside alliances while contending on territorial disputes has comparatively the same probability of going to war as having no alliances while contending on territorial disputes (.212 and .170 vs. .220, respectively),[17] which is in line with the nonsignificant logit coefficients in table 3, column three. A similar pattern holds when policy and regime disputes are examined and *both* sides have an outside alliance. However, having *one* side with an outside alliance does have a slightly higher probability of war, although these probabilities are not quite significant in that they fall within the upper 90 percent confidence interval (the upper limit of no alliance: .031 and .172 for policy and regime disputes respectively).

Lastly, while there are differences between the two periods, there are certain fundamental patterns that remain despite the sharp decline in the probability of war. One of the most persistent patterns, of course, which is revealed in table 4C, is that territorial disputes always have a much higher probability of going to war than policy or regime disputes. This is true comparing the probabilities within table 4C, as well as comparing these probabilities with the overall .094 base probability for the sample. A key pattern to note when examining the overall base probability is that, overall, regime disputes are comparatively more war prone in the relatively "peaceful" Cold War period (compared to territorial and policy disputes) than regime disputes in the more war-prone 1816–1945 period. For example, the probability of regime disputes where one side has an outside ally going to war is .162 in a period with an overall base probability of war of only .094.

Nevertheless, the generally lower probabilities of war suggest that the post-1945 period is different. Whether this is a result of the presence of nuclear weapons, the complicated structure of Cold War alliances and informal alignments, the spread of joint democratic pairs, the decline of territorial disputes, or some other variable will need further study. What seems likely, however, is that changes in the effects of some of the alliance variables may be unique to the Cold War period, a period in which the strongest states avoid war despite intense rivalry and elaborate polarizing alliances.

Separating by historical era makes it clear that the overall findings for 1816–1992 in table 3 are being driven by the earlier 1816–1945 period. The simulated probabilities make it clear that the post-1945 period is quite different from the long post-Napoleonic span that precedes it, in terms of the probability of war and the role played by politically relevant alliances, but not that played by territorial disputes. In the classic international politics period of 1816 through 1945, the effects of territorial disputes and politically relevant alliances follow the pattern predicted by the steps-to-war theoretical explanation (Vasquez 1993; Senese and Vasquez 2003). This pattern changes somewhat after 1945, especially for dyads where only one side has an outside alliance. Various theories have offered explanations as to why this period is different. Suffice it to say here that this analysis has established that it is different.

Still, it is important to remember that at least one fundamental pattern remains unchanged in the 1946–92 period and remains consistent with the steps-to-war explanation. The war proneness of territorial disputes is not affected by this system shift; only the interaction between territory and the "one outside alliance" variable is greatly affected, going from a significant positive relationship with escalation to war to a random relationship.

## CONCLUSION

The findings in the preceding analysis provide theoretically significant information on the change in the probability of war breaking out depending on whether a dyadic dispute is over territory, policy, or regime questions and whether the contenders involved have an outside alliance. For instance, in the 1816–1945 period when states contending over territory have a militarized dispute and do *not* have any politically relevant alliance, the simulated probability of their going to war is .312. If one side in the dyad has an outside politically relevant alliance, the simulated probability shoots up to .609 and if both sides in the dyad have an outside alliance, the simulated probability of war is .593.

These findings provide significant support for both the territorial explanation of war and the steps-to-war model. The analysis shows that territorial disputes have a significant impact on the probability of war and that the probability of war increases if one or both sides have outside politically relevant alliances when contending over territory. There is a statistical interaction indicating a multiplicative effect between contending over territory and having one side with an outside alliance. When both sides have an outside alliance this still increases the probability of war, but the effect is additive. The classic 1816–1945 period can be seen as the natural domain for the steps-to-war explanation, and all aspects of our hypothesis fail to be falsified by our tests.

For the post-1945 period the overall probability of war goes down, and only some of the preceding patterns hold. Territorial disputes are still the most likely to result in war, even though their absolute probability of escalating is lower. In this sense, the territorial explanation of war fits this period and the previous one, and this part of our hypothesis is consistently supported by the evidence. The theoretical expectation derived from the steps-to-war explanation that having outside alliances while contending over territory would further increase the probability of war does not hold after 1945. The alliance predictions of our hypothesis have to be rejected for this period. This means that the steps-to-war explanation is less applicable to this era. More research is necessary to see if the presence of nuclear weapons (see Sample 2000) or the Cold War alliance system may be responsible for this change in the impact of alliances and whether dyads without nuclear weapons or the Cold War alliance structure behave more like dyads in the pre-nuclear era.

Overall, the findings reported in this chapter are quite promising for the theoretical approach outlined in Vasquez (1993) and Senese and Vasquez (2003). They fit the classic international politics period (1816–1945) quite strongly. The post-1945 period is more anomalous with regard to alliances, although the results show that even in this period the territorial explanation of war holds. The differences in the two periods make it clear that historical era is potentially important, even though some of the fundamentals in terms of territory will remain. This underlines the importance of controlling for time in studies of conflict dynamics, as aspects of the Cold War period appear to be truly different from the 1816 to 1945 era. This has a host of implications for data analysis: One should never fail to control for the post-1945 period, and one should never look just at the post-1945 period if one wants to generalize about the fundamentals of world politics.

## NOTES

*Authors' Note:* The research reported in this article has been supported by NSF Grant #SES-9818557. Our thanks to Chris Leskiw for research assistance, especially in compiling the data on politically relevant alliances. Our thanks also to Paul Diehl, Marie T. Henehan, T. Clifton Morgan, Richard Tucker, and William Thompson for valuable comments on earlier analyses that helped us refine the one presented here. The responsibility for the analysis remains our own

1. This differs from Smith (1995, 1996) and much work in the realist tradition.

2. Sabrosky's (1980) finding has been criticized recently for ignoring the actual terms of alliance agreements and simply operationalizing "alliance reliability" as entering a war on the side of an ally (see Leeds, Long, and Mitchell 2000).

3. Of these there are 469 MIDs that are coded as "nonapplicable," meaning that neither member of the dyad is making a revisionist claim (typically joiners to the dispute). These are dropped from the analysis, leaving 2,576 cases.

4. Major and minor states are classified according to the conventional listing of major states by the Correlates of War Project (see Small and Singer 1982, table 2.1, 47–50; Ray 1998b, 197–200).

5. For example, the Ottoman Empire and Turkey are included in both Europe and the Middle East. Russia is included in both Europe and Asia.

6. Some realists would hold that "both sides having an outside ally" would have a lower probability of escalating to war if this resulted in a balance of power than the situation of "one side having an outside ally." The steps-to-war explanation would see "both sides having an outside ally" as having a higher probability of going to war than the case of "one side having an outside ally" but would still posit the latter as having a higher probability of war than the case where no alliances were present. In a sense, the difference between some realist explanations and the steps-to-war explanation is not over the prediction of the effect of "one side having an outside ally" but whether "both sides having an outside ally" increases or decreases the probability of war in the presence of territorial MIDs.

7. On selection effects see Fearon (1994), Morrow (1989), and the special issue of *International Interactions* edited by Reed (2002).

8. The coefficient for regime disputes with territorial disputes as the reference category for the base model in table 2 is $-1.3095$, $p = .000$. This finding also holds for both the 1816–1945 and 1946–92 periods, as well as for all the

models in table 3. The highest $p$ value is .022 for the post-1946 period for the base model.

9. Because "allied only to each other" is a perfect predictor it is dropped from the logit analysis.

10. The closest the interaction term for territorial dispute and "both sides having an outside alliance" (new2out) comes to significance is for 1816–1945 ($p = .133$) when it is the sole interaction term in the model. When two interaction terms (new1xTerr and new2out) are included, territory with "one outside alliance" is a better predictor than territory with "both have outside alliances"; hence the model with just the "one outside" interaction term is reported as the best model.

11. Simulated probabilities are calculated through use of the CLARIFY software developed by Tomz, Wittenberg, and King (2001). These estimates represent the likelihood of a given militarized dispute escalating to war.

12. The base probability is calculated by looking only at the cases in the sample, which do not include observations that have missing data: (MIDs that escalate to war)/(Total MIDs in the sample).

13. This is demonstrated by the fact that both .371 and .379 do not overlap with the upper limit of the .292 probability at the 90 percent confidence interval (which ranges from .247 to .337). However, there is no significant difference between the .371 and .379, which means that having both sides with outside alliances does not produce a higher probability of war than having one side with an outside alliance as posited by the steps-to-war explanation.

14. It is not fully consistent in that having one side with an alliance does not increase the probability of war. It should also be noted that this alliance configuration does not significantly reduce the probability of war either; it simply has no impact over having no alliances. In that sense it is similar to the findings for all alliance configurations for the full period for policy and regime disputes (table 4A).

15. The results for the miscellaneous "other" category are higher than for those of policy or regime. In this they mirror somewhat those for territorial disputes, especially for "both sides having outside alliances" and "allied to each and having one outside alliance."

16. Some have suggested that as states become more mature or pairs of democratic states spread, territorial disputes will decline, which may account for the lower probability of war in the post-1945 period. In fact, the percentage of territorial disputes (territorial MIDs/total) after 1945 does decline slightly: 34.8 percent (503/1,445) vs. 40.7 percent (461/1,131) for 1816–1945 (see Henehan and Vasquez forthcoming, table 1). Most of the decline is between major-minor and minor-minor dyads.

17. These probabilities overlap at the 90 percent confidence interval. The lower and upper limits for "no alliances" are .149 to .306.

# TOWARD A SCIENTIFIC THEORY OF WAR

*Daniel S. Geller*

The scholars most frequently credited with development of the quantitative empirical study of war include Frederick Adams Woods, Alexander Baltzly, Pitirim A. Sorokin, Quincy Wright, Lewis Fry Richardson, Karl Deutsch, and J. David Singer. Of this set, the contributions of David Singer to the scientific study of international conflict will be judged as paramount. Although Woods and Baltzly (1915), Sorokin (1937), Wright (1942), and Richardson (1960) all compiled data on wars, Singer's efforts with the Correlates of War (COW) Project stand alone. Over the last four decades, the vast majority of systematic scientific analyses conducted on the subject of international conflict have employed some component of the expansive COW Project database. Today, our empirical knowledge of the factors associated with patterns of war and peace is attributable largely to the vision of David Singer.[1]

The Correlates of War Project had its genesis in 1963 with a grant from the Carnegie Corporation to the Center for Research on Conflict Resolution at the University of Michigan. A portion of this grant went to David Singer for the study of war. As did Sorokin, Wright, and Richardson, Singer and his associate Melvin Small culled historical materials for information on war—in this case the frequency, participants, duration, and battle deaths of all wars since 1816 (Singer and Small 1972; Small and Singer 1982). Additional data sets were generated dealing with militarized interstate disputes, alliance membership, diplomatic ties, geographic proximity, territorial changes, intergovernmental organizations, civil wars, and national material capabilities (inclusive of the military, economic, and demographic dimensions of power).[2]

Singer believed that with few exceptions most previous analyses on the causes of war were insufficiently systematic and rigorous. Even the work conducted by Sorokin (1937), Wright (1942), and Richardson

(1960) was of circumscribed value due to the absence of operational definitions for war (Sorokin), legalistic criteria for identifying wars (Wright), or reliability and validity of coding categories (Richardson).[3] The Correlates of War Project database was designed in a manner to avoid such problems; it focused explicitly on the issues of consistency, accuracy, and reproducibility in data generation (as is reflected by information stored in the COW Project Data Archive), and its published products include extensive details on coding rules and sources. Singer's midrange goal for the project was to produce generalizations about the conditions associated with the onset and seriousness of war that could then be replicated and verified by subsequent research. In the end, explanatory knowledge about the causes of war would be developed that could then be applied to the purpose of eliminating war.[4] Without exaggeration, it can be said that the scientific empirical study of war has its foundation in the database of David Singer's Correlates of War Project.

## EPISTEMOLOGICAL ASSUMPTIONS IN THE SCIENTIFIC STUDY OF WAR

A fundamental objective of basic scientific inquiry is to provide explanations of empirical phenomena. For David Singer and the Correlates of War Project, the objective is to provide explanations for the occurrence and characteristics of war. In conventional language, to "explain" a phenomenon is to incorporate it within a "cause and effect" sequence—or, at minimum, to locate it within a pattern of existential regularity. It is a principal ontological assumption of the scientific search for knowledge that the phenomenal universe exhibits certain patterns or regularities and that such patterns are discernible. This focus on empirical patterns is consistent with general models of scientific explanation based on either deductive-nomological or inductive-probabilistic forms of reasoning. When an explanation of a phenomenon is provided by reference to a pattern under which the phenomenon is subsumed, this is referred to as a "covering law" explanation. Although there are substantive differences in the epistemologies of empiricist philosophers such as Hans Reichenbach (1951), Richard B. Braithwaite (1953), Karl Popper (1959), Carl Hempel (1966), and Imre Lakatos (1970), all subscribe to the covering law model of explanation in one form or another.

There are two types of covering law explanations: one based on deductive-nomological reasoning and the other based on inductive-probabilistic reasoning. Both models explain events by reference to covering laws. However, the deductive-nomothetic model employs laws of universal form, whereas the inductive model uses laws of probabilistic form. Deductive explanation implies the (internal or logical) truth of the conclusion with absolute certainty; inductive explanation implies the truth of the conclusion only with a high probability. In both cases, explanations based on covering laws can be supplemented by reference to theoretical mechanisms that underlie the patterns or regularities (Popper 1959, 59; Hempel 1966, 51, 70; Elster 1983, 29). In other words, empirical covering laws—whether of universal or probabilistic form—may be accounted for by theoretical mechanisms that refer to underlying structures and processes that produce the patterns described in the laws. Theories attempt to explain these patterns or regularities and to provide a more fundamental understanding of empirical phenomena but treat these phenomena as manifestations of underlying forces governed by the theoretical principles.

Theories contain theoretical terms (internal principles) that have no empirical referents as well as observation terms that are empirical entities or properties that the theory purports to explain, predict, or retrodict. The connection between theoretical terms and observation terms is made by correspondence rules (bridge principles). These rules cross the boundary between the unobservable structures and processes of theoretical terms and the empirical referents found in observation terms. Without correspondence rules (or bridge principles), theories would have no explanatory power and would be untestable (Hempel 1966, 72–75). It should be noted that theories also may be of either deductive-nomological or probabilistic form.[5]

The epistemology of science that David Singer holds is avowedly inductive and empirical. Criticism of this epistemological approach to the scientific study of war has coalesced around a single point: the work cannot produce "causal knowledge" or a "theory" of war. This critique is explicitly articulated in the arguments of Kenneth Waltz (1979), Alexander Wendt (1987), and David Dessler (1991), as well as the school of epistemological thought known as "scientific realism"[6] (Wendt 1987, 350–55). For example, Waltz (1979, 4–7) maintains:

The "inductivist illusion". . . is the belief that truth is won and explanation achieved through the accumulation of more and more data and the examination of more and more cases. . . . The point is not to reject induction, but to ask what induction can and cannot accomplish. Induction is used at the level of hypotheses and laws rather than at the level of theories. Laws are different from theories, and the difference is reflected in the distinction between the way in which laws may be discovered and the way in which theories have to be constructed. Hypotheses may be inferred from theories. If they are confirmed quite conclusively, they are called laws. Hypotheses may also be arrived at inductively. Again, if they are confirmed quite conclusively, they are called laws. . . . Hypotheses . . . no matter how well confirmed, do not give birth to theories. . . . Laws are "facts of observation"; theories are "speculative processes introduced to explain them" [Andrade 1957, 29, 242]. . . . Theories explain laws. . . . Theories cannot be constructed through induction alone, for theoretical notions can only be invented, not discovered.[7]

Similarly, Wendt (1987, 354) argues:

Whereas the empiricist explains by generalizing about observable behavior, the [scientific] realist explains by showing how the (often unobservable) causal mechanisms which make observable regularities possible *work*.

In Dessler's (1991, 345) view:

[C]ausal knowledge cannot be captured within the confines of the [empiricist] framework. Causal explanation shows the *generative* connection between cause and effect by appealing to a knowledge of the real structures that produce the observed phenomena, and it is this generative connection that gives the notion of cause meaning beyond that of simple regularity.

This distinction between "causal" and "empirical" science is deceptive. Modern scientific empiricist epistemology—such as that of Hempel (1966)—explicitly fuses empirical covering laws with causal theories (1966, 52–53) in the development of scientific explanations. Indeed, the stated goal of Hempel's epistemology is to produce theory that explains empirical regularity in the most basic and fundamental way, utilizing unobserved entities and processes as mechanisms.

Some of the basis for this unproductive debate over the limits of induction and the creation of causal explanation resides in the preferred sequence for theory construction and empirical observation in the development of knowledge. The arguments of Waltz, Wendt, Dessler, and the scientific realists hold that causal theorizing should proceed independently of empirical inquiry, whereas scientific empiricists believe that work begins at the level of empirical observation, proceeds to the generation of empirical (deductive-nomothetic or probabilistic) laws, and ultimately moves to the level of causal theory—explaining empirical uniformities on the basis of unobserved structures and processes. As Hempel notes (1966, 75–77):

> In a field of inquiry in which some measure of understanding has already been achieved by the establishment of empirical laws, a good theory will deepen as well as broaden that understanding. First, such a theory offers a systematically unified account of quite diverse phenomena. It traces all of them back to the same underlying processes and presents the various empirical uniformities they exhibit as manifestations of one common set of basic laws. . . . The insight that such a theory gives us is much deeper than that afforded by empirical laws; . . . for the laws that are formulated at the observational level generally turn out to hold only approximately and within a limited range; whereas by theoretical recourse to entities and events under the familiar surface, a much more comprehensive and exact account can be achieved. . . . At any rate, the natural sciences have achieved their deepest and most far-reaching insights by descending below the level of familiar empirical phenomena.

In short, modern scientific empiricist epistemology—such as Hempel's—appears fully consistent with theoretical (i.e., causal) explanation based on unobserved structures and processes. However, it anticipates that theory development will follow the identification of empirical laws. It is this epistemology that has guided Singer's research program for the Correlates of War Project.

## ANALYTIC LEVELS AND EMPIRICAL PATTERNS

### Levels of Analysis

As Ray and Wang (1998, 1) observe, the "level-of-analysis" problem is one of the most important theoretical issues in the field of international politics—an issue with fundamental ontological and epistemological implications.[8] In fact, one of David Singer's principal contributions to the study of international politics is his formulation of the level-of-analysis issue and his explication of its significance for both theory construction and empirical research in the field.

The earliest discussions of war and the level-of-analysis problem are found in Waltz (1959) and Singer (1961b); however, Singer's formulation of the issue differs from that of Waltz. Waltz, in his wide-ranging exploration of the causes of war, examines explanations that derive from the characteristics of individual human beings, the internal structure of states, and the anarchic nature of the international system. These explanatory—or causal—factors are compared and contrasted in terms of their viability as answers to the question of "why do wars occur?"[9]

Singer (1961b) is the first scholar to have employed the term *level of analysis* in the study of international relations and to have explicitly touched on its implications for both theory development and empirical research. Moreover, Singer uses the concept of level of analysis to refer to the unit of observation (i.e., the unit level of the outcome or dependent variable), whereas Waltz employs level of analysis to refer to the unit of explanation (i.e., the unit level of the explanatory or causal variable). Over the years, it has been Singer's conception of the level-of-analysis issue that has dominated quantitative empirical analysis in the field of international politics, as studies are designed to search for patterns of war at different levels of observation for the dependent variable (i.e., the state, dyad, region, or international system).[10]

### Empirical Patterns

Both deductive and inductive explanations of empirical phenomena begin with the identification of patterns. For inductively oriented empirical scientists such as David Singer, the process of explanation starts with the systematic collection of data on the phenomenon in question followed by the testing of hypotheses. Once patterns or correlates have been identified, a body of empirical generalizations about the phenomenon can be articulated. Patterns or generalizations that are particularly strong and consistent are termed "empirical laws" (Hempel [1942] 1959, 350–51; 1966, 58–69).

In 1998, Geller and Singer produced a work that identified a series of strong empirical patterns relating to the onset and seriousness of war drawn from a review of more than 500 quantitative data-based studies on international conflict. Descriptions and evaluations of empirical findings on patterns of war were grouped on the basis of the analytic level of the unit of observation (i.e., the unit level of the dependent variable). The levels of state, dyad, region, and international system were employed in this meta-analysis, and empirical regularities were identified at each level. Not surprisingly, the vast majority of the studies available for review used components of the Correlates of War Project database.[11]

Following is the list of empirical uniformities on the onset and seriousness of war classified by the levels of state, dyad, region, and international system (Geller and Singer 1998, 27–28; Geller 2000, 409–45).

FACTORS INCREASING THE PROBABILITY OF THE ONSET
(OCCURRENCE/INITIATION)[12] OF WAR

## *Level of Analysis: State*

*Power Status*
Empirical pattern: The higher the power status of a state, the greater
the probability of its war involvement.

*Power Cycle*
Empirical pattern: Passage through a critical point in the power cycle
increases the probability of war involvement for a major power.

*Alliance*
Empirical pattern: The greater the number of a state's alliance ties, the
higher the probability of its war involvement.

*Borders*
Empirical pattern: The greater the number of a state's borders, the
higher the probability of its war involvement.

## *Level of Analysis: Dyad*

*Contiguity/Proximity*
Empirical pattern: The presence of a contiguous land or sea (separated
by 150 miles of water or less) border increases the probability of war
within a dyad.

*Political Systems*
Empirical pattern: The absence of joint democratic governments increases the probability of war within a dyad.

*Economic Development*
Empirical pattern: The absence of joint advanced economic systems increases the probability of war within a dyad.

*Capability Balance*
Empirical pattern: The presence of parity in capabilities or shifts toward parity increases the probability of war within a dyad.

*Alliances*
Empirical pattern: Dyads where only one member has an external alliance tie have a higher probability of war than dyads where both
members have external ties.

*Enduring Rivalry*
Empirical pattern: The presence of an enduring rivalry increases the probability of war within a dyad.

## *Level of Analysis: Region*

*Contagion/Diffusion*
Empirical pattern: The presence of an ongoing war increases the probability of subsequent war within the same region.

## *Level of Analysis: International System*

*Hierarchy*
Empirical pattern: The presence of an unstable hierarchy among the major powers of the international system increases the probability of both major power and systemic wars.

*Number of Borders*
Empirical pattern: The greater the number of total borders in the international system, the higher the number of war participations in the system.

*Frequency of Civil/Revolutionary Wars*
Empirical pattern: The greater the frequency of civil/revolutionary wars in the international system, the higher the frequencies of interstate disputes and wars in the system.

FACTORS INCREASING THE PROBABLE SERIOUSNESS
(MAGNITUDE/ DURATION/SEVERITY)[13] OF WAR

## *Level of Analysis: State*

*Power Status*
Empirical pattern: The higher the power status of a state, the greater the probability of its involvement in severe wars.

## *Level of Analysis: International System*

*Alliance*
Empirical pattern: The presence of polarized alliances increases the probability of the seriousness (magnitude/duration/severity) of war.

In the epistemology of modern inductive science, the identification of these strong empirical patterns of war at multiple levels of analysis is a step toward the development of a scientifically derived theory of international conflict.

## TOWARD A SCIENTIFIC THEORY OF WAR

David Singer has long maintained that explanatory knowledge resides at the apex of the processes of science and that an understanding of the factors and forces that move nations into conflict constitutes a basic goal in the study of war (e.g., Singer 1976, 1979b, 1979c, 1980a, 1980b, 1986, 1995, 2000). As early as 1970, Singer speculated as to how that explanation might be shaped. Specifically, he postulated that state attributes, relational characteristics within dyads, and system-level attributes might combine in creating the conditions for war:

> It will almost certainly turn out that certain attributes do indeed make some nations more war-prone than others. . . . I would, on the other hand, expect that these attributes—in order to exercise any consistent and powerful effect—have to interact with certain *relational* variables and with the attributes of the international system at the moment. A nation must, in a sense, be in the "right" setting if it is to get into war. Finally, there is little doubt that all of these ecological factors will have to be taken into account . . . if we are ever to understand the dynamic processes of behavior and interaction which are so large a part of conflict. (1970b, 537)

Twenty-three years later, John Vasquez (1993) provided an inductive explanation of "rivalry wars" based on empirical generalizations drawn from multiple analytic levels—just as Singer had postulated. Vasquez frames his explanation in terms of a series of "steps" that culminate in war. He maintains that rivalry wars (i.e., wars between states equal in material capabilities) begin over territorial disputes. Realist foreign policy practices designed to demonstrate resolve and increase power lead to an escalation of the dispute, enhancing the position of hard-line policy proponents in both governments. As tension increases, further provocative steps are taken until one side initiates violence. These wars have, in specific cases, expanded beyond their original participants to become world wars. World wars occur through a diffusion process produced by the conjunction of three system-level attributes: a multipolar distribution of capabilities, a polarized (tight, two-bloc) alliance structure, and approximate parity in capabilities between the two blocs. According to Vasquez, world wars are only a special class of rivalry wars—subject to the same causal processes but expanding as a result of the confluence of the three system-level conditions. Thus, Vasquez has provided a compelling, empirically derived explanation for subsets of both dyadic and multistate wars based on a series of factors linked in a causal sequence.[14]

As is reflected in the work of Vasquez, there is a growing recognition of the complexity of certain types of social phenomena, and this has led to discussion among social scientists of a process termed "multiple conjunctural causality." In this process, events are the product of the intersection of several factors, and a given event can occur through several different causal paths (Levy 2000, 325). These discussions of complex conjunctive causality frequently refer, as an example, to the phenomenon of war. In retrospect, it seems that as early as 1970 David Singer intuited the direction that causal theorizing on war would take three decades later.

## Determinism, Probabilism, and the Causes of War

War is a rare event (Bremer 1995, 17; 2000, 24; Beck, King, and Zeng 2000, 22), and Stuart Bremer (1995, 18) argues that this implies something important about its causation—specifically, that it is the result of a particular or unusual concatenation of a large number of factors. He concludes that models of war that assume simple, deterministic causality will find less support in empirical analyses than models that incorporate chance and uncertainty and thus reflect the underlying complexity of this social phenomenon (12).

Fearon (1996) explores a similar line of reasoning. He speculates that certain social processes may be simultaneously characterized by both predictability and chaos: there may be a high degree of statistical regularity for a given class of phenomena, but an individual case within that class may be inherently unpredictable. For example, Helmbold (1998) demonstrates that the number of global war initiations from 1820 through 1979 is accurately represented as a Poisson process with an average rate of 0.7098 interstate war initiations per calendar year. Projecting this pattern into the twenty-first century, Helmbold predicts approximately seven interstate wars to begin in the decade 2000–2009. However, this pattern does not permit predictions about where those wars will be fought or who the participants will be. Of course, other patterns have been discovered about the probabilities of war between specific states that suggest the identities of the likely participants in those future wars. Here, Diehl and Goertz (2000, 61) examine the distributions and probabilities of conflict for rival and nonrival dyads and conclude that between 1816 and 1992 approximately 49 percent of all wars during that period occur between rival states. Goertz (1994, 208–12) calculates that enduring rivals are eight times more likely than nonrival dyads to engage in war. Therefore, a list of enduring rivals active in the year 2000 would provide a probability estimate of those dyads most likely to engage in the wars that do occur in the decade 2000–2009. However, this prediction would be irreducibly probabilistic (King, Keohane, and Verba 1994, 87), and it remains possible that no amount of information would ever permit the point prediction of a specific war—war may possess the simultaneous properties of both regular empirical patterns in general classes and extreme contingency in single events. In short, some types of social phenomena, including specific wars, may reveal an inherently limited predictability (Geller and Singer 1998).[15]

## Multiple Convergent Causal Conditions and War

The observation that wars result from a conjunction of conditions or factors is becoming more commonplace (e.g., Vasquez 1993, 1995; Bremer 1995; Wayman 1995; Geller and Singer 1998; Leng 1999; Levy 2000; Lebow 2000; Russett and Oneal 2001). As Vasquez (2000, 367) notes, the phenomenon of war is so complex that important variables—while not sufficient conditions for war—may be critical in increasing the probability of war, and it is only when multiple factors that increase the probability of war combine that war actually occurs. The same general principle guides the observation by Oneal and Russett (1999, 227) that "an understanding of any war . . . demands not a uni-causal approach but a multivariate explanation."[16]

This process of complex conjunctive causality in the occurrence of certain types of social phenomena was described explicitly by Charles Ragin (1987, 25):

> It is the intersection of a set of conditions in time and space that produces many of the large-scale qualitative changes, as well as many of the small-scale events, that interest social scientists, not the separate or independent effects of these conditions. . . . The basic idea is that a phenomenon or a change emerges from the intersection of appropriate preconditions. . . . This conjunctural or combinatorial nature is a key feature of causal complexity.

Hirschman (1970, 343) makes this argument with regard to the Russian Revolution of 1917, and, more recently, Lebow (2000, 610) presents a similar thesis dealing with the onset of World War I. However, both Hirschman and Lebow discount the value of quantitative empirical analysis as a method for understanding specific large-scale events involving social change. In contrast, King, Keohane, and Verba (1994, 10–12) note that scientific generalizations are applicable to understanding even highly unusual events that do not fall within a class of similar occurrences, and they argue that probabilistic generalizations can be useful in studying even "unique" events. Indeed, empirically derived generalizations identifying convergent causal conditions have been applied in explanations of the Iran-Iraq War of 1980 (Geller and Singer 1998), World War I (Vasquez 1993; Geller and Singer 1998; Thompson 2003), and World War II (Vasquez 1996, 1998).

In summary, there is a developing consensus on the need for a scientific explanation of war based on conjunctural causation—war understood in terms of convergent or intersecting conditions. However, it is also frequently maintained that any of several combinations of conditions might produce a given social outcome (Ragin 1987, 25)—that the complexity of certain social phenomena (such as war) is due not only to the conjunctural nature of social causation, but also to the possibility that multiple combinations of factors or conditions may produce the same outcome. This property of certain types of social phenomena is referred to as "multiple causation" or "equifinality" (King, Keohane, and Verba 1994, 87). As Ragin (1987, 26) argues, it is the conjunctive and often complex combinatorial nature of social causation that makes it so difficult to unravel the sources of major events in human affairs. In fact, if wars occur according to a multiple conjunctural causative mechanism, then the conception of necessary and/or sufficient causation in war may have to be eliminated, since no factor may be *either* necessary or sufficient for war (King, Keohane, and Verba 1994, 87; Bremer 1995, 21). This line of reasoning has led to four attempts to construct empirically derived explanations of specific wars based on the process of multiple conjunctural causation.

## Scientific Explanation of Specific Wars

Scientific explanation of particular events involves the identification of general or "covering laws" that govern those events. Empiricist philosophers such as Hempel, Popper, Braithwaite, Reichenbach, and Lakatos all refer to explanation by means of a covering law model. Hempel ([1942] 1959, 347) extends this argument close to the radical limit established by David Hume ([1748] 1894) in stating that "every 'causal explanation' is an 'explanation by scientific laws'; for in no other way than by reference to empirical laws can the assertion of a causal connection between certain events be scientifically substantiated." This position serves as the foundation for empiricist explanations of phenomena in the physical, biological, and social sciences (Guttenplan and Tamny 1971, 344). Similarly, King, Keohane, and Verba (1994, 42–43)—in their discussion of the basis for understanding "unique" historical events—contend that the best way to understand a particular event may be through the application of the methods of scientific inference to systematic patterns in similar parallel events.[17]

Scientifically derived inductive explanations of specific historical wars based on the identification of generalized patterns of war have been produced by Vasquez (1993, 1996, 1998a) and Geller and Singer (1998). These explanations emphasize the complex combinatorial nature of causation in war and describe World War I, World War II, and the Iran-Iraq War of 1980 in terms of multiple convergent or conjunctural conditions. The explanations demonstrate that these wars were specific instances of a conjunction of factors that have appeared in a larger number of cases, and, although the wars were not inevitable, they were high-probability events consistent with a broad array of empirical patterns.

## CONCLUSION

Future research may uncover a simple causal condition for war and refute the argument that wars are the product of multiple conjunctural causation. However, be that as it may, it appears that David Singer's approach toward developing an empirically grounded theory of war is progressing precisely along the lines that he framed in 1970. The research program designed by Singer for the Correlates of War Project to produce descriptive, predictive, and explanatory knowledge on international conflict is advancing in all three areas. The success of this research program is also illustrative of a broad principle of scientific epistemology: that the presumptive separation of description, generalization, and theory construction in modern empirical science—as argued by Waltz, Wendt, Dessler, and the scientific realists—is demonstrably wrong.

## NOTES

My thanks to Paul F. Diehl for his valuable comments on an early draft of this chapter. However, I am solely responsible for the views presented here.

1. See Midlarsky (2000b, 329). In addition to his work in developing the COW Project database, Singer and his initial set of collaborators produced

some of the earliest and most important large-scale quantitative empirical analyses on the war effects of: alliances (Singer and Small 1966b, 1968a), intergovernmental organizations (Singer and Wallace 1970), system-level capability concentration (Singer, Bremer, and Stuckey 1972), national cycles (Singer and Cusack 1981), and regime type (Small and Singer 1976).

2. There are numerous descriptions of the Correlates of War Project outlining its inception and development, ontological and epistemological assumptions, published works, and data sets. A few examples include Singer and Small (1972), Singer (1979b, 1980a, 1980b, 1990b), Russett (1979), Deutsch (1980), Small and Singer (1982), Vasquez (1987, 1993), Merritt and Zinnes (1990), Gochman (1990), Small (1990), Gochman and Sabrosky (1990), and Diehl (1992).

3. Merritt and Zinnes (1990, vi–vii).

4. Over the years, Singer has expressed the hope that such scientifically derived knowledge on war would be used by government leaders to produce better-formulated policy and minimize human suffering (Singer 1990a). This goal guided the studies found in Singer and Wallace (1979) and Singer and Stoll (1984).

5. See Hempel (1966, 68–69) for examples of probabilistic theories. See Geller and Singer (1998, 13–16) for a comparison of deductive and inductive forms of reasoning.

6. Characteristic of works from this perspective are Bhaskar (1979) and Wylie (1986).

7. See Vasquez (1987, 111–16) for an excellent discussion of Waltz's critique of induction. See also Chan (2002, 750) on this subject.

8. See Ray (1998b, 508–13) for a discussion of various aspects of the level-of-analysis issue, including the problem of cross-level inference.

9. Waltz (1979) elaborates his arguments and refines his analysis in a later work, arguing that answers to this question of "why war?" drawn from analytic levels below that of the international system are reductionist, and that while factors at lower levels may be useful in understanding the causes of particular wars or grasping the forces that shape foreign policy, only factors at the systemic level can provide a basic answer to the system-level question of "why do wars occur?"

10. See the tables of studies by unit of observation (i.e., unit level of the dependent variable) in Geller and Singer (1998, appendix 2, 197–201).

11. Geller and Singer (1998, appendix 2).

12. The Correlates of War Project defines an international war as a military conflict waged between national entities, at least one of which is a state, that results in at least 1,000 battle deaths of military personnel. The following definitions apply to these terms.

*War Occurrence:* A dichotomous variable indicating either the presence or absence of war for the unit of observation.

*War Initiation:* The war initiator is the state that started the actual fighting or first seized territory or property interests of another state.

13. The following definitions apply to these terms.

*War Magnitude:* The sum of all participating nations' separate months of active involvement in each war.
*War Duration:* The length in months from the inception of the war to its termination.
*War Severity:* Total battle deaths of military personnel in each war.

14. Vasquez (2002) offers empirical evidence consistent with an expanded version of his dyadic steps-to-war explanation: here he shows the increasing probability of war for dyads with the presence of a territorial dispute, external alliances, and an enduring rivalry over territory or some other issue.

15. Geller and Singer (1998, 195) propose that whereas structural factors shape the regular empirical patterns in general classes of war, limits to the predictability of specific wars may well reside in the element of human choice—which renders the final step to war indeterminate.

16. See also Russett and Oneal (2001, 176–77) and Wayman (1995, 251).

17. See also King, Keohane, and Verba (1994, 10–12), Fearon (1996, 58–59), and Garfinkel (1981, chap. 1).

# REFERENCES

Abramowitz, Milton, and Irene Stegun. 1966. *Handbook of mathematical functions.* National Bureau of Standards Applied Mathematics Series No. 55. Fifth printing, with corrections. Washington, DC: U.S. Government Printing Office.

Achen, Christopher H. 1986. *The statistical analysis of quasi-experiments.* Berkeley: University of California Press.

———. 2002. Toward a new political methodology: Microfoundations and ART. *Annual Review of Political Science,* vol. 5, ed. Nelson Polsby, 423–50. Palo Alto, CA: Annual Reviews, Inc.

Aldrich, John H., and Forrest D. Nelson. 1984. *Linear probability, logit, and probit models.* Newbury Park, CA: Sage.

Altfeld, Michael F. 1984. The decision to ally: A theory and a test. *Western Political Quarterly* 37:523–44.

Andrade, E. N. de C. 1957. *An approach to modern physics.* New York: Doubleday.

Ardrey, Robert. 1966. *The territorial imperative.* New York: Atheneum.

Axtell, Robert. 1999. The emergence of firms in a population of agents: Local increasing returns, unstable Nash equilibria, and power law size distributions. Center on Social and Economic Dynamics, Brookings Institution, Washington, DC.

Babst, Dean. 1972. A force for peace. *Industrial Research* (April): 55–58.

Badii, Remo, and Antonio Politi. 1997. *Complexity: Hierarchical structures and scaling in physics.* Cambridge: Cambridge University Press.

Bak, Per. 1996. *How Nature Works.* New York: Springer-Verlag.

Balch-Lindsay, Dylan, and Andrew J. Enterline. 2000. Killing time: The world politics of civil war duration, 1820–1992. *International Studies Quarterly* 44 (4): 615–42.

Barabási, Albert-László, and Réka Albert. 1999. Emergence of scaling in random networks. *Science* 286:509–12.

Barnard, E., and C. Botha. 1993. Back-propagation uses prior information efficiently. *IEEE Trans Neural Networks* 4:794–802.

Beck, Nathaniel, and Jonathan Katz. 2001. Throwing the baby out with the bathwater. *International Organization* 55:487–75.

Beck, Nathaniel, Jonathan N. Katz, and Richard Tucker. 1998. Taking time seriously in binary time-series-cross-section analysis. *American Journal of Political Science* 42:1260–88.

Beck, Nathaniel, Gary King, and Langche Zeng. 2000. Improving quantitative studies of international conflict: A conjecture. *American Political Science Review* 94:21–35.

Bengio, Yoshio. 1996. *Neural networks for speech and sequence recognition.* London: International Thomson Computer Press.

Bennett, D. Scott. 1997. Testing alternative models of alliance duration, 1816–1984. *American Journal of Political Science* 41:846–78.

Bennett, D. Scott, and Allan Stam III. 2000a. EUGene: A conceptual manual. *International Interactions* 26:179–204.

———. 2000b. Research design and estimator choices for analyzing interstate dyads: When decisions matter. *Journal of Conflict Resolution* 44:653–79.

———. 2000c. A universal test of an expected utility theory of war. *International Studies Quarterly* 44:451–80.

Berry, Brian, and Allen Pred. 1965. *Central place studies.* Philadelphia: Regional Science Research Institute.

Bhaskar, Roy. 1979. *The possibility of naturalism.* Brighton, UK: Harvester Press.

Bishop, Christopher. 1996. *Neural networks for pattern recognition.* Oxford: Clarendon.

Blanco, A., M. Delgato, and M. C. Pegalajar. 2000. A genetic algorithm to obtain the optimal recurrent neural network. *International Journal of Approximate Reasoning* 23:67–83.

Braithwaite, Richard B. 1953. *Scientific explanation: A study of the function of theory, probability and law in science.* Cambridge: Cambridge University Press.

Brecher, Michael, and Jonathan Wilkenfeld. 1997. *A study of crisis.* Ann Arbor: University of Michigan Press. Reprinted in paperback with CD-Rom, 2000.

Bremer, Stuart A. 1980. National capabilities and war proneness. In *The correlates of war: II. Testing some realpolitik models,* ed. J. David Singer, 57–82. New York: Free Press.

———. 1992. Dangerous dyads: Conditions affecting the likelihood of interstate war. *Journal of Conflict Resolution* 36:309–41.

———. 1995. Advancing the scientific study of war. In *The process of war,* ed. Stuart A. Bremer and Thomas R. Cusack, 1–33. Amsterdam: Gordon and Breach.

———. 2000. Who fights whom, when, where, and why? In *What do we know about war?* ed. John A. Vasquez, 23–36. Lanham, MD: Rowman and Littlefield.

Breslow, Norman. 1996. Statistics in epidemiology: The case-control study. *Journal of the American Statistical Association* 91:14–28.

Bueno de Mesquita, Bruce. 1978. Systemic polarization and the occurrence and duration of war. *Journal of Conflict Resolution* 22:241–67.

## References

———. 1981. *The war trap.* New Haven: Yale University Press.

Bueno de Mesquita, Bruce, and David Lalman. 1988. Systemic and dyadic explanations of war. *World Politics* 41:1–20.

———. 1992. *War and reason: Domestic and international imperatives.* New Haven: Yale University Press.

Bueno de Mesquita, Bruce, and James D. Morrow. 1999. Sorting through the wealth of notions. *International Security* 24:56–73.

Bueno de Mesquita, Bruce, James D. Morrow, Randolph M. Siverson, and Alastair Smith. 1999. An institutional explanation of democratic peace. *American Political Science Review* 93:791–807.

———. 2001. Testing the selectorate explanation of the democratic peace. Hoover Institution Working paper.

Bueno de Mesquita, Bruce, and J. David Singer. 1973. Alliances, capabilities, and war: A review and synthesis. In *Political science annual: An international review,* vol. 4, ed. Cornelius Cotter, 237–80. Indianapolis: Bobbs-Merrill.

Bueno de Mesquita, Bruce, and Randolph M. Siverson. 1993. War and the survival of political leaders: A comparative analysis. Presented at the Annual Meeting of the American Political Science Association, Washington, DC.

———. 1995. War and the survival of political leaders: A comparative study of regime types and political accountability. *American Political Science Review* 89:841–55.

———. 1996. Inside-out: A theory of domestic political institutions and the issues of international conflict. Working paper, Hoover Institution.

Bueno de Mesquita, Bruce, Alastair Smith, Randolph M. Siverson, and James D. Morrow. 2003. *The logic of political survival: Institutional incentives for governance.* Cambridge, MA: MIT Press.

Burkhart, Ross, and Michael Lewis-Beck. 1994. Comparative democracy: The economic development thesis. *American Political Science Review* 88:903–10.

Cederman, Lars-Erik. 1997. *Emergent actors in world politics.* Princeton: Princeton University Press.

———. 2001. Modeling the democratic peace as a Kantian selection process. *Journal of Conflict Resolution* 45:470–502.

Chan, Steve. 2002. On different types of international relations scholarship. *Journal of Peace Research* 39:747–56.

Chi, H. 1968. The Chinese warlord system as an international system. In *New Approaches to International Relations,* ed. Morton Kaplan, 403–25. New York: St. Martin's.

Cioffi-Revilla, Claudio. 1991. The long-range analysis of war. *Journal of Interdisciplinary History* 21:603–29.

———. 1996. Origins and evolution of war and politics. *International Studies Quarterly* 40:1–44.

———. 1998. *Politics and uncertainty: Theory, models, and applications.* Cambridge: Cambridge University Press.

————. 2000a. Power laws of modern warfare. Working paper. Colorado Center for Chaos and Complexity (C4), CIRES, University of Colorado, Boulder, November.

————. 2000b. War and warfare: Scales of conflict in long-range analysis. In *World system history: The social science of long-term change*, ed. Robert A. Denemark, Jonathan Friedman, Barry K. Gills, and George Modelski, 253–72. London: Routledge.

————. 2003. Many, some, few: A primer in power laws in the social sciences. Workshop on "Power Laws in the Social Sciences." Center for Social Complexity, George Mason University, Fairfax, VA, October 23–24.

Cioffi-Revilla, Claudio, and David Lai. 1995. War and politics in ancient China, 2700 B.C. to 722 B.C.: Measurement and comparative analysis. *Journal of Conflict Resolution* 39:467–94.

————. 2001. Chinese warfare and politics in the ancient East Asian international system, ca. 2700 B.C. to 722 B.C. *International Interactions* 26:1–32.

Cioffi-Revilla, Claudio, and John B. Rundle. 1999. Exploring nonlinear dynamics of extreme events in driven threshold systems. Working paper, Colorado Center for Chaos and Complexity (C4), Cooperative Institutes for Research in Environmental Sciences (CIRES), University of Colorado, Boulder, Dec. 9.

————. 2000. Modeling extreme events and scaling in driven threshold systems. Working paper. Colorado Center for Chaos and Complexity (C4), Cooperative Institutes for Research in Environmental Sciences (CIRES), University of Colorado, Boulder, December.

Claude, Inis L. 1962. *Power and international relations*. New York: Random House.

Clemens, Walter C., and J. David Singer. 2000. The human cost of war. *Scientific American* (June): 56–57.

Clinton, William. 1996. *A national security strategy of engagement and enlargement*. Washington, DC: U.S. Government Printing Office.

Collier, Paul, and Anke Hoeffler. 1998. On economic causes of civil war. *Oxford Economic Papers* 50:563–73.

Collier, Paul, Anke Hoeffler, and Mans Soderbom. 2001. On the duration of civil war. Typescript. Washington, DC: World Bank, Development Economic Research Group.

Congalton, Russell, and Kass Green. 1999. *Assessing the accuracy of remotely sensed data: Principles and practices*. London: Lewis.

Coplin, William, and Charles S. Kegley, eds. 1975. *Analyzing international relations: A multi-method introduction*. New York: Praeger.

Davis, Lawrence. 1991. *Handbook of genetic algorithms*. New York: Van Nostrand Reinhold.

Dessler, David. 1991. Beyond correlations: Toward a causal theory of war. *International Studies Quarterly* 35:337–55.

Deutsch, Karl W. 1980. An interim summary and evaluation. In *The correlates of war: II. Testing some realpolitik models,* ed. J. David Singer, 287–95. New York: Free Press.

Deutsch, Karl W., and J. David Singer. 1964. Multipolar power systems and international stability. *World Politics* 16:390–406.

Diehl, Paul F. 1992. The Correlates of War Project: A bibliographic essay, 1961–1991. *International Studies Notes* 17:21–33.

———. 1994. Substitutes or complements?: The effects of alliances on military spending in major power rivalries. *International Interactions* 19:159–76.

Diehl, Paul F., and Gary Goertz. 2000. *War and peace in international rivalry.* Ann Arbor: University of Michigan Press.

Diehl, Paul, et al. 2000. *Updating the militarized dispute data set.* Proposal to the National Science Foundation.

Dixon, William. 1993. Democracy and the peaceful settlement of international conflict. *Journal of Conflict Resolution* 37:42–68.

Eckhardt, William. 1992. *Civilizations, empires, and wars: A quantitative history of war.* Jefferson, NC: McFarland.

Elman, Miriam Fendius. 1997. Testing the democratic peace theory. In *Paths to peace: Is democracy the answer?* ed. Miriam Fendius Elman, 473–506. Cambridge: MIT Press.

Elster, Jon. 1983. *Explaining technical change: A case study in the philosophy of science.* Cambridge: Cambridge University Press.

Eulau, Heinz. 1996. *Micro-macro dilemmas in political science: Personal pathways through complexity.* Norman: University of Oklahoma Press.

Evangelista, M. 1999. *Unarmed forces: The transnational movement to end the Cold War.* Ithaca: Cornell University Press.

Fearon, James D. 1994. Signaling vs. the balance of power and interests: An empirical test of a crisis bargaining model. *Journal of Conflict Resolution* 38:236–69.

———. 1996. Causes and counterfactuals in social science: Exploring an analogy between cellular automata and historical processes. In *Counterfactual thought experiments in world politics: Logical, methodological, and psychological perspectives,* ed. Philip E. Tetlock and Aaron Belkin, 39–67. Princeton: Princeton University Press.

Foody, G. M. 1995. Training pattern replication and weighted allocation in artificial neural network classification. *Neural Computing and Applications* 3:178–90.

Foody, G. M., M. B. McCulloch, and W. B. Yates. 1995. The effect of training set size and the composition on artificial neural network classification. *International Journal of Remote Sensing* 16:170–77.

Fukuyama, Francis. 1992. *The end of history and the last man.* New York: Free Press.

Futing Liao, Tim. 1994. *Interpreting probability models: Logit, probit, and other generalized linear models.* Sage University Paper series, Quantitative Applications in the Social Sciences, 07-101. Thousand Oaks, CA: Sage.

Garfinkel, Alan. 1981. *Forms of explanation.* New Haven: Yale University Press.

Garson, G. David. 1991. A comparison of neural network and expert systems algorithms with common multivariate procedures for analysis of social science data. *Social Science Computer Review* 9:399–433.

———. 1998. *Neural networks: An introductory guide for social scientists.* London: Sage.

Gartzke, Erik. 1998. Kant we all just get along: Opportunity, willingness, and the origins of the democratic peace. *American Journal of Political Science* 42:1–27.

Geller, Daniel S. 2000. Explaining war: Empirical patterns and theoretical mechanisms. In *Handbook of war studies II,* ed. Manus I. Midlarsky, 407–49. Ann Arbor: University of Michigan Press.

Geller, Daniel S., and J. David Singer. 1998. *Nations at war: A scientific study of international conflict.* Cambridge: Cambridge University Press.

Gelpi, Christopher, and Michael Griesdorf. 2001. Winners or losers? Democracies in international crisis, 1918–94. *American Political Science Review* 95:633–47.

George, Alexander L. 1997. *Bridging the gap: Theory and practice in foreign policy.* Washington, DC: United States Institute of Peace Press.

Gibler, Douglas M. 1996. Alliances that never balance: The territorial settlement treaty. *Conflict Management and Peace Science* 15:75–97.

———. 1997a. Control the issue, control the conflict: The effects of alliances that settle territorial issues on interstate rivalry. *International Interactions* 22:341–68.

———. 1997b. Reconceptualizing the alliance variable: An empirical typology of alliances. Ph.D. diss., Vanderbilt University.

———. 1999. An extension of the Correlates of War formal alliance data set: 1648–1815. *International Interactions* 25:1–28.

———. 2000. Alliances: Why some cause war and why others cause peace. In *What Do We Know about War?* ed. John A. Vasquez, 145–64. Lanham, MD: Rowman and Littlefield.

———. 2003. Coding manual for version 2.0 of the Correlates of War formal interstate alliance data set, 1816–2000. Lexington: University of Kentucky.

Gibler, Douglas M., and Meredith Sarkees. 2002. Coding manual for v3.0 of the Correlates of War formal interstate alliance data set, 1816–2000. Typescript.

Gibler, Douglas M., and John A. Vasquez. 1998. Uncovering the dangerous alliances, 1495–1980. *International Studies Quarterly* 42:785–807.

Gleditsch, Nils Petter. 1995. Geography, democracy, and peace. *International Interactions* 20:297–323.

Gochman, Charles S. 1990. Prometheus bound: The state and war. In *Prisoners of war? Nation-states in the modern era,* ed. Charles S. Gochman and Alan N. Sabrosky, 287–308. Lexington, MA: Lexington Books.

Gochman, Charles S., and Zeev Maoz. 1984. Militarized interstate disputes, 1816–1976: Procedures, patterns, and insights. *Journal of Conflict Resolution* 28:585–615.

## References

Gochman, Charles S., and Alan N. Sabrosky. 1990. Prisoners of war? A preview. In *Prisoners of war? Nation-states in the modern era*, ed. Charles S. Gochman and Alan N. Sabrosky, 3–8. Lexington, MA: Lexington Books.

Goertz, Gary. 1994. *Contexts of international politics*. Cambridge: Cambridge University Press.

Goertz, Gary, and Paul F. Diehl. 1992. *Territorial changes and international conflict*. London: Routledge.

Goodman, Leo A., and William H. Kruskal. 1963. Measure of association for cross classification III: Approximate sampling theory. *Journal of the American Statistical Association* 58 (302): 310–64.

Gowa, Joanne. 1999. *Ballots and bullets: The elusive democratic peace*. Princeton: Princeton University Press.

Green, Donald, Soo Yeon Kim, and David Yoon. 2001. Dirty pool. *International Organization* 55:441–68.

Greene, William H. 2003. *Econometric analysis*. 5th ed. Upper Saddle River, NJ: Prentice-Hall.

Gurr, Ted R. 1970. *Why Men Rebel*. New Haven: Yale University Press.

Gurr, Ted R., and Keith Jaggers. 2000. *Polity98 Project: Regime characteristics, 1800–1998*. College Park: University of Maryland. http://www.cidcm.umd.edu/inscr/polity.

Guttenplan, Samuel D., and Martin Tamny. 1971. *Logic*. New York: Basic Books.

Hanushek, Eric A., and John E. Jackson. 1977. *Statistical methods for social scientists*. San Diego: Academic Press.

Heckman, James D. 1979. Sample selection bias as a specification error. *Econometrica* 47:153–62.

Hegre, Håvard, Tanja Ellingsen, Scott Gates, and Nils Petter Gleditsch. 2001. Toward a democratic civil peace? Democracy, political change, and civil war, 1816–1992. *American Political Science Review* 95:33–48.

Helmbold, Robert. 1998. How many interstate wars will there be in the decade 2000–2009? *Phalanx* 31 (3): 21–23.

Hempel, Carl G. [1942] 1959. The function of general laws in history. In *Theories of history*, ed. Patrick Gardiner, 344–56. Glencoe, IL: Free Press.

———. 1966. *Philosophy of natural science*. Englewood Cliffs, NJ: Prentice-Hall.

Henderson, Errol. 1998. The democratic peace through the lens of culture, 1820–1989. *International Studies Quarterly* 42:461–84.

———. 1999. Neoidealism and the democratic peace. *Journal of Peace Research* 36:203–31.

———. 2002. *Democracy and war: The end of an illusion*. Boulder: Lynne Rienner.

Henderson, Errol, and J. David Singer. 2000. Civil war in the post-colonial world, 1946–1992. *Journal of Peace Research* 37:275–99.

———. 2002. "New Wars" and rumors of "New Wars." *International Interactions* 28:165–90.

Henehan, Marie T., and John Vasquez. Forthcoming. The changing probability of interstate war, 1816–1992. In *The waning of war,* ed. Raimo Vayrynen. London: Frank Cass.

Hensel, Paul R. 1996. Charting a course to conflict: Territorial issues and interstate conflict, 1816–1992. *Conflict Management and Peace Science* 15:43–73.

———. 1998. Interstate rivalry and the study of militarized conflict. In *New directions in the study of international conflict, crises, and war,* ed. Frank Harvey and Ben Mor, 161–204. London: Macmillan.

———. 2000. Territory: Theory and evidence on geography and conflict. In *What do we know about war?* ed. John A. Vasquez, 57–84. Lanham, MD: Rowman and Littlefield.

———. 2001a. Contentious issues and world politics: The management of territorial claims in the Americas, 1816–1992. *International Studies Quarterly* 45:81–109.

———. 2001b. ICOW Colonial History Data Set, version 0.1. http://garnet .acns.fsu.edu/~phensel/icow.html#colonies (accessed June 2001).

Hensel, Paul R., and Paul F. Diehl. 1994. It takes two to tango: Nonmilitarized response in interstate disputes. *Journal of Conflict Resolution* 38:479–506.

Hermann, Margaret G., and Charles W. Kegley Jr. 1996. Ballots, a barrier against the use of bullets and bombs: Democratization and military intervention. *Journal of Conflict Resolution* 40:436–59.

Heston, Alan, Robert Summers, and Bettina Aten. 2002. Penn world table version 6.1, Center for International Comparisons at the University of Pennsylvania (CICUP), Oct.

Hirschman, Albert O. 1970. The search for paradigms as a hindrance to understanding. *World Politics* 22:329–43.

Hoffmann, Matthew. 2003. Social norm avalanches. Paper presented at the workshop on Power Laws in the Social Sciences, Center for Social Complexity, George Mason University, October 23–24.

Holland, John. 1992. Genetic algorithms. *Scientific American* 267:66–72.

Hoole, Frank, and Dina A. Zinnes. 1976. *Quantitative international politics: An appraisal.* New York: Praeger.

Hornik, Kurt, and Maxwell Stinchcombe. 1992. Multilayer feedforward networks are universal approximators. In Halbert White, ed., *Artificial neural networks, approximation, and learning theory.* Oxford: Blackwell.

Hornik, Kurt, Maxwell Stinchcombe, and Halbert White. 1990. Universal approximation of an unknown mapping and its derivatives using multilayer feedforward networks. *Neural Networks* 3:551–60.

Horvath, William J. 1965. A statistical model for the duration of wars and strikes. *Behavioral Science* 13:18–28.

Horvath, William J., and Caxton C. Foster. 1963. Stochastic models of war alliances. *Journal of Conflict Resolution* 7:110–16.

Howes, Peter, and Nigel Crook. 1999. Using input parameters influences to support the decisions of feedforward neural networks. *Neurocomputing* 24:191–206.

Hume, David. [1748] 1894. *An enquiry concerning human understanding.* Oxford: Clarendon Press.

Huth, Paul K. 1996a. Enduring rivalries and territorial disputes, 1950–1990. *Conflict Management and Peace Science* 15:7–41.

———. 1996b. *Standing your ground: Territorial disputes and international conflict.* Ann Arbor: University of Michigan Press.

———. 2000. Territory: Why are territorial disputes between states a central cause of international conflict? In *What do we know about war?* ed. John A. Vasquez, 85–110. Lanham, MD: Rowman and Littlefield.

Huth, Paul K., and Todd L. Allee. 2002. *The democratic peace and territorial conflict in the twentieth century.* Cambridge: Cambridge University Press.

Jaggers, Keith, and Ted R. Gurr. 1995. Transitions to democracy: Tracking democracy's third wave with the polity III data. *Journal of Peace Research* 32:469–82.

Jensen, John. 1996. *Introductory digital image processing. A remote sensing perspective.* Upper Saddle River, NJ: Prentice-Hall.

Jones, Daniel A., Stuart A. Bremer, and J. David Singer. 1996. Militarized interstate disputes, 1816–1992: Rationale, coding rules, and empirical patterns. *Conflict Management and Peace Science* 15:163–213.

Kacowicz, Arie M. 1994. *Peaceful territorial change.* Columbia: University of South Carolina Press.

Kaplan, Morton A. 1957. *System and process in international politics.* New York: John Wiley.

Kegley, Charles W., Jr., ed. 1991. *The long postwar peace: Contending explanations and projections.* New York: HarperCollins.

Kegley, Charles W., Jr., and Margaret G. Hermann. 1995. Military intervention and the democratic peace. *International Interactions* 21:1–21.

Kegley, Charles W., Jr., and Gregory Raymond. 1986. Normative constraints on the use of force short of war. *Journal of Peace Research* 23:213–27.

Keohane, Robert O. 1983. Theory of world politics: Structural realism and beyond. In *Political science: The state of the discipline,* ed. Ada Finifter, 541–78. Washington, DC: American Political Science Association.

King, Gary. 1986. How not to lie with statistics: Avoiding common mistakes in quantitative political science. *American Journal of Political Science* 30:666–87.

———. 2001. Proper nouns and methodological propriety: Pooling dyads in international relations data. *International Organization* 55:497–507.

King, Gary, Robert O. Keohane, and Sidney Verba. 1994. *Designing social inquiry: Scientific inference in qualitative research.* Princeton: Princeton University Press.

King, Gary, and Langche Zeng. 2000. Logistic regression in rare events data. *Political Analysis* 9:1–27.

Kinsella, David, and Bruce Russett. 2002. Conflict emergence and escalation in interactive international dyads. *Journal of Politics* 64:1045–68.

References

Kocs, Stephen. 1995. Territorial disputes and interstate war, 1945–1987. *Journal of Politics* 57:159–75.

Kohn, George C. 1986. *Dictionary of wars.* New York: Doubleday.

Krause, Volker, and J. David Singer. 1997. Patterns of alliance commitments and the risk of armed conflict involvement, 1816–1984. In *Enforcing cooperation: Risky states and intergovernmental management of conflict,* ed. Gerald Schneider and Patricia A. Weitsman, 81–103. New York: St. Martin's.

Lai, Brian, and Dan Reiter. 2000. Democracy, political similarity, and international alliances, 1816–1992. *Journal of Conflict Resolution* 44:203–27.

Lakatos, Imre. 1970. Falsification and the methodology of scientific research programmes. In *Criticism and the growth of knowledge,* ed. Imre Lakatos and Alan Musgrave, 91–195. Cambridge: Cambridge University Press.

Langer, William L. 1935. *The diplomacy of imperialism, 1890–1902.* New York: Knopf.

———. 1950. *European alliances and alignments, 1871–1890.* New York: Knopf.

Lasswell, Harold. 1936. *Politics: Who gets what, when, and how.* New York: McGraw-Hill.

Layne, Christopher. 1994. Kant or cant: The myth of the democratic peace. *International Security* 19:5–49.

Lebow, Richard N. 2000. Contingency, catalysts, and international system change. *Political Science Quarterly* 115:591–616.

Leeds, Brett Ashley, Andrew G. Long, and Sara McLaughlin Mitchell. 2000. Reevaluating alliance reliability: Specific threats, specific promises. *Journal of Conflict Resolution* 44:686–99.

Legro, Jeffrey W., and Andrew Moravcsik. 1999. Is anybody still a realist? *International Security* 24:5–55.

Lemke, Douglas. 2002. *Regions of war and peace.* Cambridge: Cambridge University Press.

Lemke, Douglas, and William Reed. 1996. Regime types and status quo evaluations: Power transition theory and the democratic peace. *International Interactions* 22:43–64.

———. 2001a. The relevance of politically relevant dyads. *Journal of Conflict Resolution* 45:126–44.

———. 2001b. War and rivalry among great powers. *American Journal of Political Science* 45:457–69.

Leng, Russell J. 1983. When will they ever learn? Coercive bargaining in recurrent crises. *Journal of Conflict Resolution* 27:379–419.

———. 1993. *Interstate crisis behavior, 1816–1980: Realism versus reciprocity.* Cambridge: Cambridge University Press.

———. 1999. Cumulation in QIP: Twenty-five years after Ojai. *Conflict Management and Peace Science* 17:133–47.

Leng, Russell, and J. David Singer. 1977. A multitheoretical typology of international behavior. In M. Bunge, J. Galtun, and M. Malitza, *Mathematical approaches to international relations.* Bucharest: Romanian Academy of Social and Political Sciences.

Levy, Jack S. 1981. Alliance formation and war behavior: An analysis of the great powers, 1495–1975. *Journal of Conflict Resolution* 25:581–613.

———. 1983. *War in the modern great power system, 1495–1975.* Lexington: University Press of Kentucky.

———. 1985. The polarity of the system and international stability: An empirical analysis. In *Polarity and war,* ed. Alan Ned Sabrosky, 41–66. Boulder: Westview.

———. 1989. The diversionary theory of war: A critique. In *Handbook of war studies,* ed. Manus Midlarsky, 259–88. Boston: Unwin Hyman.

———. 2000. Reflections on the scientific study of war. In *What do we know about war?* ed. John A. Vasquez, 319–27. Lanham, MD: Rowman and Littlefield.

Levy, Jack S., Thomas C. Walker, and Martin S. Edwards. 2000. Continuity and change in the evolution of warfare. In *War in a changing world,* ed. Zeev Maoz and Azar Gat, 15–48. Ann Arbor: University of Michigan Press.

Malin, Martin. 1997. Is autocracy an obstacle to peace? Iran and Iraq, 1975–1980. In *Paths to peace: Is democracy the answer?* ed. Miriam Fendius Elman, 373–404. Cambridge: MIT Press.

Mandelbrot, Benoit. 1977. *The fractal geometry of nature.* San Francisco: W. H. Freeman.

Maoz, Zeev. 1983. Resolve, capabilities, and the outcomes of interstate disputes, 1816–1976. *Journal of Conflict Resolution* 27:195–229.

———. 1984. Peace by empire? Conflict outcomes and international stability, 1816–1976. *Journal of Peace Research* 21:227–41.

———. 1996. *Domestic sources of global change.* Ann Arbor: University of Michigan Press.

———. 1997a. The controversy over the democratic peace: Rearguard action or cracks in the wall? *International Security* 22:162–98.

———. 1997b. The strategic behavior of nations. Paper presented at the Peace Science Society (International) meetings, Houston, Oct. 29–31.

———. 1998. Realist and cultural critiques of the democratic peace: A theoretical and empirical re-assessment. *International Interactions* 24:1–89.

———. 1999. Dyadic militarized interstate disputes (DYMID1.1) Dataset-Version 1.1. Manuscript.

———. 2000a. Pacifism, conflict proneness, and addiction: A structural history of national and dyadic conflict, 1816–1992. Paper presented at the Peace Science Society (International). New Haven, Oct. 27–29.

———. 2000b. The street gangs of world politics—Their origins, management, and consequences, 1816–1986. In *What do we know about war?* ed. John A. Vasquez, 111–44. Lanham, MD: Rowman and Littlefield.

———. 2001a. Democratic networks: Connecting national, dyadic, and systemic levels of analysis in the study of democracy and war. In *War in a changing world*, ed. Zeev Maoz and Azar Gat, 143–82. Ann Arbor: University of Michigan Press.

———. 2001b. The dyadic MID dataset, Version 1.1. (2001) http://spirit.tau.ac .il/zeevmaoz/dyadmid.html

———. 2003. Paradoxical functions of international alliances: Security and other dilemmas. In *Realism and the balancing of power: A new debate*, ed. John A. Vasquez and Colin Elman, 200–221. Upper Saddle River, NJ: Prentice-Hall.

Maoz, Zeev, and Nasrin Abdolali. 1989. Regime types and international conflict. *Journal of Conflict Resolution* 33:3–35.

Maoz, Zeev, and Bruce Russett. 1992. Alliance, contiguity, wealth, and political stability: Is the lack of conflict among democracies a statistical artifact? *International Interactions* 17:245–67.

———. 1993. Normative and structural causes of democratic peace, 1946–1986. *American Political Science Review* 87:624–38.

Maoz, Zeev, Lesley Terris, Ranan Kuperman, and Ilan Talmud. 2004. International networks and the evolution of the international system, 1816–2000. In *New directions in international relations*, ed. Alex Mintz and Bruce Russett. Lanham, MD: Lexington Books.

McGowan, Pat, Harvey Starr, Gretchen Hower, Richard Merritt, and Dina Zinnes. 1988. International data as a natural resource. *International Interactions* 14:101–13.

McKay, R. J., and N. A. Campbell. 1982. Variable selection techniques in discriminant analysis. *British Journal of Mathematical and Statistical Psychology* 35:30–41.

McLaughlin, Sara, Scott Gates, Havard Hegre, Ranveig Gissinger, and Nils Petter Gleditsch. 1998. Timing the changes in political structures. *Journal of Conflict Resolution* 42:232–42.

Meakin, Paul. 1998. *Fractals, scaling and growth far from equilibrium*. Cambridge: Cambridge University Press.

Menard, Scott. 1995. *Applied logistic regression analysis*. Beverly Hills, CA: Sage.

Merritt, Richard L., and Dina A. Zinnes. 1990. Foreword. In *Measuring the correlates of war*, ed. J. David Singer and Paul F. Diehl, v–x. Ann Arbor: University of Michigan Press.

Midlarsky, Manus I. 1981. Stochastic modeling in political science research. In *Statistical distributions in scientific work*, vol. 6, ed. Charles Taillie, Ganapati P. Patil, and Bruno A. Baldessari, 131–46. Dordrecht, Holland: D. Reidel.

———. 1988. *The onset of world war*. Boston: Unwin Hyman.

———. 1989. A distribution of extreme inequality with applications to conflict behavior: A geometric derivation of the Pareto distribution. *Mathematical and Computer Modelling* 12:577–87.

———. 1999. *The evolution of inequality: War, state survival, and democracy in comparative perspective*. Stanford: Stanford University Press.

———, ed. 2000a. *Handbook of war studies II*. Ann Arbor: University of Michigan Press.

# References

————. 2000b. Mature theories, second-order properties, and other matters. In *What do we know about war?* ed. John A. Vasquez, 329–34. Lanham, MD: Rowman and Littlefield.

————. Forthcoming. *The killing trap: Genocide, Realpolitik, and loss in the twentieth century.* Cambridge: Cambridge University Press.

Miller, Geoffrey F., Peter Todd, and S. U. Hegde. 1989. Designing neural networks using genetic algorithms. *Proceedings of the Third International Conference on Genetic Algorithm.* San Mateo, CA: 65–80.

Min, Byoung, Richard N. Lebow, and Brian M. Pollins. 2003. War, trade, and power laws in simulated worlds. Paper presented at the workshop on Power Laws in the Social Sciences, Center for Social Complexity, George Mason University, Fairfax, VA, October 23–24.

Mitchell, Sara McLaughlin, and Brandon Prins. 1999. Beyond territorial contiguity: Issues at stake in democratic militarized interstate disputes. *International Studies Quarterly* 43:169–83.

Morgan, T. Clifton, and Glenn Palmer. n.d. To protect and to serve: Alliances and foreign policy portfolios. Manuscript. Houston, TX.

————. 2000. A model of foreign policy substitutability: Selecting the right tools for the job(s). *Journal of Conflict Resolution* 44:11–32.

Morgenthau, Hans J. 1948. *Politics among nations.* New York: Knopf.

————. 1960. *Politics among nations.* 3d ed. New York: Knopf.

————. 1967. *Politics among nations.* 4th ed. New York: Knopf.

Morrow, James D. 1989. Capabilities, uncertainty, and resolve: A limited information model of crisis bargaining. *American Journal of Political Science* 33:941–72.

————. 1991. Alliances and asymmetry: An alternative to the capability aggregation model of alliances. *American Journal of Political Science* 35:904–33.

————. 1993. Arms versus allies: Trade-offs in the search for security. *International Organization* 47:207–33.

————. 2000. Alliances: Why write them down? In *Annual Review of Political Science,* ed. Nelson W. Polsby, 3:63–83.

Morrow, James D., Bruce Bueno de Mesquita, Randolph M. Siverson, and Alastair Smith. 2001. Inside-out: A theory of domestic political institutions and the issues of international conflict. Hoover Institution, working paper.

Most, Benjamin A., and Randolph M. Siverson. 1987. Substituting arms and alliances, 1870–1914: An exploration in comparative foreign policy. In *New directions in the study of foreign policy,* ed. Charles F. Hermann, Charles W. Kegley Jr., and James N. Rosenau, 131–57. London: HarperCollins; Boston: Allen and Unwin.

Most, Benjamin A., and Harvey Starr. 1980. Diffusion, reinforcement, geopolitics, and the spread of war. *American Political Science Review* 74:932–46.

————. 1984. International relations theory, foreign policy substitutability, and "nice" laws. *World Politics* 36:383–406.

————. 1989. *Inquiry, logic, and international politics.* Columbia: University of South Carolina Press.

Mosteller, Frederick, and John W. Tukey. 1977. *Data analysis and regression.* Reading, MA: Addison-Wesley.

Mueller, John E. 1989. *Retreat from doomsday: The obsolescence of major war.* New York: Basic Books.

Nishenko, Stuart P., and Christopher C. Barton. 1996. Scaling laws for natural disaster fatalities. In *Reduction and predictability of natural disasters,* ed. John B. Rundle, Donald Turcotte, and William Kline. Santa Fe Institute Studies in the Sciences of Complexity, vol. 25. Santa Fe, NM: Addison-Wesley.

Nooruddin, Irfan. 2002. Modeling selection bias in studies of sanctions efficacy. *International Interactions* 28:59–75.

Oneal, John R., Frances H. Oneal, Zeev Maoz, and Bruce Russett. 1996. Liberal peace: Interdependence, democracy, and international conflict. *Journal of Peace Research* 33:11–28.

Oneal, John R., and James Lee Ray. 1997. New tests of democratic peace: Controlling for economic interdependence, 1950–1985. *Political Research Quarterly* 50:751–75.

Oneal, John R., and Bruce Russett. 1997. The classical liberals were right: Democracy, interdependence, and conflict, 1950–1985. *International Studies Quarterly* 41:267–93.

———. 1999. Is the liberal peace just an artifact of Cold War interests? Assessing recent critiques. *International Interactions* 25:213–41.

———. 2001. Clear and clean: The fixed effects of democracy and economic interdependence. *International Organization* 52:469–86.

Oneal, John R., Bruce Russett, and Michael Berbaum. 2003. Causes of peace: Democracy, interdependence, and international organizations, 1885–1992. *International Studies Quarterly* 47:371–94.

Oren, Ido. 1995. The subjectivity of the "democratic" peace: Changing U.S. perceptions of imperial Germany. *International Security* 20:147–84.

Organski, A. F. K. 1958. *World politics.* New York: Knopf.

Palmer, Glenn, Scott B. Wohlander, and T. Clifton Morgan. 2002. Give or take: Foreign aid and foreign policy substitutability. *Journal of Peace Research* 39:5–26.

Papayoanou, Paul. 1997. Economic interdependence and the balance of power. *International Studies Quarterly* 41:113–40.

Pareto, Vilfredo. 1927. *Manuel d'économie politique.* Paris: Marcel Giard.

Parry, Clive. 1978. *The consolidated treaty series.* Dobb Ferry, NY: Oceana.

Peceny, Mark, and Caroline Beer, with Shannon Sanchez-Terry. 2002. Dictatorial peace? *American Political Science Review* 96:27–40.

Pevehouse, Jon. 2002. Democracy from the outside in? International organizations and democratization. *International Organization* 56:515–50.

Popper, Karl R. 1959. *The logic of scientific discovery.* New York: Basic Books.

Przeworski, Adam, and Fernando Limongi. 1997. Modernization: Theories and facts. *World Politics* 49:155–83.

Putnam, Robert D. 1988. Diplomacy and domestic politics: The logic of two-level games. *International Organization* 42:427–60.

## References

Ragin, Charles C. 1987. *The comparative method: Moving beyond qualitative and quantitative strategies.* Berkeley: University of California Press.

Ray, James Lee. 1990. Friends as foes: International conflict and wars between formal allies. In *Prisoners of war? Nation-states in the modern era,* ed. Charles S. Gochman and Alan Ned Sabrosky, 73–91. Lexington, MA: Lexington Books.

———. 1995. *Democracy and international conflict.* Columbia: University of South Carolina Press.

———. 1997. On the level(s): Does democracy correlate with peace? Paper presented at the Norman Thomas Lectures on Scientific Knowledge of War, Vanderbilt University, March 14–16.

———. 1998a. Does democracy cause peace? *Annual Review of Political Science* 1:27–46.

———. 1998b. *Global politics.* 7th ed. Boston: Houghton Mifflin.

———. 1999. A Lakatosian view of the democratic peace research programme: Does it falsify realism (or neorealism)? Presented at the conference Progress in International Relations Theory, Scottsdale, AZ, Jan. 15–16. In *Progress in international relations theory: Appraising the field,* ed. Miriam Fendius Elman and Colin Elman. Boston: MIT Press, 2003.

———. 2000. Democracy: On the level(s), does democracy correlate with peace? In *What do we know about war?* ed. John A. Vasquez, 299–316. Lanham, MD: Rowman and Littlefield.

———. 2001. Integrating levels of analysis in world politics. *Journal of Theoretical Politics* 13:355–88.

Ray, James L., and Yijia Wang. 1998. Integrating levels of analysis in world politics: Increased utility or exercises in futility? Paper presented at the 94th Annual Meeting of the American Political Science Association, Boston, Sept. 3–6.

Reed, William. 2000. A unified statistical model of conflict onset and escalation. *American Journal of Political Science* 44:84–93.

———. 2002. Selection effects and world politics research. *International Interactions* 28:1–3.

Regan, Patrick M. 1996. Conditions of successful third-party intervention in intra-state conflicts. *Journal of Conflict Resolution* 40:336–59.

———. 1998. Choosing to intervene: Outside interventions in internal conflicts as a policy choice. *Journal of Politics* 60:754–79.

———. 2000. *Civil wars and foreign powers: Outside intervention in intrastate conflict.* Ann Arbor: University of Michigan Press.

———. 2002. Third party interventions and the duration of intrastate conflicts. *Journal of Conflict Resolution* 46:55–73.

Reichenbach, Hans. 1951. *The rise of scientific philosophy.* Berkeley: University of California Press.

Reiter, Dan, and Allan C. Stam III. 1998. Democracy, war initiation, and victory. *American Political Science Review* 92:377–89.

Rice, Condoleezza. 2000. Promoting the national interest: Life after the Cold War. *Foreign Affairs* 79:45–62.

Richards, Diana. 2000. *Political complexity*. Ann Arbor: University of Michigan Press.

Richardson, Lewis F. 1941. Frequency and occurrence of wars and other fatal quarrels. *Nature* 148:598.

———. 1945a. The distribution of wars in time. *Journal of the Royal Statistical Society* (Series A) 107:242–50.

———. 1945b. The distribution of wars in time. *Nature* 155:610.

———. 1948. Variation of the frequency of fatal quarrels with magnitude. *Journal of the American Statistical Association* 43:523–46.

———. 1960. *Statistics of deadly quarrels*. Pittsburgh: Boxwood Press.

Ripley, B. D. 1994. Neural network and related methods for classification. *Journal of the Royal Statistical Society* 56:409–56.

Rosecrance, Richard N. 1963. *Action and reaction in world politics*. Boston: Little, Brown.

Rousseau, David L., Christopher Gelpi, Dan Reiter, and Paul K. Huth. 1996. Assessing the dyadic nature of the democratic peace, 1918–1988. *American Political Science Review* 90:512–33.

Roy, A. Bikash. 1997. Intervention across bisecting borders. *Journal of Peace Research* 34:3–14.

Rummel, R. J. 1977. *Understanding conflict and war*. Vol. 3. Beverly Hills, CA: Sage.

———. 1980. Introduction. In *The correlates of war: II,* ed. J. David Singer, xiii–xxxviii. New York: Free Press.

———. 1983. Libertarianism and international violence. *Journal of Conflict Resolution* 27:27–71.

Rundle, John B., William Klein, and Susanna Gross. 1996. Rupture characteristics, recurrence, and predictability in a slider-block model for earthquakes. In *Reduction and predictability of natural disasters,* ed. John B. Rundle, Donald Turcotte, and William Klein. Santa Fe Institute Studies in the Sciences of Complexity, vol. 25. Santa Fe, NM: Addison-Wesley.

Rundle, John B., William Klein, Kristy Tiampo, and Susanna Gross. 2000. Dynamics of seismicity patterns in systems of earthquake faults. Paper presented at the 25th General Assembly of the European Geophysical Society, April 24–29, Nice, France.

Russett, Bruce. 1979. Foreword. In *Explaining war: Selected papers from the Correlates of War Project,* ed. J. David Singer et al., 7–10. Beverly Hills, CA: Sage.

———. 1993. *Grasping the democratic peace*. Princeton: Princeton University Press.

Russett, Bruce, and John R. Oneal. 2001. *Triangulating peace: Democracy, interdependence, and international organizations*. New York: W. W. Norton.

Sabrosky, Alan N. 1976. Capabilities, commitments, and the expansion of interstate war, 1816–1965. Ph.D. diss., Ann Arbor, University of Michigan.

———. 1980. Interstate alliances: Their reliability and the expansion of war. In *The correlates of war: II. Testing some realpolitik models,* ed. J. David Singer, 161–98. New York: Free Press.

References

———. 1985. Alliance aggregation, capability distribution, and the expansion of interstate war. In *Polarity and war,* ed. Alan Ned Sabrosky, 145–89. Boulder: Westview.

Sachs, Jeffrey. 1998. International economics: Unlocking the mysteries of globalization. *Foreign Policy* 110:97–111.

Saito, K., and R. Nakano. 1998. Medical diagnostic expert system based on PDP model. *Proceedings of IEEE International Conference on Neural Networks,* 255–62. San Diego.

Sambanis, Nicholas. 2001. Do ethnic and nonethnic civil wars have the same causes? A theoretical and empirical inquiry (Part 1). *Journal of Conflict Resolution* 45:259–82.

Sarkees, Meredith. 2000. The Correlates of War data on war: An update to 1997. *Conflict Management and Peace Science* 18:123–44.

Sarle, Warren. 1994. Neural network and statistical models. *Proceedings of the Nineteenth Annual SAS Users Group International Conference,* Cary, NC, 1–13.

———. 1995. Stopped training and other remedies for overfitting. *Proceedings of the Twenty-seventh Symposium on the Interface of Computing Science and Statistics,* Fairfax, VA, 352–60.

Sartori, Anne E. 2002. Enduring facts about enduring rivals. Paper presented at the annual meeting of the American Political Science Association, Aug./Sept., Boston.

———. 2003. An estimator for some binary-outcome selection models without exclusion restrictions. *Political Analysis* 11:111–38.

Schrodt, Phillip. 1991. Prediction of interstate conflict outcomes using a neural network. *Social Science Computer Review* 9:359–80.

Schroeder, Manfred. 1991. *Fractals, chaos, power laws.* New York: Freeman.

Schroeder, Paul W. 1976. Alliances, 1815–1945: Weapons of power and tools of management. In *Historical dimensions of national security problems,* ed. Klaus Knorr, 227–62. Lawrence: University Press of Kansas.

Senese, Paul D. 1996. Geographic proximity and issue salience: Their effects on the escalation of militarized interstate conflict. *Conflict Management and Peace Science* 15:133–61.

———. 1997. Between disputes and war: The effect of joint democracy on interstate conflict escalation. *Journal of Politics* 59:1–27.

———. 2002. Reciprocal contingency: Territory and proximity. Paper presented at the annual meeting of the Peace Science Society (International), Tucson.

Senese, Paul D., and John A. Vasquez. 2001. The effect of territorial disputes and politically relevant alliances on the probability of war, 1816–1992: Testing for interactions. Paper presented at the ISA Hong Kong convention of international studies, July 28.

———. 2003. A unified explanation of territorial conflict: Testing the impact of sampling bias, 1919–1992. *International Studies Quarterly* 47:275–98.

Simmons, Beth A. 1999. See you in "court"? The appeal to quasi-judicial legal processes in the settlement of territorial disputes. In *A road map to war:*

*Territorial dimensions of international conflict*, ed. Paul F. Diehl, 205–37. Nashville: Vanderbilt University Press.

Simon, Herbert. 1957. *Models of man.* New York: Wiley.

Singer, J. David. 1958. Threat perception and the armament-tension dilemma. *Journal of Conflict Resolution* 2:90–105.

———. 1961a. The relevance of the behavioral sciences to the study of international relations. *Behavioral Science* 6:77–92.

———. 1961b. The level of analysis problem in international relations. *World Politics* 14:77–92.

———. 1963. Inter-nation influence: A formal model. *American Political Science Review* 57:420–30.

———. 1965. Data-making in international relations. *Behavioral Science* 10: 68–80.

———. 1966. The behavioral science approach to international relations: Payoff and prospect. *SAIS Review* 10:12–20.

———. 1968. Man and world politics: The psycho-cultural interface. *Journal of Social Issues* 24:127–56.

———. 1969a. The global system and its sub-systems: A developmental view. In *Linkage politics: Essays in national and international systems,* ed. James N. Rosenau, 21–43. New York: Free Press.

———. 1969b. The incomplete theorist: Insight without evidence. In *Contending approaches to international politics,* ed. Klaus Knorr and James Rosenau, 62–86. Princeton: Princeton University Press.

———. 1970a. Escalation and control in international conflict: A simple feedback model. *General Systems Yearbook* 15:163–75.

———. 1970b. From *A study of war* to peace research: Some criteria and strategies. *Journal of Conflict Resolution* 14:527–42.

———. 1971. Modern international war: From conjecture to explanation. In *The Search for World Order,* ed. A. Lepawsky, E. H. Buehrig, and H. D. Lasswell, 47–71. New York: Appleton-Century-Crofts.

———. 1972a. The Correlates of War Project: Interim report and rationale. *World Politics* 24:243–70.

———. 1972b. *The scientific study of politics: An approach to foreign policy analysis.* Morristown, NJ: General Learning Press.

———. 1972c. Theorists and empiricists: The two-culture problem in international relations. In *The analysis of international politics,* ed. James N. Rosenau, Vincent Davis, and Maurice A. East, 80–95. New York: Free Press.

———. 1976. The Correlates of War Project: Continuity, diversity, and convergence. In *Quantitative international politics: An appraisal,* ed. Francis W. Hoole and Dina A. Zinnes, 21–42. New York: Praeger.

———. 1977. The historical experiment as a research strategy in world politics. *Social Science History* 2:1–22.

———, ed. 1979a. *The correlates of war I: Research origins and rationale.* New York: Free Press.

References

———. 1979b. Introduction. In *The correlates of war: I. Research origins and rationale*, ed. J. David Singer, xi–xix. New York: Free Press.

———. 1979c. The scientific study of politics: An approach to foreign policy analysis. In *The correlates of war: I. Research origins and rationale*, ed. J. David Singer, 133–44. New York: Free Press.

———. 1979d. Social science and social problems. *Society* 16:49–56.

———. 1980a. Conflict research, political action, and epistemology. In *Handbook of political conflict*, ed. Ted R. Gurr, 490–99. New York: Free Press.

———. 1980b. Introduction. In *The correlates of war: II. Testing some realpolitik models*, ed. J. David Singer, xiii–xxxviii. New York: Free Press.

———. 1982. Confrontational behavior and escalation to war, 1816–1980: A research plan. *Journal of Peace Research* 19:37–48.

———. 1985. The responsibilities of competence in the global village. *International Studies Quarterly* 29:245–62.

———. 1986. Research, policy, and the correlates of war. In *Studies of war and peace*, ed. Oyvind Osterud, 44–59. Oslo: Norwegian University Press.

———. 1989. The making of a peace researcher. In *Biographical reflections of thirty-four academic travelers' journeys through world politics*, ed. J. Kruzel and J. N. Rosenau, 213–29. Lexington, MA: Lexington Books.

———. 1990a. *Models, methods, and progress in world politics: A peace research odyssey.* Boulder: Westview.

———. 1990b. One man's view: A personal history of the Correlates of War Project. In *Prisoners of war? Nation-states in the modern era*, ed. Charles S. Gochman and Alan N. Sabrosky, 11–27. Lexington, MA: Lexington Press.

———. 1990c. Reconstructing the Correlates of War data set on material capabilities of states, 1816–1985. In *Measuring the correlates of war*, ed. J. David Singer and Paul F. Diehl, 53–71. Ann Arbor: University of Michigan Press.

———. 1991. Democracy, disputes, and war: The two-body problem. Memo, Correlates of War Project, University of Michigan, Ann Arbor.

———. 1995. Metaphors and models in the explanation of war. In *The process of war*, ed. Stuart A. Bremer and Thomas R. Cusack, 227–32. Amsterdam: Gordon and Breach.

———. 1999. The correlates of war. In *The encyclopedia of violence, peace, and conflict*, ed. Lawrence Kurtz. San Diego: Academic Press.

———. 2000. The etiology of interstate war: A natural history approach. In *What do we know about war?* ed. John A. Vasquez, 3–21. Lanham, MD: Rowman and Littlefield.

Singer, J. David, Stuart A. Bremer, and John Stuckey. 1972. Capability distribution, uncertainty, and major power war, 1820–1965. In *Peace, war, and numbers*, ed. Bruce M. Russett, 19–48. New York: Free Press; Beverly Hills, CA: Sage.

Singer, J. David, and Thomas R. Cusack. 1981. Periodicity, inexorability, and steersmanship in international war. In *From national development to global community: Essays in honor of Karl W. Deutsch,* ed. Richard L. Merritt and Bruce M. Russett, 404–22. London: George Allen and Unwin.

Singer, J. David, and Susan D. Jones. 1972. *Beyond conjecture in international politics: Abstracts of data-based research.* Itasca, IL: F. E. Peacock.

Singer, J. David, and Paul Ray. 1966. Decision making in conflict: From interpersonal to international relations. *Bulletin of the Menninger Clinic* 30: 300–312.

Singer, J. David, and Melvin Small. 1966a. Formal alliances, 1815–1939: A quantitative description. *Journal of Peace Research* 3:1–32.

———. 1966b. National alliance commitments and war involvement, 1815–1945. *Peace Research Society (International) Papers* 5:109–40.

———. 1968a. Alliance aggregation and the onset of war, 1815–1945. In *Quantitative international politics: Insights and evidence,* ed. J. David Singer, 247–86. New York: Free Press.

———. 1968b. Formal alliances, 1816–1965: An extension of the basic data. *Journal of Peace Research* 6:257–82.

———. 1972. *The Wages of War, 1816–1965: A Statistical Handbook.* New York: John Wiley.

———. 1974. Foreign policy indicators: Predictors of war in history and in the state of the world message. *Policy Sciences* 5:271–96.

Singer, J. David and Richard J. Stoll, eds. 1984. *Quantitative indicators in world politics: Timely assurance and early warning.* New York: Praeger.

Singer, J. David, and Michael Wallace. 1970. Intergovernmental organization and the preservation of peace, 1816–1965: Some bivariate relationships. *International Organization* 24:520–47.

———, eds. 1979. *To augur well: Early warning indicators in world politics.* Beverly Hills, CA: Sage.

Siverson, Randolph M., and Joel King. 1979. Alliances and the expansion of war. In *To augur well,* ed. J. David Singer and Michael D. Wallace, 37–49. Beverly Hills, CA: Sage.

———. 1980. Attributes of national alliance membership and war participation, 1815–1965. *American Journal of Political Science* 24:1–15.

Siverson, Randolph M., and Harvey Starr. 1991. *The diffusion of war.* Ann Arbor: University of Michigan Press.

Siverson, Randolph M., and Michael P. Sullivan. 1983. The distribution of power and the onset of war. *Journal of Conflict Resolution* 27:473–94.

Small, Melvin. 1990. History and the Correlates of War Project. In *Prisoners of war? Nation-states in the modern era,* ed. Charles S. Gochman and Alan N. Sabrosky, 29–39. Lexington, MA: Lexington Books.

Small, Melvin, and J. David Singer. 1969. Formal alliances, 1816–1965: An extension of the basic data. *Journal of Peace Research* 6:257–82.

———. 1976. The war-proneness of democratic regimes, 1816–1965. *Jerusalem Journal of International Relations* 1:50–68.

———. 1982. *Resort to arms: International and civil wars, 1816–1980.* Beverly Hills, CA: Sage.

———. 1990. Formal alliances, 1816–1965: An extension of the basic data. In *Measuring the correlates of war,* ed. J. David Singer and Paul F. Diehl, 159–90. Ann Arbor: University of Michigan Press.

Smith, Alastair. 1995. Alliance formation and war. *International Studies Quarterly* 39:405–25.

———. 1996. To intervene or not to intervene: A biased decision. *Journal of Conflict Resolution* 40:16–40.

Snyder, Glenn H. 1984. The security dilemma in alliance politics. *World Politics* 36:461–95.

———. 1997. *Alliance politics.* Ithaca: Cornell University Press.

Sorokin, Gerald L. 1994a. Alliance formation and general deterrence: A game-theoretic model and the case of Israel. *Journal of Conflict Resolution* 38: 298–325.

———. 1994b. Arms, alliances, and security tradeoffs in enduring rivalries. *International Studies Quarterly* 38:421–46.

Sorokin, Pitirim A. 1937. *Social and cultural dynamics.* Vol. 3, *Fluctuation of social relationships, war, and revolution.* New York: American Book Company.

Starr, Harvey, and Benjamin A. Most. 1976. The substance and study of borders in international relations research. *International Studies Quarterly* 20: 581–620.

Strahler, A. H. 1980. The use of prior probabilities in maximum likelihood classification of remotely sensed data. *Remote Sensing of Environment* 10: 135–63.

Suzuki, Susumu, Volker Krause, and J. David Singer. 2002. The Correlates of War Project: A bibliographic history of the scientific study of war and peace, 1964–2000. *Conflict Management and Peace Science* 19:69–107.

Thompson, William R. 1995. Principal rivalries. *Journal of Conflict Resolution* 39:195–223.

———. 1996. Democracies and peace: Putting the cart before the horse? *International Organization* 50:141–74.

———. 2003. A Streetcar named Sarajevo: Catalysts, multiple causation chains, and rivalry structures. *International Studies Quarterly* 47:453–74.

Thompson, William R., and Richard Tucker. 1997. A tale of two democratic peace critiques. *Journal of Conflict Resolution* 41:428–54.

Toland, John. 1970. *The rising sun.* New York: Random House.

Tomz, M., J. Wittenberg, and G. King. 2001. CLARIFY: Software for interpreting and presenting statistical results. Version 2.0. Cambridge: Harvard University, June 1. http://gking.harvard.edu/.

Vasquez, John A. 1987. The steps to war: Toward a scientific explanation of correlates of war findings. *World Politics* 40:108–45.

———. 1993. *The war puzzle.* Cambridge: Cambridge University Press.

———. 1995. Developing a strategy for achieving greater cumulation in peace research. In *The process of war,* ed. Stuart A. Bremer and Thomas R. Cusack, 241–49. Amsterdam: Gordon and Breach.

———. 1996. The causes of the Second World War in Europe: A new scientific explanation. *International Political Science Review* 17:161–78.

———. 1997. The realist paradigm and degenerative versus progressive research programs: An appraisal of neotraditional research on Waltz's balancing proposition. *American Political Science Review* 91:899–912.

———. 1998a. The evolution of multiple rivalries prior to World War II in the Pacific. In *The dynamics of enduring rivalries,* ed. Paul F. Diehl, 191–224. Urbana: University of Illinois Press.

———. 1998b. *The power of power politics: From classical realism to neotraditionalism.* Cambridge: Cambridge University Press.

———. 2000. What do we know about war? In *What do we know about war?* ed. John A. Vasquez, 335–70. Lanham, MD: Rowman and Littlefield.

———. 2002. The probability of war, 1816–1992. Presidential address presented at the Forty-third Annual Convention of the International Studies Association, New Orleans, March 24–27.

———. 2003. The new debate on balancing power: A reply to my critics. In *Realism and the balancing of power: A new debate,* ed. John A. Vasquez and Colin Elman, 87–113. Upper Saddle River, NJ: Prentice-Hall.

Vasquez, John A., and Colin Elman, eds. 2003. *Realism and the balancing of power: A new debate.* Upper Saddle River, NJ: Prentice-Hall.

Vasquez, John A., and Marie T. Henehan. 2001. Territorial disputes and the probability of war, 1816–1992. *Journal of Peace Research* 38:123–38.

Vieira, C. A. O., and P. M. Mather. 1999. Techniques of combining multiple classifiers in remote sensing. *Proceedings of the Twenty-fifth Annual Conference and Exhibition of the Remote Sensing Society,* Aberystwyth: University of Wales (Sept.): 387–94.

Waal, Frans de. 1989. *Chimpanzee politics.* Baltimore: Johns Hopkins University Press.

Waldrop, M. Mitchell. 1995. *Complexity.* New York: Simon and Schuster.

Walker, Thomas. 2000. Peace, rivalry, and war: A theoretical and empirical study of international conflict. Ph.D. diss., Rutgers University.

Wallace, Michael D. 1985. Polarization: Towards a scientific conception. In *Polarity and war,* ed. Alan Ned Sabrosky, 95–113. Boulder: Westview.

Wallace, Michael, and J. David Singer. 1970. Inter-governmental organization and the preservation of peace, 1816–1964: Some bivariate relationships. *International Organization* 24:520–47.

Waltz, Kenneth N. 1959. *Man, the state, and war.* New York: Columbia University Press.

———. 1964. The stability of the bipolar world. *Daedalus* 93:881–909.

———. 1967. International structure, national force, and the balance of world power. *Journal of International Affairs* 21:215–31.

———. 1979. *Theory of international politics.* Reading, MA: Addison-Wesley.

Ward, Michael D. 1982. Research gaps in alliance dynamics. *Monograph series in world affairs* 19:3–95. Denver: University of Denver.

## References

Wasserman, Stanley, and Katherine Faust. 1994. *Social network analysis: Methods and applications.* Cambridge: Cambridge University Press.

Wayman, Frank W. 1984. Bipolarity and war: The role of capability concentration and alliance patterns among major powers, 1816–1965. *Journal of Peace Research* 21:61–78.

———. 1990. Alliances and war: A time-series analysis. In *Prisoners of war? Nation-states in the modern era,* ed. Charles S. Gochman and Alan Ned Sabrosky, 93–113. Lexington, MA: Lexington Books.

———. 1995. Purpose, process, and progress in the study of war. In *The process of war,* ed. Stuart A. Bremer and Thomas R. Cusack, 251–58. Amsterdam: Gordon and Breach.

Wayman, Frank W., and T. Clifton Morgan. 1990. Measuring polarity in the international system. In *Measuring the correlates of war,* ed. J. David Singer and Paul F. Diehl, 139–58. Ann Arbor: University of Michigan Press.

Wayman, Frank W., J. David Singer, and Gary Goertz. 1983. Capabilities, allocations, and success in militarized disputes and wars, 1816–1976. *International Studies Quarterly* 27:497–515.

Weede, Erich. 1996. *Economic development, social order, and world politics.* Boulder: Lynne Rienner.

Weinberg, Gerald. 1975. *An introduction to general systems thinking.* New York: Wiley.

Weiss, Herbert K. 1963. Stochastic models for the duration and magnitude of a "deadly quarrel." *Operations Research* 11:101–21.

Wendt, Alexander. 1987. The agent-structure problem in international relations theory. *International Organization* 41:335–70.

Werner, Suzanne. 2000. The effects of political similarity on the onset of militarized disputes, 1816–1985. *Political Research Quarterly* 53:343–74.

Wesley, James Paul. 1962. Frequency of wars and geographic opportunity. *Journal of Conflict Resolution* 6:387–89. Reprinted in *Theory and research on the causes of war,* ed. Dean G. Pruitt and Richard C. Snyder, 229–31. Englewood Cliffs, NJ: Prentice-Hall, 1969.

Wilkinson, David. 1980. *Deadly quarrels: Lewis F. Richardson and the statistical study of war.* Los Angeles: University of California Press.

Woods, Frederick, and Alexander Baltzly. 1915. *Is war diminishing? A study of the prevalence of war in Europe from 1450 to the present day.* Boston and New York: Houghton Mifflin.

Wright, Quincy. 1942. *A study of war.* Chicago: University of Chicago Press.

Wylie, Alison. 1986. Arguments for scientific realism: The ascending spiral. *American Philosophical Quarterly* 23:287–97.

Wyss, Max, and Stefan Wiemer. 2000. Change in the probability for earthquakes in Southern California due to the Landers magnitude 7.3 earthquake. *Science* 290:1334–38.

Yao, Xin. 1999. Evolving artificial neural networks. *Proceedings of the IEEE* 87 (9): 1423–47.

References

Zacher, Mark. 2001. The territorial integrity norm: International boundaries and the use of force. *International Organization* 55:215–50.

Zeng, Langche. 1999. Prediction and classification with neural network models. *Sociological Methods and Research* 27:499–524.

Zipf, George K. 1949. *Human behavior and the principle of least effort.* Cambridge, MA: Addison-Wesley.

# CONTRIBUTORS

Bruce Bueno de Mesquita is Senior Fellow at the Hoover Institution at Stanford University and Silver Professor of Politics at New York University.

Claudio Cioffi-Revilla is Professor of Computational Social Sciences and Director of the Center for Social Complexity, George Mason University.

Paul F. Diehl is Professor of Political Science and University Distinguished Teacher/Scholar at the University of Illinois at Urbana-Champaign.

Daniel S. Geller is Professor of Political Science and Chair of the Political Science Department at Wayne State University and a Consultant with the Office of Technology and Assessments, U.S. Department of State.

Errol A. Henderson is Associate Professor of African/African-American Studies and Political Science at Pennsylvania State University, and is Associate Director of the Correlates of War Project.

Volker Krause is Assistant Professor of Political Science at Northern Arizona University.

Monica Lagazio is a Lecturer in Political Studies at the University of the Witwatersrand, South Africa.

Douglas Lemke is Associate Professor of Political Science at Pennsylvania State University.

Zeev Maoz is Professor of Political Science and Head of the Graduate School of Government and Policy at Tel-Aviv University, Israel.

Manus I. Midlarsky is the Moses and Annuta Back Professor of International Peace and Conflict Resolution at Rutgers University.

James Lee Ray is a Professor of Political Science at Vanderbilt University.

Patrick M. Regan is Associate Professor of Political Science at Binghamton University.

Bruce Russett is Dean Acheson Professor of International Relations and Director of United Nations Studies at Yale University, and Editor of the *Journal of Conflict Resolution.*

Paul D. Senese is Assistant Professor of Political Science at the University at Buffalo, SUNY.

John A. Vasquez holds the Harvey Picker Chair of International Relations at Colgate University.

# INDEX